Air Defence Artillery
in Combat,
1972 to the Present

To
Harpreet, Prabhleen and Gurleen

Air Defence Artillery in Combat, 1972 to the Present

Mandeep Singh

AIR WORLD

First published in Great Britain in 2020 and reprinted in 2021 and
2022 by
Pen & Sword Air World
An imprint of
Pen & Sword Books Ltd
Yorkshire – Philadelphia

ISBN 978 1 52676 204 7

A CIP catalogue record for this book is
available from the British Library.

Printed and bound in the UK by
CPI Group (UK) Ltd, Croydon, CR0 4YY

Pen & Sword Books Limited incorporates the imprints of Atlas,
Archaeology, Aviation, Discovery, Family History, Fiction, History,
Maritime, Military, Military Classics, Politics, Select, Transport, True
Crime, Air World, Frontline Publishing, Leo Cooper, Remember
When, Seaforth Publishing, The Praetorian Press, Wharncliffe
Local History, Wharncliffe Transport, Wharncliffe True Crime
and White Owl.

For a complete list of Pen & Sword titles please contact

PEN & SWORD BOOKS LIMITED
47 Church Street, Barnsley, South Yorkshire, S70 2AS, England
E-mail: enquiries@pen-and-sword.co.uk
Website: www.pen-and-sword.co.uk

Or

PEN AND SWORD BOOKS
1950 Lawrence Rd, Havertown, PA 19083, USA
E-mail: Uspen-and-sword@casematepublishers.com
Website: www.penandswordbooks.com

Contents

Abbreviations

Above Ground Level	AGL
Airborne Early Warning	AEW
Aircraft	ac
Airborne Warning and Control System	AWACS
Air Defence	AD
Air Defence Artillery	ADA
Air Defence Direction Centre	ADDC
Air Defence Operations Centre	ADOC
Air Force	AF
Ante Meridiem	AM
Anti-Aircraft	AA
Anti-Aircraft Artillery	AAA
Anti-radiation Missiles	ARM
Anti-Tank Guided Missile	ATGM
Armour	Armr
Armoured	Armd
Artillery	Arty
Battery	Bty
Beyond Visual Range	BVR
Brigade	Bde
Fuerza Aérea Argentina	FAA
Central Intelligence Agency	CIA
Colonel	Col
Combat Air Patrol	CAP
Commando	Cdo
Commander	Cdr
Control & Reporting	C&R
Continuous Wave	CW
Division	Div

Electronic Counter Measures	ECM
Electronic Intelligence	ELINT
Electronic Warfare	EW
Electronic Warfare Officers	EWO
Forward Looking Infra-Red	FLIR
Her Majesty's Ship	HMS
Homing All the Way Killer	HAWK
Infantry	Inf
Infra-red	IR
Integrated Air Defence System	IADS
Identification Friend or Foe	IFF
Israeli Air Force	IAF
Israeli Defence Forces	IDF
Mark	Mk
Missile	Msl
Non-Commissioned Officer	NCO
North Atlantic Treaty Organisation	NATO
Precision guided munition	PGM
Operation	Op
Photo-reconnaissance	PR
Post Meridiem	PM
Prisoner of War	PoW
Radar	Rdr
Radar-Surface to Air Missile	R-SAM
Radar Warning Receiver	RWR
Reconnaissance	Recce
Remotely Piloted Vehicle	RPV
Man-portable Air Defence System	MANPADS
Mobile Observation Unit	MOU
Palestine Liberation Organization	PLO
Royal Air Force	RAF
Royal Navy	RN
Special Air Service	SAS
Standard Operating Procedure	SOP
Surface to Air Missile	SAM
Suppression of Enemy Air Defence	SEAD

Squadron	Sqn
Television	TV
Trinitrotoluene	TNT
United Nations	UN
United Nations Security Council	UNSC
United States Air Force	USAF
United States Marine Corps	USMC
United States of America	USA
Unmanned Aerial Vehicle	UAV
Vertical/Short Take-Off and Landing	V/STOL
Very Low Observability	VLO

Introduction

The first two decades following the Second World War saw the ground-based air defences challenge the air forces and emerge as a force to be reckoned with. It saw the growth and maturing of surface-to-air missiles as the most feared and respected component of an air defence system. Starting from the efforts made by Nazi Germany, the initial developmental efforts were made to counter jet aircraft, but the real development took place in the early fifties, ostensibly to counter the threat of long-range jet bombers carrying nuclear weapons.

The US was the first to develop an operational surface to air missile; it deployed the Nike Ajax in 1954, designed to counter the conventional bomber aircraft flying at high subsonic speeds and altitudes above 15,000 metres. The Soviet Union followed a year later with the S-25 Berkut system (SA-1) entering operational service on 7 May 1955. It was a static system used for the air defence of Moscow. The basic design of the S-25 was used to develop the smaller but more mobile and effective S-75 Dvina (SA-2) which entered service in 1957. The early surface-to-air missiles were aimed to counter the high-flying reconnaissance aircraft and the jet-powered nuclear-armed bomber and it was no surprise that the first successful use of SAM was against a Taiwanese Martin RB-57D Canberra high-altitude reconnaissance aircraft which was hit by a Chinese-operated S-75 near Beijing on 7 October 1959 – over six months before the much publicised shooting down of Francis Gary Powers' U-2 in 1960. The SA-2 would go on to claim several Taiwanese-piloted and operated aircraft to include at least five U-2s besides several RB-57s and drones as well as another US U-2 over Cuba in 1962.

The SA-2 was supplied to almost forty countries and remains in service to date with over twenty of them. It is just one of the many surface-to-air missiles which have proliferated and are in frontline service worldwide. It was to become one of the most widely deployed and used surface-to-air missiles in history. This is not surprising as the Soviet Union was at the forefront of SAM development – and today Russia is following suit. The reasons for this are varied, but one of the main factors is the need to have a credible and effective, yet affordable, counter to the technologically superior US air power. Missiles are cheaper, easier to maintain and operate than the vast fleet of aircraft required to defend an airspace, and more so in case of absence of access to cutting-edge aviation technology. The development of a range of missiles to include both strategic and tactical, as also the man-portable missile system, by the Soviet Union (now Russia) is a manifestation of the same.

The impetus for development of missile systems was not always to counter high-flying bombers but was also the need to have an effective weapons system that could be used with ease by the foot soldiers. Based on the experiences of the Second World War when the infantryman relied on his machine gun for anti-aircraft protection, and its failure to defend against the modern jet combat aircraft, the USA started developing a man-portable air defence system and, after various concept designs, the Redeye missile system, an Infra-Red (IR) guided man-portable air defence system, was selected for development. Though the work on the project had started in the fifties, it entered operational service only in 1968. The Soviets introduced their version of the man-portable missile, the Strela-2, a 'tail-chaser' like the Redeye, one year later. Along with the SA-2, it became one of the most widely used SAMs and has been used in almost all conflicts since the 1970s and remains in service even today.

The first combat employment of surface-to-air missiles was during the Vietnam War, which was also the debut of the SA-2 when a Dvina missile shot down a USAF F-4C aircraft on 24 July 1965. The Dvinas went on to claim over 31 per cent of US aircraft shot down in the war. Although anti-aircraft (AA) guns were the leading cause of US aircraft losses, a large number of aircraft claimed by the guns were facilitated by the SAMs as they forced the aircraft to fly lower – into the AA guns' fire envelope.

During the Six Days War of 1967, the SA-2, operated by Arabs, failed to make any impact as it did not shoot down any Israeli aircraft during the entire war. The tactical employment of the Israeli Air Force, plus the intelligence about the SA-2 gained through the USA, were the reasons for the relative failure of the surface-to-air missiles. Making its debut also during the war was the HAWK, a US missile held and operated by Israeli Air Defences, which shot down an aircraft – although it was a case of friendly fire claiming one of the Israeli aircraft which had strayed over the Negev Nuclear Research Centre.

The wars in South Asia in the sixties and seventies were an exception as the surface-to-air missiles made no impact during the wars fought by India and Pakistan. India had introduced the (then) Soviet SA-2 missile in 1963–4 and reportedly used it during the two conflicts with Pakistan but without any success. Pakistan, on the other hand, had no surface-to-air missile in its inventory. It was only much later, during the Kargil War in 1999, that surface-to-air missiles made their impact when the use of man-portable missiles by Pakistan forced the Indian Air Force to revisit and revise their tactical employment of aircraft and gunships. On 21 May 1999 an Anza missile (a Chinese copy of the Soviet SA-7 missile) fired by Pakistani troops hit an Indian Air Force Canberra PR.57 aircraft and damaged its right engine. The Indian Air Force lost a MiG-21 and a Mi-17 armed helicopter to the MANPADS which led to the fitting, and use, of flares by all fighter aircraft and withdrawal of the slow-moving Mi-17s from the fire-support role. Further, the fighter aircraft operated from outside the lethal threat envelope of the shoulder-fired missiles. Pakistan reportedly fired more than 100 missiles during the operation but not a single Indian aircraft was lost or damaged after these measures were adopted.

The shoulder-fired missiles had earlier been used in the longstanding conflict in the Siachen glacier also. Though the terrain and weather conditions in the region severely restrict the use of missiles in the region, the man-portable missiles have occasionally been used by both sides. Amongst the more notable instances are the downing of a Pakistani helicopter carrying the then Force Commander Northern Areas of the Pakistani Army by India using an Igla missile on 1 August 1992, and the use of MANPADS by Pakistan to shoot down an Indian Mi-17 in 1996 in the same sector.

The most extensive use of surface-to-air missiles has been in the Middle East. After the disastrous debut in the Six Days War, the SAMs made their presence felt in the later stages of the War of Attrition when Egypt used the SA-2 and the newly acquired SA-3s to establish a 'missile box' that took a heavy toll of Israeli aircraft. Between 30 June and 3 August, nine Israeli aircraft were shot down, and three more damaged. These included four F-4 Phantoms shot down on a single day (18 July).

Adding to its woes was the latest Soviet surface-to-air missile system, the SA-6, a highly mobile, tracked missile system which claimed at least one F-4 on 3 August 1970. The war ended on 8 August with the ceasefire agreement as part of the Roger Plan, but Israel had no counter to the new threat.

The War of Attrition was in a way the harbinger of things to come but the Israelis were too confident, to the point of being complacent, to see the writing on the wall. They underestimated the lethality and effectiveness of the missiles – dismissive of the nature of threat posed by the SAMs. 'We have countered the Arab air defences in the past and will do so in the future' seemed to be the refrain.

However, what was apparently overlooked was that there were no technical inputs on the new radar and missiles and, as a result, no countermeasures were available to the Israeli Air Force. Such was the state of affairs when Egypt and Syria launched the Ramadan War on 6 October 1973. This was the war which brought surface-to-air missiles to the centre stage. Egyptian and Syrian air defences shot down almost fifty Israeli aircraft in the first three days alone – almost one fourth of Israel's combat aircraft. Israel lost 104 aircraft during the war and, for the first time, more aircraft were lost to surface-to-air missile than any other cause.

The age of surface-to-air missiles had dawned.

It was not that in all the wars that followed the missiles would be the leading cause of attrition but the central role played by the missiles was critical to the success, or failure, of the air campaign – and the result of a conflict as it happened during the Beka'a Valley campaign of 1982 when Israel destroyed almost the entire Syrian Air Defence network, including nineteen SAM batteries, in just twenty-four hours. The Israeli Air Force claims:

The IAF's most stunning achievement in the war was the destruction of the Syrian SAM array in the Lebanese Beka'a Valley, within a matter of hours. This operation was accompanied by a massive air battle, in which 25 Syrian planes – most of them MiG-23s - were shot down. *The Syrian air defense was effectively nonexistent from that day on.*

It is interesting to note that Israel claimed to have destroyed SA-9 missile batteries also which are Infra-Red (IR) guided missiles and do not use radar guidance – raising questions about the credibility of such claims. The Israeli claims again come into question when the 'effectively non-existent' air defences shot down two US aircraft over Lebanon on 4 December 1983, just a year and half after the Israeli operations. The US Navy had launched the strikes against Syrian air defences *after* they had fired at a US reconnaissance aircraft carrying out a mission in support of US Marines in Lebanon. While it may be possible to supress, or even destroy, radar-guided missile systems, it is difficult to effectively supress all ground-based air defences, especially the guns and IR guided-missile systems. Time and again, this lesson was to be learnt by the adversary air forces the hard way. Lebanon 1983 was no exception.

One of the factors that make the suppression of air defences difficult is the deliberate switching off of the systems to prevent them being detected. This was also experienced during the First Gulf War when Iraq selectively used its air defence missiles, as can be observed, in three distinct phases when the coalition air forces suffered losses to the Integrated Air Defences System (IADS). Also, the IADS proved to be more resilient than earlier appreciated: it was suppressed but was at no stage totally ineffective. The reason, as during other conflicts, was the use of AA guns and IR SAMs to continue causing attrition. The tendency to believe that suppressing radars, and radar-guided missiles, is adequate suppression has cost the air forces many an aircraft. Even in this age of the missile, the guns and small arms are a major contributory factor of attrition. This was seen in Afghanistan also, during the Soviet Afghan War from 1979 to 1989. Contrary to popular belief, it was the *Dooshka* (as the 12.7mm DShK heavy machine gun was commonly called) that was the most effective air defence weapon. Stingers came only in 1986 and did cause considerable attrition but the losses to the *Dooshka* remained high.

This raises another issue – the claims of effectiveness of air defence systems, and of SAMs in particular. As with air forces, the air defences also have the tendency of exaggerating claims of kills achieved. A few examples would suffice. Claims made regarding effectiveness of Stingers in Afghanistan are one prime example. First supplied to the Mujahideen in 1986, it was claimed by the US that they were 'shooting down one Soviet aircraft every day' and that the Stingers made the continued Soviet air operations almost an impossibility, leading to their withdrawal in 1989. All such claims are contrary to available facts – if facts as available from all sources are considered. Most, if not all, claims of the Stinger kills were by Mujahideen with no corroborative evidence. The claimed performance was way better than even the performance of trained soldiers under test conditions, whereas the Mujahideen were using the Stingers in combat conditions, under fire from the Soviets.

The claims about the Stinger's performance are open to question as the Soviets were already using flares as early as 1983 when the SA-7 was first used by the Mujahideen. Flare dispensers mounted on the upper fuselage of the aircraft were a standard practice and, by spring 1983, Soviet helicopters and fixed-wing aircraft were routinely dropping decoy flares and altering their tactics as countermeasures to MANPADS. The Stingers were a new element in the war but did not change the nature of air operations and, after an initial spike in losses, Soviet air losses came down to pre-Stinger level. The figures for losses to MANPADS are quite revealing in this – from a high of twenty-seven aircraft lost in 1987, only six were lost to similar weapons in 1988. The lowering of the loss rate was due to better tactics and the adoption of countermeasures by the Soviets. The losses to *Dooshkas*, as percentage of total losses, remained high – almost half of all losses were to 12.7mm and 23mm guns.

Similar exaggerated claims were also made by the British during the Falklands War when the Rapier missile was initially credited with shooting down fourteen Argentine aircraft with six probables. This was later revised to four, with only one of the four as a confirmed kill. Only one Argentine aircraft, a Dagger A of Grupo 6 of the Argentine Air Force (*Fuerza Aérea Argentina* – FAA), was confirmed as a Rapier kill. It was shot down at San Carlos on 29 May 1982. The other three were attributed to the other air defence systems deployed at/around San Carlos – the

Sea Wolf, Sea Cat, Blowpipe and small arms, as well as T (Shah Sujah's Troop) Battery. The exaggerated claims were apparently made to show the Rapier in good light and the revised assessment was not publicly revealed as it 'could have a serious adverse effect on sales' prospects for Rapier, which is the staple revenue-earner for BAe's Dynamic Group'.

The tendency to over-hype a system's performance was again on display in the Gulf War. From the announcement of having destroyed the Iraqi air defences to the performance of Patriot missiles, claims of superlative performance were made. The later campaign in Bosnia and the more recent war in Syria also exemplify the same. The lapse in assessment of a system's performance may lie in the incorrect, or incomplete, analysis of the facts available. Facts, after all, can be read, presented and interpreted in different ways. It depends on (selective) picking of data and facts and the inherent bias that may exist. Taking the case of aircraft 'lost' to air defence systems, it generally includes only the number of aircraft shot down and not the aircraft damaged, although an aircraft severely damaged may not be available for the rest of the war (campaign) and should be considered as a 'loss' for all practical purposes. In the Gulf War, the coalition air forces 'lost' thirty-eight aircraft to Iraqi air defences. Another forty-eight were damaged, making a total of eighty-six casualties. This still represents a negligible attrition rate but the figure of thirty-eight losses does not give the complete picture, however imperfect it may be, of IDAS. Similarly, Patriot missiles were used to counter the Scuds – and were effective, if the initial assessment is considered. The only failure of the Patriot was supposed to be the Scud attack on Dahran, Saudi Arabia, on 11 February 1991 when it did not intercept the incoming Scud missile. What is generally glossed over is that 158 Patriot missiles were fired during the war – and the number of successful intercepts is still not known. Therein lies the problem in technical assessment of its performance although as a psychological weapon it excelled and achieved its aim.

This aspect is important and needs to be borne in mind for the effectiveness of an air defence system cannot be known by crunching numbers only. The number of aircraft shot down does not tell whether an air defence system was effective or not, nor does the number of missiles fired give that. The number of aircraft shot down or damaged is a secondary factor for an air force may still degrade enemy ground forces even after suffering huge losses as the Israeli Air Force did in the Yom Kippur War. A better method may be in assessing the impact the air defences had on the performance of the adversary air force. If it impeded the air operations or degraded the strike missions and *defended* its own forces from being degraded, the air defence system was effective.

Chapter 1

Yom Kippur War 1973

'They forgot that it was not their genius but our failure that handed them victory in 1967 on a plate.'
(Mohamed Heikal, Egypt's Minister of Information in 1973[1])

Egypt and Syria attacked Israel in a surprise move on 6 October 1973. This was a war like none before as it was the first time since 1939 that a country was going to war relying on a ground-based air defence system for control of the air. Realising that an outright win against Israel was not a realistic objective, the aim of going to war was not total annihilation of Israel but a more modest one – to defeat Israel in a battle. As Muhammad Hassanayn Heikal, a member of Nasser's inner circle put it,[2]

> I am not speaking of defeating the enemy in war *(al-harb)*, but I am speaking about defeating the enemy in a battle *(ma'arka)* … the battle I am speaking about, for example, is one in which the Arab forces might … destroy two or three Israeli Army divisions, annihilate between 10,000 and 20,000 Israeli soldiers, and force the Israeli Army to retreat from positions it occupies to other positions, even if only a few kilometres back. … Such a limited battle would have unlimited effects on the war.

The war was a manifestation of the longstanding but unfulfilled desire to avenge the humiliation of the stinging loss suffered during the Six Days War. The War of Attrition had failed to avenge the defeat and, in spite of the massive military aid, especially the surface-to-air missiles (SAMs), the war ended on 7 August 1970 with no change to the frontiers and no real commitment to peace.

Just before the ceasefire and in the days following it, Egypt pushed more SAM batteries into the area along the canal. From a low of fifteen in August 1970, Egypt had forty to sixty SAM batteries by November 1970. The lethality of this air defence layout had been faced by Israel when it tried to use the American ECM pods with its Phantom aircraft to try to avoid the SAMs and lost six of its aircraft in just two days in July.[3] This loss was soon forgotten by Israel and she was to pay dearly for this lapse

The War of Attrition was followed by diplomatic efforts to break the stalemate and give Egypt a honourable exit but, after the failure of these efforts, Egypt realised that the military option was the only way to break the stalemate. As it went about developing its military capabilities, special emphasis was laid on air defences. The Soviet Union supplied Egypt with additional quantities of ZSU-23-4Bs, SA-3s, SA-6s and advanced electronic command, control, and radar equipment.[4]

With the infusion of Soviet military hardware, Egypt had built a formidable air defence and air force with 770 combat aircraft. Over 400 MiG-17s and -21s were the most numerous of fighters with Egypt, besides the 120 Su-7. Egypt had eighteen Tu-16 bombers that were equipped to carry the KELT air-to-surface missiles, giving Egypt a deep-strike capability. In addition, it had ten Il-28 bombers and over forty Il-14 and An-12 transport aircraft. It had a sizeable helicopter fleet with over 140 Mi-4/-6/-8 helicopters.[5] To better defend its air force, Egypt had the aircraft distributed across thirty-five airfields, besides preparing protective hangarettes for aircraft, additional runways, and special teams for runway repair.

The Egyptians had organised their air defence force into a separate air defence command. Egyptian Air Defence forces included approximately forty SA-2 and eighty-five SA-3 missile batteries as well as about forty mobile SA-6 batteries.[6] The majority of these batteries were deployed in a twenty-three-kilometre-wide belt along the Suez Canal, with some batteries providing point defence of the Aswan Dam, Alexandria, and Cairo West air base.[7] These batteries were supplemented by fifty control centres and 180 radar sites. The total number of early warning, acquisition, and fire-control radars was said to have been over 400.[8] There was also an integrated network of visual observers to provide low altitude detection.[9]

The SA-2 and SA-3 were the known component in the air defence network. The Israelis had encountered the SA-2 during the Six Day War and the SA-3 during the latter part of the War of Attrition. The Israelis knew the technical specifications of the two missiles and had their counters in place, with the US-supplied electronic warfare equipment to jam both of them. Plus, the evasive tactics refined by the US Air Force in Vietnam had all been passed on to the Israelis and they were confident that they could operate in a hostile SA-2 and SA-3 environment. The 'unknown' amongst the missile systems was the SA-6, a tracked missile system mounted on a PT-76 chassis with a slant range of twenty-four kilometres. The radar unit had good frequency agility and, more importantly, there was no electronic counter measure (ECM) developed as yet which could jam the SA-6 radar.

Each SA-6 firing unit was based on five tracked vehicles: one central radar unit for both acquisition and tracking of targets and missile guidance; and four launcher vehicles with three ready to fire missiles. The SA-6 launchers were controlled by the radar unit and could not launch missiles independently, except in unguided mode. The launchers were deployed around the radar unit and generally fired a salvo of two missiles (only two of the available twelve missiles being fired at a time).[11] Moreover, each firing unit could engage only one target at a time, thus limiting the overall target handling capability of the SA-6. The biggest advantage of the system was its mobility as it could move along the mechanised units and fire after five minutes of deploying, unlike the time taken by the semi-mobile SA-3 to move, deploy and be ready to engage targets.

An additional element of this command was six to nine squadrons of MiG-21 fighters dedicated to the air defence role and under the air defence commander's control. The low altitude spectrum of this air defence system and the Egyptian front-line forces was covered by in excess of 1,300 pieces of anti-aircraft artillery divided into about 800 ZSU-23 and ZU-23 rapid-fire cannon and approximately 500 57mm guns.[12] The ZSU-23-4 Schilka was the most formidable of the AA guns; based on a tracked chassis of a PT-76 tank (the same as that of the SA-6), it was a four-barrelled gun system that could fire over 4,000 rounds per minute. The Schilka could fire on the move with the 'Gun Dish' radar giving it all-weather capability.[13]

Egypt also had a large number of 85mm and 100mm anti-aircraft guns for defence of its bases and static installations. Lastly, hundreds of SA-7 shoulder-fired heat-seeking missiles went into battle to supplement those already formidable defences, most of which were fitted with infra-red filters that did not react to flares. The Egyptians, moreover, mounted the SA-7 missiles in banks of eight on military vehicles to increase their mobility and rate of fire. These were very effective; as one Skyhawk pilot shot-down said,[14] 'Once that thing gets behind you, it's all over.'

As part of the overall air defence plan, Egyptians constructed 650 individual launcher platforms with dummy launchers and missiles, along with concrete shelters for men and ammunition. Many of the dummy and real sites were manned alternately to confuse the Israelis. In addition, the sites were well protected by embankments and with reinforced concrete structures covered with a layer of sand 4–5-metres thick providing protection from bombs. The SAM sites were assigned three to four ZSU-23-4 Schilka AA guns and detachments of the man-portable SA-7s. The Schilkas were located 200 to 300 metres from the SAM launchers with the Strela-2 positioned at a distance of about five to seven kilometres along the likely low-level approaches to the site.

The Syrian Air Force had about 275 to 360 combat aircraft that included 200 MiG-21s, eighty MiG-17 and eighty Su-7s, with thirty-six Mi-4/6/8 helicopters. Also, a squadron of new Su-20 fighter-bombers was available in Syria.[15] These aircraft had armament similar to the Egyptians. The uncertainty of these figures can be attributed to the large-scale increases acquired from the Soviet Union between April and October 1973. Most aircraft were distributed to eight major airfields in Syria, and these had been prepared for war with one- and two-plane hangarettes, additional runways, and repair crews. Sections of highway had also been surveyed for emergency landings.

Like Egypt, Syria also organised its surface-to-air missile batteries and anti-aircraft artillery into a separate air defence command under the control of Colonel Ali Saleh. This command was built around approximately thirty-two SA-6 batteries and twelve to twenty SA-2 and SA-3 batteries.[16] In addition, anti-aircraft artillery pieces numbering about 900 guns including 160 ZSU-23, 260 ZU-23, and 300 57mm guns provided low-altitude defence. These guns were supplemented by hundreds of SA-7 shoulder-fired missiles. An estimated 100 radars supported this system along with necessary control and command sites.

Added to the arsenals of these major Arab combatants were aircraft from Iraq and Libya. Libya during the war contributed about forty-eight newly acquired Mirage fighter-bombers which were flown by Egyptian pilots in strikes. Iraq operated approximately twenty-five of its MiG-21 fighters in Egypt, starting about one year prior to the war, and deployed MiG-21, Su-7, and MiG-17 aircraft to the Syrian front in support of its ground forces. Immediately just prior to the outbreak of war Iraq also received a squadron of supersonic Tu-22 bombers. The Jordanian Air Force, comprising of two squadrons of F-104 fighters and two squadrons of Hawker Hunters, did not participate in the war against Israel.[17]

Israel had a total of 390 combat aircraft distributed amongst four Mirage squadrons with seventy-five aircraft; four F-4E/RF-4E Phantom squadrons with about 115 aircraft; five A-4 Skyhawk squadrons with 175 aircraft; and an upgraded Super Mystère squadron with twenty-five aircraft.[18] At the outbreak of war, Israel was relatively well equipped to deal with the SAM threat as the Phantoms had ALQ 71, 87 or 101 ECM pods with the passive warning systems. However, the electronic warfare (EW) systems had two operational deficiencies – they were initially not capable of recognising SAM-6 CW radar signals, and they did not have any associated self-defence chaff and flare dispensers. The chaff/flare dispensers were fitted on only a fourth of the Skyhawks, although they did have limited quantities of Shrike anti-radar missiles and first-generation Walleye and HOBO precision guided munition (PGM). These aircraft were deployed throughout Israel and the Sinai on about twenty airfields.[19]

The ground-based air defences included twelve batteries of HAWK missiles, each with six launchers and had an inventory of 400 missiles, deployed in both Israel and the Sinai with about five to six for covering the Suez front. Israel had about a thousand[20] AA guns of 20, 30, and 40-millimetre calibres, used both in static and mobile roles. Emplaced guns were used to defend critical targets, including HAWK batteries. The Israelis used either 40mm radar-directed Bofors or captured Russian built 37mm and 57mm cannon for protection of the air bases.[21] For the field formations, twin 20mm guns placed on an upgraded power-operated

M55 mount, with several hundred of these mounted on modified half-track chassis, were used. In addition, Israel had 300 captured Soviet 37mm and S-60 57mm AA guns and numerous ZSU-2 twin and the ZSU-4 quadruple 14.5mm gun mounts.[22] Unlike Egypt and Syria, the Israeli ground-based air defence systems were part of its air force.

The October War did not start unexpectedly, even though the Israelis were caught unaware, surprisingly, with intelligence being available of a build-up – probably because of too much intelligence. The period preceding the Arab offensive was one of build-up and intelligence gathering by the Arabs. On 18 August 1973 a pair of Egyptian Su-7BMK reconnaissance aircraft crossed the Suez Canal at low altitude and, going deeper by several kilometres into Sinai airspace, turned back. Such sorties were often repeated by the Egyptians under the guise of training flights. Soviet MiG-25s and Tu-16K-11-16 with 'Ritsa' reconnaissance and intelligence aircraft meanwhile were used to locate and pinpoint the Israeli air defence sites in the Sinai. The Soviet MiG-21R and Su-7BMK of 123 Aviation Brigade were also used for this purpose.[23]

As the Arabs were preparing for the offensive, skirmishes did take place with the Israeli forces, the more prominent of which was the incident on 13 September 1973 when twelve Syrian MiGs were shot down by Israel. The previous encounter between the two air forces was in January when Israeli planes attacking radar and military installations in Syria shot down six MiG-21s. The incident reinforced the general consensus in Israel that the Arabs would not launch any offensive, although the Syrian missile system was reportedly strengthened following the incident. In the south, Egypt mobilised a large number of reserves on 27 September, the twenty-third time they had mobilised reserves in 1973. Another group was mobilised on 30 September, and the group of 27 September was de-mobilised.[24] On 2 October, Syria moved forward its bridging equipment, fighter aircraft and SAM batteries. In the south, Egyptian bridging equipment was also observed advancing and crossing spots were being prepared in the Egyptian Third Army sector.[25] The Egyptian Air Force kept up its activities, checking the readiness of Israeli air defences; on 5 October 1973 a single MiG-17 twice invaded the airspace over Sinai, provoking the activity of enemy air defences with a Soviet Tu-16K-11-16 tracking the Israeli radar activity. This continued till the morning of

6 October when a MiG-21R flew along the canal on its regular route. The Arabs had managed to keep up a 'normal' front and were now ready for their strike.

At five minutes past two in the afternoon of 6 October, Egypt and Syria launched a co-ordinated air strike on Israel. The targets attacked in the south by 250 Egyptian aircraft – MiG-2ls, MiG-19s, and MiG-17s – included the Israeli air bases at Bit Cifgafa, El Arish, Ras Nasrani and Bir et-Tamada, command posts, artillery gun positions, ten HAWK missile batteries, armoured concentrations and logistics centres.[26] The Egyptians damaged the runways on at least three air bases besides destroying two early-warning sets and causing some damage to two of the HAWK batteries. Operations at the Rafidim and Bir et-Tamada airports were temporarily suspended while the control centre was damaged, and the communications antenna was shut down for several hours. The strafing Egyptian aircraft were met by intense fire from the AA guns at the air bases but they failed to hit any Egyptian aircraft. The only instance of a serious challenge by the Israelis was at Ras Nasrani where a flight of F-4 Phantoms shot down seven Egyptian aircraft. Otherwise the Egyptians suffered only light losses during the day.[27]

These raids were accompanied by Kelt missiles launched by Tu-16s at artillery and armoured concentrations and command centres in Sinai. Simultaneously two Tupolevs launched Kelt missiles at radar stations in central Israel. The Israeli radars managed to detect the Egyptian Tu-16 bombers in time and alert the air defences with several Kelts being shot down by anti-aircraft (AA) guns but not before two radar stations were destroyed. One of the Kelts fired towards central Israel was shot down by a Mirage while the second fell harmlessly into the sea.[28]

As the Egyptian Air Force was carrying out the strike against multiple targets, Egyptian infantry and armoured forces crossed the Suez Canal as special commando forces were flown in dozens of Mi-8 and Mi-6 helicopters to Sinai to seize control of road junctions, to attack and destroy supply convoys and reserve forces, and to seize strategic points. In the southern sector, an Israeli Hawk battery in the Ras Sudar area identified helicopter waves moving east between Ras Sudar and Abu Rudes. The request of the battery commander to open fire was not confirmed for some time and by the time the permission was granted the first wave of helicopters had already passed. The HAWK battery could only engage the second wave, shooting down one helicopter. A second helicopter, hit by the debris of the first, was also destroyed.[29] The much-vaunted communication and command channels of Israel had also failed.

A second air strike by the Egyptian Air Force had been planned initially but, based on the assessment that sufficient damage had been done, it was not carried out. As the Egyptians were aware of the limitation of their air force, and its inability to provide an air defence cover, the Egyptian army limited the initial bridgeheads to twelve to fifteen kilometres east of the canal, ensuring that the forward most elements were also well within the range of their SAMs on the west bank. The entire plan thus hinged on the restrictions imposed by the air defence umbrella provided by the SAMs – the first time that the ground-based air defences were dictating the operational plans of any army.

By mid-afternoon, the Israeli Air Force had directed its efforts against the Egyptian crossings over the canal although it had expected to first concentrate its effort on destroying the Egyptian air-defence system. But taken back by the sheer speed of the Egyptian operation, the Israeli Air Force was forced to focus instead on the Egyptian ground troops. As the Egyptians were well within the SAM umbrella, Israeli pilots were forced to operate while facing a concentrated fire of not only the SA-6 but of AA guns and the man-portable SA-7 as well. The Israeli aircraft were met by a barrage of AA fire and salvoes of SAMs. The Israeli electronic counter measures (ECM) were only partly effective against the SAM-2s and SAM-3s but were completely powerless against the SAM-6s. The experience was described by a Skyhawk pilot as follows:[30] 'It was like flying through hail. The skies were suddenly filled with SAMs and it required every bit of concentration to avoid being hit and still execute your mission.'

In this, the SA-7s got their first kill, just two hours after the crossing of the canal, of an F-4 Phantom which came in low to attack the Egyptian bridgehead.[31] The SA-6 missiles were the most lethal of all; they had been encountered before, during the last stages of the War of Attrition, but, for most, they were an unknown factor and the pilots were at a loss against them. Adding to their woes was the sheer volume of fire, as if a barrage of missiles had been fired. Faced with the lethal anti-aircraft fire, many pilots dropped their bombs at safer distances, missing the targets altogether. Israel lost at least ten aircraft in the afternoon. Shocked by the unexpected losses, Israel suspended all aerial operations just after 1600 hours and resumed them after an hour with the pilots ordered to strike from a flank, keeping fifteen kilometres away from the canal zone – the outer limit of the Egyptian air defence SAMs.

In the north, Syrian MiGs attacked Israeli Defence Forces' (IDF) positions along the Golan Heights, as well as the forces stationed on the barbed wire and rear bases in the Golan Heights, while its three divisions attacked the Israeli positions. The Israeli air defences, including a HAWK missile battery at Mount Hermon, were taken by surprise and only one Syrian aircraft was shot down in the first wave.[32] Syrian commandos, airlifted in Mi-8 helicopters, assaulted and captured the electronic surveillance outpost on Mount Hermon in a fiercely fought battle, dealing a blow to the Israeli electronic early warning capability in the sector.[33]

Faced with a prospect of its defences crumbling in face of the Syrian offensive, Israel had to fall back on its air force that swung into action to try and stem the Syrian advance. The Syrian air defences had not been neutralised as yet, but the threat was so grave that Israel went ahead with the close support missions.

The Syrian air defences were, however, lagging behind the advancing armour and could only shoot down three Israeli aircraft. Included in this was an A-4 Skyhawk shot down by a SA-2 missile during the attack on Birkat Ram – the first Israeli aircraft to be shot down during the war.[34] The combined efforts of Israeli ground forces and the air force were unable to hold the Syrians who had advanced almost twenty kilometres beyond the 1967 ceasefire line by nightfall.[35]

Operation TAGAR, the plan to supress the Egyptian air defences, was launched on 7 October with raids against Egyptian airfields at Beni-Suef, Bir Arido, Tanta, Mansurah, Shubrah-hit, Genaclis and Kutamich. With the Egyptian aircraft protected inside the hangarettes, all the Israeli Air Force could do was crater the runways, losing five aircraft to the Egyptian defences. This was only the first part of TAGAR – targeting the airfield and AAA defences. The SAMs were yet to be attacked when the Israeli Air Force was asked to shift its efforts and support the ground troops. Its efforts to attack the pontoon bridges and the formations across the Suez also met the same fate. The SAM batteries, especially the SA-6s, took a heavy toll. As the Israeli aircraft tried to evade the SA-6s, they came within the lethal envelope of SA-7 and the AA guns who were no less effective. In all, Egypt claimed to have shot down fifty-seven Israeli aircraft in the first two days, while admitting a loss of twenty-one aircraft.[36] Operation TAGAR had been a failure with the Egyptian air defences, especially its SAM batteries, remaining intact. The Israeli Air Force then generally kept away from the Egyptian air defences for a few days.

The situation in the north was, however, more grim for Israel. Syrian formations threatened to break through the Israeli defences which were thinly held. The Israeli Air Force was called in to try and hold off the Syrian advance, but was met with a determined Syrian air defence network which exacted a heavy toll of Israeli aircraft. One of the close support missions called in at dawn lost all the four A-4 Skyhawks of the first wave to Syrian missiles. The second wave fared no better as it lost all its aircraft, again to the SAMs. The local infantry commander declined to call for any more air support.

As per initial plans, the Israeli Air Force was to carry out Operation CHALLENGE 4 against the Egyptian air defences but, faced with increasingly threatening ground offensive in the north, the Israeli Air Force realised that neutralising the SAM batteries in the Golan Heights area had to be the top priority so that it could have the freedom to support its ground forces. CHALLENGE 4 was thus given up for Model 5 – to target the Syrian air defences. The Model 5 was launched at 1130 hours.

The attack on the Syrian missile batteries was planned to be carried out by the F-4 Phantoms while the AA guns defending the SAMs were to be attacked by the A-4 Skyhawks. During the day (7 October) dozens of sorties were carried out to soften and destroy the Syrian air defences. Unknown to the Israelis, the Syrians had moved most of their SAM and AA batteries in the night. As a result, most of the targets attacked by the Israeli Air Force were locations already vacated by the Syrians. Israel lost six Phantoms during the day, four of them of One Squadron alone with ten more damaged.[37]

Most of the damaged aircraft were hit by ZSU-23-4B air defence artillery guns, which were especially lethal at low altitude. Two crewmen were killed and nine captured by the Syrians.

The operation had been hampered by lack of electronic warfare Bell 205 helicopters which had been placed in Sinai for TAGAR against the Egyptian air defences and could not be moved to the Golan Heights area. To make matters worse, only one SAM battery could be hit during the day.

One tactic used by the Israelis was to 'entice the Syrian missilemen to fire repeatedly at their planes and try and dodge the missiles'.[38] The SAM sites firing the missiles were then detected and located by aircraft behind friendly lines and subjected to artillery fire. This tactic was effective only against the SA-6 which had less range than the improved SA-2 but, as mentioned earlier, even so Israelis could target and destroy only two SAM batteries during the day.

A more effective method to try and attain ascendancy was to attack the Syrian airfields and re-supply columns during the time the SAM batteries temporarily exhausted their missile stocks. Playing an important role in this was the Chukar unmanned aerial vehicle (UAV). Israel had procured twenty-seven Northrop Chukars in December 1971 for this purpose only – to act as an aerial decoy for enemy anti-aircraft systems, making it easier for the combat aircraft to locate and destroy the missile batteries.

The Chukars were launched in the north for the first time on 7 October, towards the Golan Heights, and fooled the Syrians into thinking that a massive air strike had begun against their AA positions. As the Syrian air defences opened up, they were subjected to strikes by air and artillery.[39] Following the failure of the operation, the Israeli Air Force was forced to change its tactics and it did not try again to use its full force on the missile batteries until the end of the war. Only selective batteries, impeding the planned mission flight routes, especially batteries in the northern sector of the Golan Heights, were thereafter attacked to contain attrition to acceptable limits.

While Model 5 was being carried out and was not even two hours into its execution, the Israeli General Staff started receiving reports of a sharp deterioration in the situation of the ground forces in the south as a result of which the air effort had to be diverted to the Suez area. The Egyptians had not only consolidated and expanded the bridgeheads but had attacked the Israeli defences and captured the strongholds of Hatznit, Oracle and Milano.

At 1307 hours the air force was asked to split its attacks on both fronts. Immediately on receipt of the order, the Israeli Air Force began to attack areas on the southern front, including the canal, Shlofa, Budapest, Ismailia, Kantara, Port Said and Pirdan, as well as the bridges on the canal. Coming up against the Egyptian air defences again, the Israeli Air Force suffered heavy losses to the combination of SA-6s and the ZSU-23-4B guns with SA-7 missiles. As the SA-6 had a much better low-altitude capability than the SA-2 and SA-3, the earlier tactics of going low did not help evade the air defences. Plus, the concentration of Schiklas and SA-7s, putting up a co-ordinated fire, added to the overall anti-aircraft fire. The Israelis found the going tough against the Egyptian air bases also as they were better prepared as compared to the Six Days War. The Egyptians bases were now defended by four to six missile sites and batteries of AA guns. The air defence aircraft, on combat air patrol in the rear areas, added an additional tier to the air defences – something not experienced before. Israel carried out forty-four sorties by the F-4 Phantoms, with Mirages as top cover, to attack seven Egyptian bases but faced with determined air defences could not achieve much success. The Israelis lost twenty-two aircraft on day two – most to ground-based air defences. In the Golan heights alone, Israel had lost fourteen aircraft from 272 sorties. Egypt on the other hand lost four aircraft from forty sorties in support of their ground troops.[40]

By 8 October Egypt had built up a considerable force across the Suez Canal with over a dozen bridges acting as the lifeline. Repeated attempts by Israel to destroy the bridges had failed, not only because of severe attrition caused by the Egyptian air defences but because the Egyptians had planned for such an eventuality. If a span of the pontoon bridges was damaged or destroyed, it was soon replaced, putting the bridge back into action. The Israelis lost seven aircraft to the SAMs and AA guns while attacking targets along the canal.[41] It was equally bad while providing support to the Israeli counter-attack launched by two divisions to evict the Egyptian army from their bridgeheads. Not only did the counter-attack fail but two aircraft were shot down by the Egyptian air defences, besides damaging others.[42]

The only success Israel achieved was at Port Said which was not covered by the main Egyptian air defence network. It had its own air defence based on the ZSU-23-4B quad-23mm guns, other anti-aircraft guns, and missiles. Most were these housed in brick-lined, igloo-like shelters banked with sand as protection against blast. The Israelis managed to strike the twin bridges linking the city with the causeway to the south and put them out of action.

Israel had received additional electronic warfare (EW) equipment by the 8th but it was of no use against the SA-6s. They tried instead using decoy balloons of plastic, twelve to eighteen inches in diameter, carried in the ECM pods or strapped beneath the Phantoms. Coated with radioactive reflecting material, they also showed up on radar screens and attracted heatseeking missiles – a method known in the jargon as 'radar echo enhancement'. It had only limited use and the Israeli pilots started using 'jinking', the sudden evasive manoeuvre to evade the SAMs – as practised by US pilots during the Vietnam War. Israeli tactics were to dive onto a SAM battery directly from a great height. As the SA-6 missile is initially slow to accelerate, this manoeuvre had some success as the pilot's manoeuvre only brought him into range of another battery, so that by the fourth manoeuvre, he had lost all altitude and was caught by the ZSU guns.

The Egyptian Air Force on its part launched more attacks on Israeli forward air bases, HAWK missile sites and communication centres during which Israel claimed to have downed seventeen Egyptian aircraft. The situation in the North was marginally better for Israel as the Syrian advance had been contained although the air force suffered a number of losses to the Syrian air defences. With an improvement in the situation, Israel resumed its practice of attacking the enemy air bases and hit the airfields at Hulhul, Nazariah, Sykel, Damir and Blay. So stiff was the opposition by the Syrian air defences that the air advisor to Northern Command informed the commander that, under such circumstances, it was not possible to assist in any meaningful way (*although*) the air strikes would be carried out as required by the ground forces.

By the morning of 9 October, Israel had lost forty-nine aircraft – fourteen Phantoms, twenty-eight Skyhawks, three Mirages and four Super Mystères. The Israeli attempt to recapture Mount Hermon, however, failed in face of stiff resistance by Syrian forces. Syria added a new dimension to the air battle when it launched several FROG (Free

Rocket Over Ground) long-range rockets at Ramat David air base on 9 October. By then Israel claimed to have regained control of the air in the Golan Heights sector with only the ground-based air defences challenging the Israeli Air Force. Israel claimed that even the intensity of SAMs fired had reduced, with fewer missiles being fired.[43]

The FROG attack, however, presented a new challenge and Israel decided to strike at a strategic target inside Syria, for which purpose the General Staff Headquarters in Damascus was selected. In order to reduce the threat of Syrian air defences, the Israeli Air Force decided to route the strike package through Lebanon and therefore first attacked the Lebanese radar station at Barouk, which had been linked to the Syrian air-defence network. Eight F-4 Phantoms from each of three squadrons had been tasked for the strikes of which only the first from 119 'Bat' Squadron reached Damascus owing to heavy cloud cover in the target area.[44] The Phantoms struck the General Staff Headquarters and other buildings. Major Arnon Levushin, the leader of the mission, recounts the mission as:[45]

We approached Damascus, and from above it seemed like a big village town. I felt the silence in the air. It's hard to explain this atmosphere. We were going to attack in surprise – and we succeeded. We passed an anti-aircraft position that rotated the barrels and did not have time to fire, a Strela shoulder missile passed in the air near my plane, and went on, now we are just above the target.

I first entered the forest and the rest … followed me. The surprise was perfect. The sirens do not work before the first bomb hits the heart of the camp. The Phantoms drop the bombs one by one. The vulnerability is accurate. The General Staff buildings are smoky, unmistakable, and now our mission is to move away as fast as we can, the surprise is already behind us, and at that very moment all the huge flak that was there began to spit fire at us from all the tools. The shooting was random without direction, but the quantity did its job: one of our planes was hit directly and fell in Syrian territory.

The Syrian air defences were quick to open up and shot down four of the seven Phantoms although Israel admits to a loss of only one with another damaged.[46] Jordan also claimed to have downed two Israeli aircraft as they traversed its airspace.[47] In a separate incident, Israeli air defences claimed to have shot down five Syrian Mi-8 helicopters as they were being used to land Syrian commandos in the Golan Heights area.[48]

There were reports that, by 9 October, over 1,000 SAM missiles on the combined Syrian and Egyptian fronts had been fired to date and the Syrian SAM-6s ceased firing through 'a near exhaustion of missiles' with the Syrians withdrawing some of their forward launchers to the Damascus Plain.

The Israeli air operations in the south were spread over very large areas: Port Said, Wadi Mahbuk, Mitla, Suez, Dwyer-Soir, Kantara, Firdan, Ismailia, Shlofa, Jedi Junction, Furth-Chronicle, Chinese Farm, Ras-Suder, the stronghold of Budapest and Ophir, with targets including missile batteries and anti-aircraft batteries. Egyptian air defences claimed to have shot down sixteen Israeli aircraft.[49] The day ended with a loss of nineteen aircraft for Israel – the second highest loss in a day since the war had started. Only on 7 October had Israel suffered a greater loss, of twenty-two aircraft, in a single day.[50]

Israelis suffered more aircraft getting damaged by SA-7s as both Egypt and Syria were using their vehicle-mounted SAM-7s, firing them in salvoes of eight at a time, in greater numbers. This firing procedure tended to nullify evasive movement by Israeli pilots and resulted in more aircraft being hit.

The next day, 10 October, Egypt moved more SAM and anti-aircraft batteries, and armour across the canal to beef up its anti-aircraft and anti-armour defences. Israeli air strikes at the bridgehead and other targets in Quwaysina and Abu-Hamed were met with intense air defence fire, shooting down six Israeli aircraft.[51] With the ground situation almost at a stalemate in the south, the Israeli focus during the day was again on the Golan Heights as they carried out 230 air sorties, attacking not only the tactical targets but also air bases and strategic targets in depth. Israel attacked missile sites in Sasa, Tel Shams and the Khmer region, claiming to have destroyed one SAM battery for the loss of an aircraft although the crew managed to eject safely. The helicopter sent to rescue the crew was also shot down by the Syrian air defences.[52]

Unlike the south, the Israeli Air Force was challenged in the air, not only by the Syrian Air Force but also by Iraqi Hawker Hunter aircraft who claimed to have shot down sixteen aircraft, both by fighters and ground-based air defences. Syria on its part claimed forty-three kills.[53] To make up for the losses and the acute shortage of the military hardware, the re-supply from the Soviet Union picked up during the day.

On 11 October consolidation was carried out by both sides along the canal with air strikes by the Egyptian and Israeli Air Forces on select targets. With the situation improving for Israel in the north, the focus was shifting to the Sinai with air strikes on Egyptian armour and infantry in Ismailia and the missile batteries at Port Said. The Egyptian Air Force retaliated with strikes on the area between Qantara and Ismailia. Israel lost two aircraft in Sinai with a helicopter shot down by an air defence missile. In a fratricide incident, an Egyptian helicopter was hit by anti-aircraft fire.[54]

The Golan Heights saw the Israeli ground troops advance, pushing back the Syrians although suffering serious losses both in the air and ground. The air defences continued to take a heavy toll of Israeli aircraft and, although the missile batteries were attacked by Israel, the results could not be ascertained. The next day the Israeli Air Force supported the ground forces in pushing the Syrian formations further back, targeting missile sites and airfields. Sixteen Syrian and Iraqi aircraft were shot down during the day. Meanwhile, the Egyptian Army was expanding the bridgehead, preparing for a breakout. Its air force attacked several Israeli troop concentrations and radar sites.

The Israelis had come to terms with the SA-6 by then, devising new tactics to evade it, using a combination of chaff and a violent jinking action. Spotters were used to pick up the SAM sites so that they could be taken out. The losses meanwhile were adding up on both sides. Israel had reportedly lost seventy aircraft in the first week with losses for Syria and Egypt of eighty aircraft each. Six aircraft were lost by Iraq during the same period.[55]

Jordan entered the war on 15 October with its 40 Armoured Brigade joining the Syrian forces. The heaviest fighting was in the Golan Heights area with a renewed Israeli drive pushing back the Syrians. The Syrian Air Force on its part focused on air defence and generally kept away from the forward areas. Israel lost three aircraft in the Golan Heights to Syrian AA fire.[56] Egypt launched an offensive, breaking out from the bridgehead on 14 October. The Second and Third Egyptian Armies attacked eastward in six simultaneous thrusts over a broad front, leaving behind five infantry divisions to hold the bridgeheads. As the attacking forces did not have SAM cover, the Egyptian Air Force was tasked with their defence. Though the Egyptian forces seized the Khatima, Giddi and Mitla passes, this was to prove a costly lapse as the Israeli Air Force, without having to contend with the Egyptian air defences, could operate freely and support the ground troops. Over 100 sorties were carried out against Egyptian ground troops while the Israeli Air Force also renewed its attacks on the SAM batteries and airfields on the west of the canal. This was exactly as per the Israeli plan which had by then had given up its efforts to push back the Egyptians and instead allowed them to advance – tempt them into an ambush, in an area beyond the air defence cover, and then use the air and armour in a combined operation to destroy the Egyptian ground troops.

The Israeli plan worked, and they caught the Egyptians without an effective air defence cover, giving the air force a free run engaging the Egyptian tanks. The SA-6 batteries that the Egyptians had managed to move across the canal were not effective due to technical reasons – they reportedly had problems in calibration. The Egyptian Air Force had started the day with early morning raids against targets in Sinai, including HAWK missile batteries and electronic jamming stations. The Egyptian air raid in the Beluzah area was met by the HAWK Battery in Abu Samra which fired five missiles, shooting down only one of the two attacking aircraft. In the Golan Heights area, two A-4 Skyhawks attacking a Syrian post on Tel-Hara were shot down by Syrian air defences.

The Egyptians had lost over 250 tanks on 14 October but in spite of the heavy losses, continued their offensive on the 15th only to be met by a buoyant Israeli Air Force which repeatedly attacked the Egyptian formations in absence of any opposition from ground-based air defences. The SAM batteries, on both sides of the canal, continued to be attacked. The losses to SAM had come down to two to three per day by now as the countermeasures adopted by the Israelis were taking effect. In the Golan Heights area, the losses on both sides were far less than before – even the intensity of air activity had come down with Syrian Air Force being on the defensive.

The Egyptians were forced back on the 16th by a strong Israeli counter-attack supported by the air force. The Israeli paratroopers managed to drive a wedge in the Egyptian forces and secure a foothold on the west of the canal. By dawn on the sixteenth, Israel had two battalions (one tank and one paratrooper) on the west bank. Taking advantage of the bridgehead as a launchpad, the Israeli raiding parties destroyed three SAM batteries and some supply dumps.

The idea to raid the SAM batteries by ground troops had come when the Israeli Air Force turned down the request for close air support by the armoured formation across the canal. The air force told General Avraham Adan, the commander of the Israeli armoured division, that 'the anti-aircraft missile batteries in the area made this (close air support) impossible'.[32] It was then the Israeli decided to assault the surface-to-air missile batteries, destroying three of them. Another four SAMs were destroyed by a small Israeli force of twenty-seven tanks and seven armoured vehicles which had moved out on a reconnaissance sortie westward and then southward from the bridgehead.

This had an unintended result as the Egyptians decided to move back some other forward missile batteries to prevent them from being attacked or captured, giving the Israelis an opening to operate in, and not only provide the much needed close support to ground troops but also provide a corridor through which to strike deep inside Egypt.

The move back by the SAM batteries was also prompted by the shelling of the missile sites by the Israeli long-range artillery. The Israeli bridgehead was attacked by the Egyptians using both its artillery and the air force and, in the ensuing air battle, Egypt lost ten MiG-17s to Israeli fighters and ground fire, in addition to ten other aircraft. Egypt on its part claimed to have downed eleven Israeli aircraft during the day. The main opposition to Israeli Air Force during the day was by Egyptian air defences only.[57]

Israel received twenty-five F-4 Phantoms and some A-4 Skyhawks from the US to make up for the heavy losses suffered to date. The military hardware provided included much-needed new electronic-warfare equipment for use against the SAMs. Israel had constructed a bridge across the canal by the morning of the 17th and was able to hold the bridgehead in spite of a strong Egyptian effort to push it back. Israel lost five aircraft during the day to Egyptian air defences. By the 18th, Israel had a division-sized force on the west bank, supported by its air force. Egypt put in all its might to attack the bridgehead, even using armed helicopters but, in face of heavy losses to Israeli fighters and ground fire, could not sustain the effort. With a number of SAM and anti-aircraft batteries destroyed over the past few days by Israeli ground troops, the only opposition to the Israeli Air Force in the air was from the Egyptian Air Force, which was a much-improved force than that of 1967. It claimed to have shot down fifteen aircraft and three helicopters although the Israelis admitted to losing only six. These six were all lost during 'Operation CRACKER 22 – the SAM suppression mission carried out by Israel on 18 October.[58]

The operation was carried out jointly by Phantoms and Skyhawks with the aim of destroying the SAMs deployed in the Kantara area where six SA-2 and SA-3 batteries had been identified with additional SA-6s in ambush deployment mode. The first wave was tasked to supress the AA batteries defending the SAMs, so that the follow-up waves could take on the SAMs. As the first wave approached the target area, the AA guns opened up, destroying two of the F-4 Phantoms. The second wave, of twelve A-4 Skyhawks, suffered a hit from an SA-6, severely damaging it and forcing it to abort the mission. Three more Skyhawks in the wave were not so fortunate as they were shot down by the SAMs. Israel lost three more aircraft and had a couple more damaged before the operation was over. In all, six aircraft were lost and three damaged although the operation was considered a success as Israel claimed to have destroyed all six SAM batteries and freed the area of any missile threat.

Meanwhile Syrian jets attacked Israeli positions in the Golan Heights and, as the Israeli Air Force was focusing on supporting the operations in the south, it was only the air defence forces that offered resistance to Syrian air raids in the Golan Heights area.

On 19 October Israeli ground troops destroyed more Egyptian SAM batteries, creating a gap in the air defence layout and giving the Israeli Air

Force the much-needed freedom to operate. This was contested by the Egyptian Air Force but without any success.

Egypt kept hitting the Israeli bridgehead and, in the ensuing operations, air battles went on all throughout 20 October with Egypt claiming fifteen Israeli aircraft and Israel on its part claimed eleven Egyptian aircraft. Almost all the losses were to air combat as most of the Egyptian ground air defences had been suppressed around the bridgehead area.

Israeli troops expanded their bridgehead on the east bank of the Suez Canal on 21 October pushing back the Egyptian defences further by a distance of twenty-five to thirty kilometres from the canal, along a front almost forty kilometres wide. Its air force claimed to have 'almost total freedom of action', following the destruction of dozens of Egyptian surface-to-air missile batteries. Most of the missile batteries destroyed were the static SA-2s and SA-3s although some of the mobile SA-6 missiles were also destroyed. The main focus of Israeli forces remained destroying Egyptian anti-aircraft missiles as well as engaging and destroying as many enemy tanks as possible.[59]

One indication of the thinning of the Egyptian air defence cover was that by the 21st the vehicles of the Egyptian Third Army had started moving 300 metres apart, from the earlier fifty metres, to minimise the loss to an air strike. By then even the ground troops were well aware that the 'umbrella' protecting them from the Israeli Air Force was no longer effective.

The capture of some airfields on the west bank by Israel helped them bring in supplies and sustain the operations across the canal. Israel claimed to have shot down seven Egyptian aircraft for the loss of three of its own while Egypt claimed twenty-five aircraft. In the north Israel launched a concerted effort to regain Mount Hermon, supported by its air force which had two main tasks – a massive air attack on the outposts and roads leading to Mount Hermon, and the landing of a brigade by helicopters. The entire operation took place in face of stiff resistance by the Syrians who tried to reinforce their positions by moving in reinforcements by helicopters but, after a number of them were shot down, gave in. After a bitterly fought battle Mount Hermon, at times called 'The Eyes of Israel', was back in Israeli control

Egypt lost eleven aircraft to Israeli fighters and anti-aircraft fire while Israel reportedly lost twelve aircraft. As per some sources Israel by then had received forty-eight additional Phantom aircraft and reportedly some of them were even piloted by volunteer reservists or regular United States Air Force (USAF) pilots.[60]

The United Nations sponsored ceasefire came into effect on sundown on 22 October, bringing a halt to the hostilities, only for it to be broken by both sides. Israel tried to encircle the Egyptian Third Army and also capture the town of Suez. In the north Syria tried to advance towards Mount Hermon but was contested by Israeli Air Force. After having encircled the Third Army, Israel agreed to a ceasefire, effective 1700 on 24 October, although its efforts to capture Suez town had been defeated by the Egyptian Army. The Yom Kippur war thus ended after sixteen days of hard, bitter fighting which many a time saw the fortunes of air forces and air defence fluctuate.

Due to relatively high initial loses, the IAF deliberately held back its squadrons during days five to ten of the war to keep its serviceable inventory of fast jets safely beyond a red line of 225 aircraft, the minimum number of serviceable aircraft assessed necessary to maintain air supremacy over Israel. Therefore, the average number of fast jet combat sorties generated during the 1973 war was only about 600 per day, about two-thirds of which were attack sorties. The daily sortie generation was about 40 per cent below pre-war expectations and the effectiveness of attack sorties against static fortified positions was far lower than had been anticipated. By the end of the war, Israelis had launched fifty Mavericks and claimed forty-two hits with five deliberate misses[61] but had managed to destroy only three of thirty-three SAM systems and damage five others.[62] Strafing, so effectively used in 1967, was all but negated by SA-7s fired against Israeli Air Force aircraft that were not yet fitted with self-defence decoy flares.[63]

One major factor that helped Israel achieve air superiority early on in the 1967 war was the spectacular success they achieved in their pre-emptive strikes on Arab air bases. It was not so this time around. It was not that they did not apply the required effort – between 8 and 14 October the Israeli Air Force delivered more than 100 air strikes on Arab airfields, supported by the simultaneous suppression of SAM sites and AA batteries in and around the targets. The attack groups usually consisted of eighteen to twenty-six F-4 Phantoms, Mirages and, sometimes, Skyhawk aircraft. The groups of repeated attacks comprised six to eight aircraft. On 7 October alone, forty-four sorties of F-4s, with Mirages for top cover, hit seven Egyptian bases. Again on the 10th, 130 sorties attacked five Syrian and two Egyptian bases.[64] Yet they did not achieve the desired results, primarily due to better air defences at these, unlike the pervious war of 1967. Most of the air bases were protected by four to six SAM sites and AA guns of varying calibre making them a much more difficult target. Also, the Arabs kept their air defence aircraft on combat air patrol (CAP) in the rear areas. Although not as effective as the Israelis', they had to be countered in order to penetrate to the bases.[65]

Even while operating against the field armies, the Israeli Air Force was not prepared to efficiently suppress the dense SAM array at the beginning of the war and took time to come up with a way to counter the Arab air defences. The task was made difficult by not only the radar-guided AA and SA-7s used en masse to defend the SAM sites but also a lack of real-time intelligence; the SAMs, especially the SA-6, changed their location often. The high mobility of the SA-6s gave them an advantage of re-locating immediately after an engagement to an alternative site. Major General Yahya al-Sanjak of Egyptian Air Defence Forces, who participated in the Yom Kippur War, recollects:[66]

We hit the Israeli aircraft with air defence missiles, and shot them down and then withdraw quickly to another exchange site, and when the other aircraft came to bomb the location of the battalion from which the missile was launched, you cannot find anything by targeting the same battalion from another place ...

The failure of Operation DUGMAN 5 meant that the Israeli Air Force did not attempt another mass operation against SAMs for the remainder of the war.[67] In many cases, when the Israeli aircraft reached the target area, the SAMs would have moved to a new location with the Israelis ending up attacking empty dug-outs. This was more the case in the Golan Heights than in the south. In one instance, when the pilot realised that the SAM site was a dummy and as he attempted to attack a real battery, he was hit at low altitudes by AA guns protecting the site. Following the failure of the operation, Israelis only selectively attacked batteries that disturbed the flight routes, especially batteries in the northern sector of the Golan Heights.[68]

Eventually, it was a combination of air and ground action against the SAMs that gave the Israeli Air Force an opening to provide effective close air support. Only after the armour rolled back the Egyptian SAM defences, did the Israeli attrition rate fall. It was not the Israeli Air Force that 'defeated' the Egyptian air defences but the ground troops. As many as thirty-four missile batteries, about one-half of the Egyptian SAMs defending the canal, were claimed to have been destroyed by the Israeli armoured formations.[69] Unlike the south, Syrian air defences were never truly degraded and denied the Israeli Air Force the freedom of action over the area covered by it. The major drawback was the positioning of the SAMs and the fact that they were not moved to cover the Syrian troops with the progress of the battle. This lapse gave limited openings to the Israelis that were well exploited. Even so, it was more of a stalemate in the Golan Heights area, thanks to the effective air defence cover.

The war saw a very high rate of attrition, though the details of total losses suffered by both sides in the air vary according to different sources. The most common assessment for Israeli losses varies between 102 and 128 aircraft, with the official Israeli accounts giving a figure of 102 to include fifty-three A-4 Skyhawks, thirty-two F-4 Phantoms, eleven Mirages and six Super Mystères, the majority of which were to anti-aircraft weapons.[70] The breakdown, as assessed by US Army Combined Arms Centre in its Study, is as follows:[71]

Cause	F-4	A-4	Mystère	Mirage	Helicopters	Others
SA-2, -3, -6	9	27	1	2	1	–
AAA	9	12	2	4	3	1
SAM & AAA	1	1	1	–	–	–
SA-7	–	2	1	–	–	–
SA-7 & AAA	1	2	–	–	–	–
Technical	4	–	1	3	1	–
Interception	3	–	–	–	–	–
Unknown	3	6	–	1	–	–
Other	2	3	–	1	–	–
Total	32	53	6	11	5	2

(US Army Combined Arms Centre, 'Analysis of Combat Data – 1973 Mideast War')

The majority of Israeli losses, a total of forty-nine came from SAMs, either operating alone or with AA. SAMs alone shot down forty aircraft; of this number twenty-eight were destroyed by SA-6s, making it the most effective SAM with the SA-2 and SA-3 claiming six aircraft each.[72] The number of missiles fired to achieve these kills is estimated to be have been between 2,000 to 3,000; fifty to seventy-five missiles were fired to achieve one kill giving them the same effectiveness as experienced in the Far East.[73] However, the SA-6 fared better with a lesser number of missiles fired to achieve a greater number of kills. Though the US records do not give any details, the Russians claim that the SA-6 shot down sixty-four Israeli aircraft, i.e. about half of the total Israeli aircraft shot down during the war, with just ninety-five missiles. On the first day itself, SA-6s claimed 40 per cent of kills by the Arabs.[74]

The SA-7 was used in large numbers, with some reports suggesting almost 5,000 of them having been fired during the war. About three to six A-4E/H and one Mystère were shot down by the SA-7 with twenty-seven A-4s and one F-4 damaged. The small payload and the limited capability against manoeuvring aircraft made it difficult for the SA-7 to achieve a greater number of kills although its use did make it difficult for the Israeli Air Force to provide close support to its ground troops.[75] The Arab AA artillery did reasonably well with thirty-one kills to their credit, besides damaging many more. They shot down a large number of drones also – Israel lost a total of fifteen during the war: five Chukars and ten Firebees with only two operational Firebees left at the end of the war.[76]

The Arab claims are, understandably, quite different from the generally accepted figure of Israeli losses. Egypt claimed to have destroyed a total of 149 Israeli aircraft by SAMs alone, including 101 aircraft by S-75 with twenty-one by S-125s and only twenty by the newer SA-6 missiles. The other seven were claimed to have been downed by SA-7s. Syria, on its part, claimed a total of 173 kills of which 155 were by SAMs. Again, Syria claimed that the S-75 and S-125 were more effective than the new SA-6 with only forty-two aircraft being shot down by the Kvadrats and the older two missile systems claiming ninety-one aircraft. Syria also claimed that the man-portable SA-7s shot down eighteen aircraft. The exaggeration notwithstanding, the lower number of kills credited to SA-6s is quite contrary to the fact that even Israel acknowledged the SA-6 to be the more potent and lethal of the SAMs.[77]

The details of the kills attributed to SA-2s and SA-3s are as follows:

	Engagements	Number of Missiles fired	Kills claimed
Egypt			
SA-75MK	140	400	90
S-75	29	88	8
S-75M	3	8	3
S-125	61	174	21
Syria			
S-75MK	50	116	26
S-75	60	139	32
S-125	72	131	33

One major failure of Arab air defences was the large number of fratricide incidents. The details of numbers of aircraft lost in these accidents is not known although it is believed that a large proportion of the fifty-nine Arab aircraft lost to 'unknown' causes were due to fratricide.[78]

In this respect the Israeli air defence performed better with HAWKs having more stringent control. They fired only when positive identification was made, thus bringing down the possibility of fratricide.

The Arab losses were quite severe with over 500 aircraft lost during the war, the main cause being air combat. Only twenty-two aircraft were destroyed on the ground with 334 aircraft being claimed by Israel in air combat. Fifty-nine were lost to unknown causes, of which fratricide was a major factor.[79]

Cause	Numbers lost	Remarks
Air combat	334	
Destroyed on ground	23	During raids on air bases
SAM crew served (HAWK)	22	
AAA	78	Including 42 by 20mm AA guns with field formations
Unknown	59	
Other	22	
Total	516	480 fixed-wing and 36 helicopters

Twenty-two aircraft were claimed by HAWK missiles from only thirty-two engagements using sixty-three missiles. In fifteen engagements no kills were achieved although twenty missiles were fired and, in three engagements, the Arab aircraft managed to evade the HAWK missile, suggesting that it could be outmanoeuvred.[80] The AA guns shot down seventy-eight Arab aircraft, of which the majority (forty-two) were by 20mm AA guns with the field formations, but they failed to shoot down any Arab aircraft during the raids on Israeli air bases. They however did shoot down nine of the twenty-six Kelt missiles.[81]

Overall, the air defences performed well during the war with the Arab air defences thwarting the Israeli efforts to use their air force in support of the ground operations on both fronts. In face of the stiff opposition from ground defences, the Israeli Air Force struggled throughout to impose itself on the ground battle.[82] Two reactions by the Israelis typified the acknowledgement of the greater importance of air defences. Firstly, as Eric Weizmann said, the 'missile [had] bent the aircraft's wing' and Chaim Herzog, a career soldier and later president of Israel, who commented in his post-war analysis:[83] 'The role of the plane in war has changed ... *To a degree air power will not be as influential as it has been and will affect the battlefield less than it did.*'

Later analyses have tried to downplay the success of Arab air defences but, as the Patriot was considered to be a success in the Gulf War in spite of its failure to counter the Scuds, the Arab air defences in the Yom Kippur War had given the Arabs a badly needed win over Israel.

Chapter 2

Iran-Iraq War

The Iran-Iraq War was one of the bloodiest and longest wars of the twentieth century with the origins of the conflict going back centuries although the immediate trigger for the long-drawn-out war was the Ayatollah's attempts at fomenting unrest in the Shi'ite regions of Iraq. After several weeks of border skirmishes, Saddam Hussein finally made the decision to invade Iran, launching a full-scale offensive on 22 September 1980 with a pre-emptive strike against ten Iranian airfields and radar stations near the Iraqi frontier,[1] hoping to replicate the Israeli strikes in the Six Day War of 1967. The results were not what Saddam Hussein had expected as the strike caused only minor damage.

It was not that Iraq did not have a well-equipped air force. Iraq had about 300 combat aircraft in nineteen squadrons, including twelve Tu-22 bombers, ten Il-28 light bombers, eighty MiG-23 Floggers, forty Su-7Bs, forty Su-20s, 115 MiG-21s and fifteen Hawker Hunters,[2] making it one of the largest air forces in the region, and much better equipped than the rival Iranian Air Force. But these numbers hid more than they revealed. Poor maintenance with old, vintage aircraft meant that some squadrons had mission-capable rates as low as 20 per cent.[3] Adding to the woes was the shortage of pilots and all that Iraq could muster on the opening day of the war was a total of eighty sorties.[4] Not only was the overall sortie generation rate low, the allocation of aircraft to targets was marred by poor planning. It was as if the entire exercise was of a token effort with just three Iraqi aircraft allotted to strike Tehran.[5]

This was grossly insufficient to make a serious impact. Iraq did manage to destroy some radar stations but the strike on Iranian air bases was a complete failure as the Iranian aircraft, housed in hardened shelters,[6] were left unscathed. Lack of intelligence about the Iranian air bases and wrong selection of weapons to target the hardened shelters were the two main reasons why the Iraqis failed to cause any damage.

The frustration of the Iraqi pilots was summed up by Major General 'Alwan Hassoun 'Alwan al-Abousi;[7]

> I flew several sorties on 22 and 23 September. When we arrived over the Iranian bases, I was looking for aircraft on the ground but could not find anything. Shahrokhi Air Base is large with three runways and many shelters, but there were no aircraft!

It was not a particularly impressive start by the Iraqi Air Force. Moreover, the Iraqi Air Force failed to carry out any battle damage assessment after their initial strikes, as a result of which the follow-on missions were just random strikes with no bearing on the overall aim of degrading Iranian air capability.[8] The lackadaisical Iraqi effort had no impact at all on the Iranian capability. And Iran hit back almost instantaneously, the first counter-strike being launched within two hours of the Iraqi attack. Iran had a modern air force, equipped entirely with over 440 United States aircraft that included 188 F-4G/F Phantoms, 166 F-5E/F Tigers, seventy-seven F-14A Tomcats and fourteen RF-4E Phantoms, plus the 200 AH-1J Cobra attack helicopters with its army.[9]

Leading the counter-attack were the Iranian Air Force Phantom IIs, four of which were the first to strike Rashid, an air base south of Baghdad. This was not the first combat use of F-4 Phantoms by Iran against Iraq as they had been employed previously in August-September, in the run up to the war, and Iran had even lost some to Iraqi surface-to-air missiles.[10] During the raid on Rashid 'not a single round was fired, nor any SAM launched' and the Phantoms exited without any casualties or damage.[11] It was followed up with a strike by another four-ship package against Shoaibah air base. The Iraqi air defences failed to detect the Iranian Phantoms during their low-altitude ingress and offered no resistance at all. This was surprising as Iraq had a sizeable air defence network with over seventy batteries of Soviet SAMs (SA-2, SA-3, SA-6, SA-7, SA-9 and SA-14) and sixty Roland SAM systems. It also had over 4,000 anti-aircraft guns of various calibres.[12]

There were multiple reasons why the Iraqi air defences failed to react. Most of the Iranian pilots had been trained by the United States Air Force and were professionally very competent. They adopted a very low-level flight profile during their approach to the targets, making it difficult for the Iraqi radars to detect them in time. Plus, they attacked the targets from multiple directions, no two aircraft coming in from the same direction. This did not allow the Iraqi air defences to even traverse the guns or the SAMs to lock on to the aircraft.[13]

The major damage caused was at Shoaibah and, following the raid, Iraq moved its newly-received MiG-25s to a base farther west, near the border with Jordan. These were followed up by a further fifty sorties by the Phantoms against targets that included naval and air bases, and two Silkworm missile sites. Iran claims not to have lost any aircraft during the strikes on 24 September.[14]

With 140 combat aircraft, Iran launched a more concerted air attack on 23 September against multiple targets. As Iran did not have any anti-radiation missiles (ARMs), the only way to ensure some survivability from air defences was to fly at very low level, using terrain to mask their approach. This time around they were met by intense, but inaccurate, anti-aircraft fire over Baghdad. Iran lost three F-4Es to Iraqi air defences although Iraq claimed, in an obvious exaggeration, that its air defence downed sixty-seven Iranian aircraft on the first day itself.[15]

In these conflicting claims, what is not disputed is that the Iranian aircraft seemed to have arrived unhindered over Iraqi targets, as if the entire Iraqi air defence command and control system had collapsed or was incompetent.[16]

Even in instances when the Iranian aircraft were detected or reported by the Iraqi air defence network, the main command posts failed to identify the hostile aircraft in time, further degrading the capabilities of the SAMs and AAA to engage the targets.[17] While Iraq failed to cause much damage to the attacking Iranian aircraft, Iran managed to destroy fifteen Iraqi aircraft on the ground and damaged eight air bases.[18]

Iraqi air defences, like the air force, faced multiple problems. The large number of SAMs and AA guns notwithstanding, Iraq did not have adequate number of radars which limited the surveillance capability; long-range detection capability was practically absent. An important target would have a small mobile radar that could detect targets up to fifty kilometres away but that was of no use against the low-flying Iranian aircraft. Poor maintenance and unreliable equipment also meant that the radars were not functional at times.[19] To try and achieve two layers of observation, Iraq maintained a series of visual observation posts for early warning, but poor training made the warning received from them suspect and counter-productive at times. Iraqi air defences shot down sixteen of their own aircraft in the initial days of the war.[20]

Taking advantage of its professionally competent air force, Iran had discovered that a low-flying group of two, three, or four F-4s could hit targets almost anywhere in Iraq. Using this advantage, it carried out a number of air strikes in the initial days, without suffering any major losses from Iraqi air defences. Even in the instances when a SAM was fired, the Iranian pilots were able to avoid them using American tactics developed in Vietnam.[21]

As Iraq found its SA-2s and SA-3s to be ineffective in countering the Iranian Air Force, it moved some of the SA-6s to cover the strategic targets in the rear, leaving both the front-line formations and the strategic targets with not enough missile systems to be an effective deterrent.[22]

As the ingress and egress were both at low level to avoid Iraqi radars and SAM defences, the greater danger to Iranian aircraft was from their own AA gunners who were as well, or as poorly, trained as the Iraqis. Lack of effective command and control, added to the panic that afflicted poorly-trained Islamic revolutionary guardsmen, made the foot soldiers shoot at anything that flew over their heads.[23]

One major air strike during which the Iraqi air defence failed badly was carried out by the Iranian Air Force on 30 September, just a week after the start of the war. Four F-4 Phantoms struck the Iraqi nuclear reactor at Osirak. The reactor building site had a multi-layered air defence cover with an SA-6 battery located about two kilometres to the south-east, three Shelter Roland 2 SAMs sited all around the reactor and about thirty 23mm and 57mm radar-guided AA guns protecting it.[24] The four F-4 Phantoms were able to jam the SA-6 radars only. To avoid the Rolands, the Iranians adopted a low profile while approaching the objective and exited the target area after just one pass. They were able to get back without any loss although they caused only minor damage to the reactor building. The attack, however, again exposed the chinks in the Iraqi air defences.

One reason given for the failure of the Iraqi air defence to react to an Iranian air strike on the Osirak nuclear reactor is that they feared a repeat of the fratricidal incidents on 23/24 September when its air defences had shot down a number of their own aircraft.[25]

With a rudimentary air defence set-up, plagued by poor equipment reliability and manned by ill-trained personnel, such losses were not wholly unexpected. With the risk of fratricide being high, Iraq had adopted a system wherein the areas defended by air defence weapon systems were a free-to-fire zones for those weapons and where the Iraqi Air Force was prohibited from operating. Any aircraft over the designated areas, which included Baghdad and Basra, were assumed to be hostile and the air defence weapons were free to engage them. This made the Iraqi air defence aircraft carry out combat air patrols outside these 'free-fire' areas to intercept the incoming Iranian aircraft within the CAP area. The downside of this arrangement was that the Iranians faced only one defensive tier at a time but, as Iraqi air defence gunners shot down an Iraqi Il-76 aircraft over Baghdad itself on 22 September,[26] it was still the best possible method of exercising control over the air defence system. Another reason was the strict adherence to fire-control measures with the firing by air defence weapons restricted rather than kept free, especially when the approach routes of Iranian aircraft were not known. The following incident, as narrated by Lieutenant General Ra'ad Hamdani, formerly a corps commander in Saddam Hussein's Republican Guard, describes the downside of shutting down the anti-aircraft defences:[27]

I remember an incident in the middle of one battle, when I was on top of a hill and saw two Iranian Cobras [attack helicopters] coming from behind our forces and firing at ground targets. They were flying so low that I could actually see the pilot and his long beard. I gave orders for the ground forces to respond, but they replied [that] they had orders to do nothing, because everything was shut down, so that they could not use their anti-air capabilities.

But as the same report also mentions that the Iraqi soldiers equipped with the SA-7s found it difficult to differentiate a friendly from an enemy aircraft, the only option was to clamp down on the anti-aircraft defences any time the Iraqi aircraft or helicopters were in the air. One report suggesting the dismal state of affairs mentions that a common method employed to alert Popular Army units on air defence duty was to play patriotic songs on the radio. Not having much faith on their capabilities to identify friendlies from the foes, they were ordered to fire only when they saw the missiles being fired at the aircraft.[28]

Following the Iranian air raids in the initial days, Iraq dispersed its aircraft in Jordan and other Gulf states.[29]

The Iraqi air attacks carried out in the early days of the war suffered from lack of intelligence and poor planning and, at times, the Iraqi aircraft returned with their bomb loads as the assigned targets could not be located by them.[30] The losses to the Iranian Air force and the air defences only made it worse.[31] The Iranian air defence forces were equally lethal, although much smaller than the Iraqis. Iran had some 1,800 23mm, 35mm, 40mm, 57mm, and 85mm towed AA pieces with 100 ZSU 23-4 and ZSU 57-2 self-propelled guns.[32] An unspecified number of HAWK and Rapier missile systems were also held by Iraq as were the man-portable SA-7s and about 300 RBS-70 missile systems,[33] but Iranian SAMs were not integrated with Iranian ground force units. Greater reliance on fighter aircraft, in spite of such a large number of weapons systems, was primarily due to the abysmal state of readiness of the SAM system[34] – in any case, no long-range/high-altitude SAMs were held by Iran. By an estimate, Iraq had lost almost 17 per cent of its air force by October.[35] The deep incursions by the Iraqi Tu-22 Blinder bombers against the Iranian cities were also given up when two of them were shot down by the Hawk missile system on 29 October.[36]

These losses, which were in equal measure due to the Iranian fighter aircraft and ground-based air defence weapons, with the fear of Iranian retaliatory attacks, against which Iraq seemed defenceless, made Iraq scale down the air operation, making air operations and use of air defence systems rather low key during much of the early part of the war.

The fear of Iranian retaliation came true as Iranian Air Force F-4 Phantoms raided Baghdad regularly, the raids being carried out by a single F-4 flying at low level with apparent impunity. Iraqi air defences managed to shoot down only one F-4 while the Iraqi Air Force MiG-23s claimed a second F-4.[37]

Holding back the use of air force and limiting its use against selected targets was but an obvious option for Iraq. Here also, Iraq under-utilised its resources as the fear of retaliatory Iranian action remained real enough. This caution was not ill-placed as the raid by Iran on Al-Walid airfield in April 1981 exposed the chinks in the Iraqi air defence network. Located on the border with Jordan, it housed a few transport squadrons and a squadron of MiG-21s, as well Hawker Hunters. Eight Iranian F-4 Phantoms attacked the air base on 4 April 1981 and claimed to have destroyed forty-eight Iraqi aircraft and two radar stations without suffering any loss. Iraqi air defence commanders claimed that the incoming raid was picked up by its radars – but no Iraqi aircraft contested the raid and even the anti-aircraft fire was reportedly weak and ineffective.[38]

In such a scenario, the two sides got down to a series of raids and counter-raids after the initial strike at the strategic targets. Barring a few, the raids/counter-raids were without any strategic or even tactical aim. With its own limited air defences incapable of deterring the Iranians,[39] Iraq was cautious to a fault and continued to be on the defensive, not partaking in any aggressive air actions lest the Iranians hit back. Furthermore, Iraqi pilots were reluctant to attack targets protected by surface-to-air defences or to get into air-to-air combat as a result of which Iraq only attacked undefended and relatively insignificant targets.[40]

With the Iranian air defence radars hardly effective due to a combination of lack of spares and battle damage, it was not so difficult to find such targets, but only if Iraq wanted to do so. Lack of radar cover also meant a lack of early warning for the Iranian air defences as a result of which most of the surface-to-air missiles, the HAWKS and Rolands, were not able to challenge the Iraqi aircraft but, whenever opportunity arose, HAWKS proved to be quite lethal and were responsible for quite a few kills. The only means to provide air defence in such cases were the AA guns and shoulder-fired SA-7s – something akin to the Iraqi situation.

In 1981, the inadequacies of Iraqi air defence were exposed once again when Israel attacked the Osirak nuclear facility.[41] After the air strike Iraq added tethered balloons on 300-metre-long cables with high-tension wires around the site to upgrade its defence but it was too little, too late to make any difference. The Iraqi Air Force was by then reduced to sporadic raids on strategic Iranian targets with no integration with ground forces. The retaliatory strikes by Iran may have been carried out by a token force of two to four aircraft even on important targets but were more effective as the Iranians were more aggressive and had better aircraft, displaying the reach of the Iranian Air Force.[42] The lack of control over its air defence weapons aggravated the problems. Even when attacked by just two to four aircraft, all the weapon systems would fire without any control, filling up the sky with anti-aircraft rounds. Rapid depletion of ammunition was a factor that could not be glossed over and neglected by Iraq and played a major role in determining its use of air defence systems.

Poor performance of SA-2 and SA-3 notwithstanding, Iraqi air defences were not totally ineffective. There are reports which suggest that Iraqis started the practice of anticipatory firing by its ZSU-23-4Bs, forcing the attacking aircraft to fly through a curtain of lead. By one estimate, Iran lost about a hundred aircraft by the end of 1981.[43] During the same period, Iraq is estimated to have lost eighty aircraft, the majority of them to AA guns and HAWKs.

Iraq had approached France for military hardware to shore up its air defences and by the end of 1981 had received the Crotale missile system. At almost the same time it also received the Roland missiles. This move was in part prompted by difficulties faced in integrating and using the Soviet SA-2 and SA-3 missile systems. Infrequent Iranian air raids added to Iraq's problems as it found it difficult to continuously maintain a high degree of alert without burning out the missile electronics.[44]

The new missile systems gave a much need impetus to Iraqi air defences although both the Crotale and Roland were not integrated into a system but were used in stand-alone mode. This could have given the Iraqis the confidence to resume air raids over Iran but, in early 1982, the Iraqi Air Force was repeatedly grounded during purges and was used very selectively against strategic targets and in support of ground forces. In these strikes, Iraq suffered very heavy losses to Iranian air defences[45] – the total losses amounted to 175 aircraft by the summer of 1982.[46] A large number of the losses were avoidable, caused by their own air defences, due to lack of integration between army and air force: while the air force managed the early-warning systems, the surface-to-air weapons were controlled by the army, resulting in frequent system breakdowns.[47]

Iraq had to revisit its policy of selective use of the air force when Iran launched the counter-offensive, Operation FATH-OL-MOBIN (Quranic phrase meaning 'Undeniable Victory' or 'Manifest Victory') in March 1982, forcing Iraq to use its air force against Iranian ground formations. As a departure from the past practice when it hardly used its air force in support of the army, the Iraqi Air Force provided extensive close support carrying out over 100 sorties per day during selected periods, for example, during the battle of Khorramshahr in May 1982. It was not something that the air force was too pleased about and the air support was provided rather reluctantly as the Iraqi Air Force was not too confident about the ground-based air defence forces' ability to ensure security of its aircraft.

One reason for the Iraqi Air force's reluctance was its not too favourable experience in the Yom Kippur War when it had lost over forty aircraft to Israeli Air Force and surface-to-air weapons.[48] The fears of the Iraqi Air Force came true as, in face of intense anti-aircraft fire and the SA-7 with the ground troops, the close support was not very effective and Iraq lost a number of aircraft.[49] To provide air defence for its ground troops, Iran had moved the HAWK missiles and it was these missiles that claimed the majority of Iraqi aircraft felled during the battle, shooting down six aircraft and damaging six more.[50]

The importance of having an air defence cover for the ground troops was once again emphasised when the Iranian advance went beyond the cover of HAWK missile system and, faced with a rout, Iraq decided to apply its air power to try and stem the Iranian forces. With no air force or ground-based air defence to oppose it, the Iraqi Air Force pounded the Iranian armour for thirty-six hours, destroying over 100 tanks. But regretfully for Iraq, even this did not hold the Iranians who evicted Iraq from its positions in southern Iraq. The Iranian Army captured a large cache of armaments left behind by the Iraqis, including an SA-6 battery. It was duly taken back to the rear by Iran who used the captured equipment to study it and develop countermeasures against the SA-6.[51]

Iran did not carry out any substantial close support missions as it had neither an organisation to support such missions nor the required number of aircraft for the task. The Iranian Air Force, however, did carry out limited battlefield air interdiction missions. Moreover, lack of spares was hitting the Iranians badly and they were hard pressed to keep their aircraft serviceable. In time, close support missions by Iran were primarily carried out by the AH-1J Cobra helicopters. Iraq responded by November when the ZSU-23-4B Schilka gun systems were moved forward to cover the field army units and soon they started downing the Cobras.[52] Estimates are that each side lost 250 helicopters in the war, the bulk of these to the Soviet ZSU 23-4 23mm system.[53]

The battle of Dehloran, ending in its recapture, was another successful operation for Iran and had a major impact on the air battle as the Iranians re-activated and improved the radar and SAM sites at the Dehloran heights, co-ordinating the SAM nets and anti-aircraft artillery with the Iranian Air Force, resulting in downing of at least twenty-seven Iraqi aircraft between March and June 1982 in the Dehloran theatre alone.[54] The Iraqi Air Force suffered a further loss when it was tasked to attack Iranian troop concentrations and air bases in April 1982. The ZSU-23-4B anti-aircraft guns and the shoulder-fired SA-7s shot down at least twenty Iraqi aircraft and helicopters.[55] Iraq was down to about 175 aircraft at this stage, including the Mirage F-1s.

The Iranian offensives in 1983 failed to achieve any substantial success, relying on more massive 'human wave' attacks.[56] The Iranian Air Force, with no more than seventy operational fighter aircraft at any given time, was of no support to the Army and it was again the helicopters that provided the close air support, a number of them being lost to the Schilkas. Not being able to make any headway, Iran refined its tactics with time to negate the Iraqi advantages of heavy firepower and having defence in depth, by carrying out assaults in marshy and hilly areas. These were regions where Iraq could not effectively employ its armour and heavy artillery. This change yielded favourable results as Iran made rapid gains. With a numerically smaller army, Iraq resumed the air offensive in January 1983 but lost over eighty aircraft while destroying only forty of Iran's.

In 1984 Iran launched Operation KHEIBAR with the aim of capturing the Basra-Baghdad highway, cutting off Basra from Baghdad and setting the stage for an eventual attack upon the city. The operation was launched through the Hawizeh marshes which were crossed by the Iranians using motorboats and transport helicopters in an amphibious assault. The vital oil-producing Mainoon Island was attacked by landing troops via helicopters onto the islands and severing the communication lines between Amareh and Basra. The Iraqis responded in kind but lost eight helicopters in the operation. Iran had captured the islands by 27 February but suffered a serious setback as the Iraqi Air Force shot down forty-nine of fifty Iranian helicopters transporting Pasdaran troops.[57] As Iraq was unable to launch successful ground attacks against Iran, it used the now expanded air force to carry out strategic bombing against Iranian shipping, economic targets, and cities to damage Iran's economy and morale.

The Iraqi Air Force had been strengthened by 1985 with Iraq becoming the first country outside the Soviet Union and Czechoslovakia to receive the Su-25 Frogfoot and the first outsider to receive the MiG-29 Fulcrum. The Soviet MiG-23s and Su-17/20/22s, as well as the Chinese F-7s, enabled the Iraqi Air Force to renew the air offensive although its efficacy was marred by the tactics adopted by Iraqi pilots. To avoid the Iranian air defences, Iraqi pilots flew at 10,000 to 20,000 metres, effectively degrading the bombing effort as the desired ordnance release altitude was between 1,000 and 3,000 metres. The Iranian air defences may not have been very successful against the high-altitude Iraqi air intrusions but they continued to chip away at the Iraqi Air Force and limited the damage caused by the Iraqi air raids.[58] The continued attrition resulted in unilateral cessation of air raids, not to be resumed until 1984 when Iraq received the Mirage F-1s from France. The arrival of the Mirage F-1 and the associated weapons systems, however, added a new dimension to the air war – and air defence. Included in the military aid package were the AS-30L air-to-surface missiles and Exocet missiles that gave the Iraqis the capability to hit targets from stand-off ranges, beyond the reach of Iranian air defence weapons. The Iraqi attacks on Kharg Island using the AS-30 laser-guided bomb for the first time in August meant that the Iranian air defences were not able to counter the Iraqi air raids.

Faced with the new stand-off threat, and fearing for the defence of its capital, Iran moved back some of its air defence systems from its key oil installations in order to beef up the air defences of Tehran.[59] The move back of Iranian air defence systems resulted in Iraq suffering lower losses during the follow-up attacks on Iranian installations. This was partly due to use of the newly-acquired electronic warfare systems by Iraq. The air defence system most targeted with considerable success by Iraq for degradation was the I-HAWK system.[60]

With the armies deadlocked in a stalemate with limited gains, the degraded Iranian defences meant that, from then on, the improved Iraqi Air Force played a more visible, and effective, role.

Its renewed offensive on Iranian population centres led to the 'War of the Cities' in 1985. The results of its action were telling on Iran and were having the desired political effect. Iraq used Tu-22 Blinder and Tu-16 Badger strategic bombers, escorted by Mig-25 Foxbats and Su-22 Fitters, to carry out the long-range raids on Iranian cities, including Tehran. With its air force weakened by losses and lack of spares, Iran deployed, first, the F-4 Phantoms and, eventually, the F-14s to combat the Iraqis. Carried out in a now-on-now-off manner, it was a tactic of putting pressure on Iran and yet staying out of the reach of Iranian defences to contain its own attrition although its losses continued to mount. The gaps in Iranian air defences meant that there were enough 'blind spots' that could be used for ingress by Iraq and, as there were not enough air defences to fully protect all cities, the raids manged to hit the population centres, which in any case did not require precision strikes. The air defences at some of the centres, notably Arak, Ahvaz and Tehran, however, did take a heavy toll of Iraqi aircraft.[61] The losses notwithstanding, the raids succeeded in achieving their aim of pressurising Iran.

The retaliation by Iran caused serious damage with the raids on Baghdad and other cities resulting in deaths of thousands of people. On the battlefield, the two sides were still caught in a stalemate and it was only in 1986 that Iraq, enthused with military and financial aid, decided to go on an offensive, the first of which was the attempt to retake Majnoon Islands, failing which Iraq went back to the 'War of the Cities' in March. The Iranian response was the use of Scuds for the first time to target Iraqi cities.

To beef up its air defences, Iran revised its tactics, creating killing fields by integrating interceptors and SAMs. The supply of new air defence weapons like the 200 RBS-70 missile system illicitly acquired by Iran and the supply of HAWK spares under the Iran-Contra deal meant that Iran once again had an effective air defence system.[62] The supply of HAWK spares to Iran meant that Iran still had a potent, and working, air defence system and it continued to take a toll of Iraqi aircraft. Iraq reported losing nine aircraft to the HAWK system during the Al-Faw offensive alone, with over forty aircraft falling to the HAWK during the entire duration of the war.[63] The supply of spares did not last long, however, and, again, Iran found it difficult to maintain the Hawk missiles system. This had a direct effect on its capability to provide an effective air defence – leaving the skies free for the Iraqi air force.

Iran launched the Al-Faw offensive in 1986 across the Shatt al-Arab river aiming to capture the strategic Al-Faw peninsula, which connects Iraq to the Persian Gulf. The Iranians defeated the Iraqi defenders, capturing the tip of the peninsula, including Iraq's main air control and warning centre covering the Persian Gulf. Iraq could not use its air power effectively during the critical initial phase of the battle due to inclement weather and it was only after 14 February that it could carry out air strikes against Iranian targets, taking heavy losses in the bargain. Iraq lost fifteen to thirty aircraft during the first week of Wal Fajr 8 while Iran claimed to have shot down roughly seven Iraqi fighters a day, mostly by the ground-based air defences even as Iraq claimed to have shot down several of Iran's remaining F-4s. One reason for the high rate of Iraqi losses was their practice of attacking at unusually low altitudes.

Wal Fajr 8 was followed by another offensive, Wal Fajr 9, against the Kurdish area of Iraq while its main forces were still involved in the attack on Al-Faw. Iraq on its part launched a major counter-attack but, after the Iraqi attack on Majnnon failed, it turned back to use of air power, launching a new wave of bombing, extending the range of its air strikes against Iran's oil targets, including a raid the Iranian facilities at Sirri Island for the first time. On its part, Iran countered by firing its first Scud missile at Iraq in thirteen months, evidently targeting the Iraqi refinery at Dowra.

The much-weakened Iranian forces got much needed fill-up as they received the Chinese-made SA-2 surface-to-air missiles in 1986 along with twenty Contraves Skyguard anti-aircraft fire-control systems from

Switzerland. These were, however, not enough to secure Iran from the Iraqi Air Force which continued to fly long-range attack missions. All Iran could do was carry out a limited number of attack and air defence sorties, although largely unopposed, with few successful kills of Iraqi aircraft. The Iraqi use of its air force was still not strong enough to yield decisive results.

Iran received 235 HAWK assemblies by November 1985 but it did not have a major effect on the Iranian capabilities initially as it did little to stop or inhibit Iraq from continuing its air raids. One target of the Iraqi raids in November was in fact a HAWK missile site near Dezful. Iraq though lost as many as ten aircraft in November with Iran claiming that nine out of ten of its surface-to-air missiles scored kills.

The most likely reason was that the US arms shipments were finally allowing Iran to make its HAWK defences more effective. The improvement in Iranian defences was apparent in keeping the Iraqi Air Force at bay as they tried to attack Kharg Island, suffering increasing losses to HAWK missiles.[64] The Iranian Air Force, on the other hand, was reduced to as few as forty fully-operational fighters capable of air defence missions, and a total of eighty to a hundred operational aircraft. The worst affected was the F-14 fleet, of which only seven were reportedly operational, none with functioning radars.

Iran launched a new offensive called Karbala 4 on the night of 23/24 December but suffered reversals although it did not stop its efforts to launch new offensives, Karbala 5 and 6. Karbala 5 was directed against Basra while the next offensive, Karbala 6, was directed against the area north of Baghdad between Qasr-e-Shirin and Sumar. Karbala 5 was by far the most important of these offensives, aimed to strike across the border near Basra, cutting off Basra and Faw from the rest of Iraq.

To contain the Iranian offensive, Iraq did not hold back its air force and carried out extensive close support missions. These were strongly countered by Iranian air defences who shot down fifty Iraqi aircraft during the first two months of 1986 – about 10 per cent of its operational force. The re-activated HAWK units positioned in Kharg Island and in the rear of its forces attacking Basra seem to have proved rather effective in blunting the Iraqi air offensive.[65]

The Iranian pressure on Basra was severe enough to force Iraq to revive the 'War of the Cities'. Iran could do little to retaliate except launch more Scud attacks giving Iraq a limited victory, though it came at a considerable cost as it lost sixty-nine aircraft by the end of January. As Iran rarely flew air defence sorties, most of these losses were to short-range air defences and a mixture of maintenance problems and pilot error. Iraq lost three more aircraft in February – at least one to a surface-to-air missile. Iran had only a limited number of operational strategic surface-to-air missile units and, as a result, it was only the HAWK that offered some modicum of resistance, claiming a number of Iraqi aircraft flying at high altitude.[66]

The Karbala offensives were the last major land offensives by Iran in 1987 and their failure marked the end of its attempts to win the war. One major reason was the large number of casualties and the growing public pressure which restricted the options available to Iran. Things were bad for Iraq also which had lost at least seventy aircraft since the beginning of Karbala 4 with average losses going up to seven aircraft in a week. More critical than the aircraft was the loss of trained pilots that Iraq could ill afford to lose. Accordingly, it scaled down its air operations when the Iranian offensive had run out of steam.

Lack of precise and detailed data about the weapon performance makes a realistic and accurate assessment of the air defence systems difficult, although the available information suggests that the most effective ground-based air defences during the war were anti-aircraft guns, and short-range air defence systems including man-portable missile systems. Comparably, the large number of medium-range missile systems deployed by both Iran and Iraq were not effective. The SA-7 was the most widely used missile system and, even though the vast majority of the missiles fired did not hit a target, its performance was reportedly better than that of the SA-2 and SA-3 in the Yom Kippur War as one kill was obtained per twenty-to-thirty missiles fired as compared to fifty-to-seventy missiles fired for a kill in case of SA-2. However, it needs to be remembered that this kill rate had more to do with the low-level tactics used by the aircraft and the widespread proliferation of such missiles than the actual efficacy of SA-7. Still, it forced the helicopters to fly higher, bringing them in to the range of ZSu-23-4B gun systems. Similarly, it limited the ability of aircraft to fly over target areas long enough to identify and hit targets effectively. The weapon systems were used more in stand-alone mode, rather than as part of an integrated network. This degraded their efficacy and made intrusions by enemy aircraft that much easier.

Iran had the more effective HAWK surface-to-air missile system but its use was curtailed due to lack of spares – and effective use of electronic-warfare equipment by Iraq. Only with the resumption of supply of spares under the Iran-Contra deal was Iran able to put the HAWKs back into use in 1986–87 with disastrous results for Iraqi pilots. Even so, it was used for point-defence and not as an integrated weapons system which limited its overall effectiveness. The most widely used SAM was the SA-7 and the locally assembled copies of the same were available in large numbers and were more effectively used by Iran. Cordesman even refers to it as an area defence weapon because of its widespread use although it was a point-defence system. Iran had a limited quantity of Short Tiger Cat SAMs and Oerlikon cannon to defend its air bases, but their performance is not known.

Anti-aircraft guns were widely used by both sides, more to degrade effectiveness of the opponent's air-to-ground operations than to destroy the aircraft. They were extensively used in an anti-personnel role also. The most effective of all the anti-aircraft guns was the ZSU-23-4B gun system which was equally effective against attack helicopters. Both sides continued to build up their anti-aircraft gun inventory through the war. Iraq increased its inventory from about 1,200 guns in 1980 to over 4,000 in 1985. The main source of anti-aircraft artillery (AAA) were China and the Soviet Union, with China alone providing over 1,100 57mm Type 59 and 14.5mm (ZPU-4) guns between 1983 and 1988. The AAA was used for both the field army units and at the major economic and military installations. The twin-barrelled 23mm AA guns were frequently used at defensive strongpoints and near headquarters in direct fire roles.[67]

The 118 57mm AA guns supplied by Hungary also added to the anti-aircraft capability of Iraq although they were used in a dual role against ground targets as well. Similarly, Iran had 1,900 anti-aircraft guns in 1980 which increased to over 2,800 in 1988.[68]

The increase in anti-aircraft guns did not deter the much-weakened Iranian Air Force from continuing with their tactics of low-level air attacks, albeit with limited success. To counter this, Iraq purchased the mobile low-altitude SA-8 and SA-13 surface-to-air missile systems, deploying the SA-8 in the rear areas to cover the corps and divisional headquarters and the SA-13 with the front-line formations although it had numbers sufficient for only armoured division only. The Rolands were deployed at the air bases and the chemical production plants at Al Qaim and Samarra.[69]

The long-drawn-out war did not have the air forces and, as an extension, the air defences play a major role, but even the limited use of air defences bring out some relevant lessons. It is not only the air defence weapons that determine the efficacy of an air defence system but equally important are maintenance, ensuring adequate spares and training, as also the seemingly simple and unimportant air recognition procedures.

A unified command-and-control system over entire air defence resources is important to ensure its optimum performance. The Iraqi practice of having the air force control the early-warning radars while putting the missile systems under army control undermined the overall efficacy of air defences with disastrous results. The designation of 'free to fire' areas and keeping the air force away from such zones may have been necessary to control fratricide but it effectively degraded Iraq's air defence capability by half.

The basic lesson that can be drawn from the war is that merely having a large inventory of modern air defence weapons does not add up to an effective air defence system.

Chapter 3

Soviet Afghan War

On 25 September 1986 a group of specially trained Mujahideen fired Stinger surface-to-air missiles at three Mi-24 Hind gunship helicopters as they came in to land at the Jalalabad airfield. While one helicopter fell stricken, a second was damaged but managed to land. This was the first time Stingers had been used in the long-drawn-out war and for many analysts it marked an important milestone when the Soviet control of the air was seriously challenged for the first time and forced the USSR to withdraw from Afghanistan. Some have called it the 'Stinger effect' but like all claims about wars and warfare, the claim is more smoke and mirrors.

The Soviet Union invaded Afghanistan in December 1979 to extend support to the puppet regime of Babrak Kamal and, like all invaders, got caught up in the quagmire of Afghanistan, only to stay on for almost a decade. Considering the size and spread of Afghanistan, the Soviet military presence was not large. Coupled with the low military presence, the terrain necessitated the extensive use of aircraft for almost all operations and, with the mountains and winding valleys spread all over, it was the helicopter that was to play the more important role in air operations.

The regular motor rifle units that had moved into Afghanistan suffered heavy losses in the first year and were replaced with additional airborne units in 1980 as Soviets changed to a more offensive strategy, adding more airpower to support the ground operations. The Soviet Air Force had a modest presence in Afghanistan in 1979–80 with about 130 fixed-wing aircraft and sixty helicopters but, with increasing reliance on helicopters, their number soon increased to over 300 and they were being used for almost all operations.[1] The most common helicopters were the Mi-4, Mi-6, Mi-8s, and the Mi-24 gunships. The fixed-wing aircraft inventory also increased with the introduction of several squadrons of

MiG-21s and Su-17s. The Soviets tried out many aircraft in Afghanistan, including the Yak-38 and Su-25 Frogfoot.[2] Of these latter two, Frogfoot saw extensive service and earned a reputation for being a sturdy and dependable close-support aircraft.[3] However, the aircraft of choice was the Mi-24 gunship which became the most feared weapon system for its formidable firepower. It was used by both the Soviets and the Afghans, and usually operated in pairs with one Hind attacking the Mujahideen while the other kept a watch for any hostile fire. Depending on the target, the number of Hinds could increase from four to eight for continuous attack on the objective.[4]

With an extensive use of and reliance on both the fixed- and rotary-wing aircraft, control of the air was vital for the success of all Soviet operations and, in the initial phase of the occupation, there was not much of an opposition to Soviet air operations by the Mujahideen. The tactics employed by the Soviets in the early days of the invasion do not reveal fear of any anti-aircraft weapons as small arms were the best that the Mujahid could use.[5] The low threat level made the Soviet pilots adopt reckless tactics at times as evident in the practice of establishing a high orbit over the target area. With an effective anti-aircraft weapon in the hands of the Mujahideen, that would have proved to be suicidal for the Soviets.

Armed only with small arms and heavy machine guns, the only effective method available to the Mujahid to inflict attrition was to attack air bases, using RPG-7s and mortars. The Mujahideen did achieve some success during such raids but it was not a serious threat – as yet. On the other hand, the extensive use of Mi-24 gunships gave an edge to the Soviets and was proving to be the most valuable weapon in their arsenal. It was much feared and respected by the Afghans as the Soviets used them extensively and ruthlessly against the Mujahideen with 'its firepower and mobility and initial invulnerability putting the guerrillas on the defensive'.[6]

What the Mujahideen lacked was a weapon to take on the Hinds although it was not long before the situation changed with the influx of SA-7s and heavy machine guns. These were first provided by China and Pakistan in June 1980 when the missiles were delivered as part of a military aid package given by China, routed through Pakistan.[7] The availability of SA-7s to the Mujahid meant that, for the first time, they had a weapon that they could use with ease and inflict attrition. The SA-7 was quite effective at first and shot down a number of aircraft. A first-generation air defence missile system, the SA-7 Grail had limited capabilities only against slow-flying aircraft and was prone to rudimentary counter-measures like flares. Even in case of a direct hit, its rather small warhead (only 1.17kg including a 370gm TNT charge) meant that the damage caused was not necessarily fatal. Yet the missile was a serious enough threat as it was easily portable, could be used by almost any trained person, under almost all conditions anywhere, and did not require any technical expertise or a large support system. The early kills achieved by the SA-7 were partly due to the poor tactical training of the Soviet pilots as they failed to adapt and change their tactics in view of the new threat.[8]

As the losses to SA-7s mounted, the Soviets started flying low, adopting a nap-of-the-earth(NOE) flight pattern though it had an unexpected consequence – a spate of accidents followed as the crews were not trained for NOE flying in mountains.[9] A common enough accident was the tail rotor hitting the ground but soon the Soviets learnt how to handle the helicopters in the narrow, winding valleys.

One of the simplest and most effective measures adopted by the Soviets was the installation of rear-view mirrors in the helicopters, which allowed pilots to monitor the rear hemisphere to detect the SA-7s and take evasive action. As a result, the Mi-8's vulnerability from attacks by SA-7 reduced almost by half. Additionally, exhaust deflecting skirts were installed on the engine nozzles to disperse the hot stream of exhaust gases, thereby reducing the heat signature of the helicopters and their vulnerability to the SA-7s.[10]

Another change was the adoption of flares as a defensive measure by Soviet aircraft and helicopters although the larger transport aircraft were not yet fitted with the defensive suite and remained vulnerable to the man-portable missiles. The Mujahideen were quick to note this vulnerability of the transport aircraft and targeted the lumbering aircraft more than the helicopters.[11]

Although the SA-7 was now available to the Mujahideen, the most common anti-aircraft weapon in their arsenal remained the 12.7mm DShK and 14.5mm KPV heavy machine guns. These were relatively elementary anti-aircraft weapons but could be very dangerous at low level, especially below 4,500 feet. The Mujahideen were quite proficient in using them to carry out ambushes and scored quite a few hits as well. The overall impact and the attrition caused was rather limited, however, as the Mujahideen were woefully short of the heavy machine guns with only thirteen in the entire Panjshir valley in 1982. It was only by 1984 that the Mujahideen could build up their inventory of anti-aircraft machine guns with supplies coming in mainly from China and the number of heavy machine guns in the Panjshir valley alone went up to 250 by the end of 1984.

The normal tactic of using these weapons was to fire them from ambush sites, e.g. from caves against passing aircraft, from mountaintops downwards or from fire positions sited away from the target on likely approach routes. The Mujahid, at times, used to offer bait to lure the Mi-24 gunships into an ambush. One of the favoured air defence ambush tactics was to deploy the heavy machine guns into caves along the walls of canyons. As the helicopters would fly down, through the canyon, the machine guns were used to fire across it, filling the air with bullets, trapping the helicopters in crossfire.[12]

The Mujahid positioned mountain air defence mounts and heavy machine guns, such as the DShK, on the commanding heights, occupying the most important position in the Mujahideen fire plan. As the air defence weapons were the prime targets for the Soviet helicopters, the Mujahideen camouflaged the heavy machine-gun sites and built trenches that resembled vertical mine shafts to protect them. The DShK positions, although camouflaged, had no permanent overhead cover so that it could fire at both ground and air targets. Often these positions were made of concrete and had special slit trenches to protect the personnel. Main positions were connected by slit trenches on all sides and were used to protect personnel from aircraft and helicopter gunship attack. To protect the anti-aircraft weapons, they were kept in special fortified hidden positions and moved to the firing positions only when necessary. As these fixed sites were not suitable to engage all targets, the Mujahid resorted to man-packing the machine guns and engaging the aircraft from alternative sites. Salvo fire from small arms, using improvised mounts, was used to amplify the effect of the heavy machine-gun fire. These were deployed, dispersed, and echeloned in lines to subject the aircraft to continuous fire from different direction, opening up on a given signal when an aircraft or helicopter was on a bombing run, or when they were pulling out from a bombing run. In order not to give away their positions, tracer ammunition was not used.[13]

One of the more successful uses of the Dooshkas by the Mujahideen was carried out in the early years of the war in the Kale Kanesake valley.

In July 1982 Soviet troops carried out a raid on a Mujahid base in the Kale Kaneske canyon. Three Mi-24 gunships took the Mujahids by surprise as they flew down the canyon. The DShKAs sited on the high ground were not able to engage the Hinds and it was only when they were manhandled and fired off-the-shoulder were the Mujahids able to hit the Hinds, bringing down one and damaging another. The incident is described by the local Mujahideen commander thus:[14]

> At noon in July, about a month after the DRA officer's visit, three Soviet helicopter gunships suddenly flew down the canyon and fired at the caves and structures of our base. Our DShK machine guns were all positioned on the high ground and could not engage aircraft flying below them in the canyon. The gunships were severely damaging our base. Khodai-Rahm was one of the DShK gunners. Physically, he was a weak person, but he took the 34-kilogram weapon off the mount, hoisted it on his shoulder and fired down into the canyon. He hit two of the helicopters, one of them in the rotors. That helicopter gunship climbed to the top of the mountain and then the rotors quit turning. The pilot baled out, but he was only 50 meters above the mountain and he and the helicopter crashed onto the mountain southern wall near the interior mouth of the canyon. The second damaged helicopter managed to escape, while the third helicopter attacked the Mujahideen DShK gunners. Khodai-Rahm was killed by the third helicopter.

The shooting down of the Hind could not be celebrated for long as Soviet fighter-bombers came over and started bombing the Mujahid base. They were followed by Soviet troops who landed about three kilometres away. A pitched battle went on for eight days after which the Soviets withdrew having inflicted heavy losses.

One flaw in the Mujahids' siting and use of the Dooshkas during this particular battle was that the heavy machine guns were not dug in along the canyon walls for then they could have been able to fire across the canyon, inflicting heavier casualties on the helicopters. For the damage these heavy machine guns could cause, they were always a prized catch for the Soviets and some of the raids were specifically carried out to seize them. As Ahmad Jalali, a Mujahideen commander recollects,[15]

> We had brought a number of heavy anti-aircraft machine guns into the area, particularly the 14.5mm single-barrelled machine guns. The enemy was concerned about the presence of these air defence weapons. One of the objectives of the offensive was to seize our air defence weapons that were becoming a hindrance to their air raids.

The raids to seize and confiscate the Dooshkas being not so common an occurrence, the preferred tactic was to supress the anti-aircraft Dooshkas using a team of Su-25s and Su-17s. The Su-25 Frogfoots had been introduced in Afghanistan in 1980 and were first used operationally soon after arrival in the country. Developed as a specialised *Shturmovik* armoured assault aircraft to provide close air support for the Soviet ground forces, Afghanistan was in a way the proving ground to test, evaluate and refine the aircraft. After the successful evaluation during Operation ROMB, the Su-25 became as successful and feared as the Mi-24 Hind. It enabled the Soviets to expand their area of operations due to it providing better and more effective air cover for the ground troops than any other fixed-wing aircraft. The first Frogfoots were located at Shindand and operated with two 800-litre external fuel tanks to extend their range with the S-24 rocket being the payload of choice for use against the Mujahids.

Initially it was seldom used alone and usually operated with the Su-17 Fitters against pre-planned targets. The Su-17s were used to detect and mark the targets with smoke bombs and strafe the Mujahid positions to supress the anti-aircraft weapons, especially the Dooshkas. The Fitters were followed by Su-25s to drop bombs on the targets marked by the smoke bombs.[16]

The Su-25 with its tremendous firepower came to be feared and respected by the Mujahideen, the only aircraft to command this respect alongside the Hinds. With time the Mujahids had to adapt and change their tactics and work out new methods of countering the threat.[17] The Su-25 was a frequent target for Mujahideen anti-aircraft fire and surface-to-air missiles and suffered some hits from ground fire but the first aircraft was not shot down until January 1984.

Facing a challenge in the air for the first time, Soviets took some time to adapt and change. Even after the Mujahedeen had started using the heavy anti-aircraft machine guns, the Mi-24 pilots would press on with their raids in ravines and narrow valleys where the threat of anti-aircraft fire was high. Partly out of a false sense of security in their armoured gunships, the Hind pilots continued with the attacks in face of the ack-ack fire. Due to lack of space to manoeuvre and take evasive action, they would be sitting ducks.[18]

Another costly lapse the helicopter pilots made during raids was to attack positions vacated by the Mujahideen as the rebels used to cover these positions with heavy machine guns and, as soon as the helicopter would 'attack' the vacated post, it would be met with a hail of fire. It was only after the losses started mounting that the Soviets started following defensive measures to control attrition.

In later years, the Mujahideen used the air defence 'nomadic ambush' widely to combat Soviet aviation. These ambushes were established close to airfields at the ends of the take-off and landing strips and also on the likely flight routes of aircraft and helicopters.

Another Mujahideen tactic was to raid air bases or to use rockets and mortars to destroy aircraft while on the ground, at their bases. In one of the biggest such raids, the Mujahideen reportedly destroyed twelve aircraft of the Soviet 355th Independent Helicopter Regiment at Jalalabad air base when the defecting Democratic Republic of Afghanistan (DRA) troops let guerrillas inside the perimeter of the air base. In another major raid, Mujahideen shelled Bagram air base on the night of 13/14 July 1984 for three hours with Chinese 107mm unguided rockets and a variety of mortars. Although no permanent damage was caused, the base was closed for fixed-wing operations for a day.[19]

The success in raids and ambushes notwithstanding, the Mujahids faltered and failed also at times in countering the helicopter threat. Helicopters were most vulnerable when landing. An assault force hitting the helicopters as they came in to land, firing upon them from all sides, would have been an effective way to deal with them, but the Mujahideen often failed to establish air defence and/or minefields on likely landing zones in advance, giving away the advantage to the Soviets.[20] While the heavy machine guns were the favoured anti-aircraft weapons, losses to the man-portable and lightweight SA-7s were mounting with the Mujahideen claiming to have shot down eight Mi-8 helicopters in an operation in Paktia province in 1983.[21]

1984 marked a turning point in the air war in Afghanistan. In spite of attempts by the Mujahideen to attrite Soviet air forces, the Soviet Union had faced no serious opposition in the air thus far. The situation changed with an increased supply of air defence weapons to the Mujahideen, amongst them more SA-7 missiles, reportedly acquired from Palestine Liberation Organization (PLO) stocks in Lebanon, and approximately 2,000 heavy machine guns from China.[22]

The Mujahid used SA-7s very effectively for 'nomadic ambush'. These ambushes were established close to airfields at the ends of the take-off and landing strips and also on the likely flight routes of aircraft and helicopters. With an increased availability of SA-7s, the number of aircraft shot down while taking-off/landing at the air bases increased in 1984. On 28 October 1984 a Soviet An-22 Cock heavy transport was shot down using a SA-7 just after it took off from Kabul airport. In another ambush an Afghan Airlines DC-10 with 300 passengers aboard was hit by an SA-7 although it managed to land safely.[23]

The Soviets were quick to adopt counter-measures and pilots of both fixed-wing aircraft and helicopters routinely started using infra-red decoy flares.[24] To ensure safety of the transport aircraft, helicopter flare-ships were used to orbit the airport prior to take offs and landings to deploy flares to neutralize the threat of SA-7s.[25] In addition, the aircraft adopted a higher flight profile, releasing the ordnance from higher altitude.[26] As an added safety measure, the Soviets moved back their electronic intelligence (ELINT) aircraft and long-range bombers from Shindand to the Soviet Union.[27]

A new dimension to the air defence battle in Afghanistan was added in mid-1984 with 20mm Oerlikon anti-aircraft cannon. Part of a CIA-funded programme, about forty to fifty of these cannon were supplied to the Mujahideen in face of stiff opposition by the rebels as the bulky guns were of no practical use to any insurgent group. They had to be deployed in threes to be effective, an almost impossible proposition in the mountains. As a result, these remained as more of a prestige weapon with some Mujahideen commanders.[28]

By the end of 1984 all Soviet operations against the Mujahideen were centred around air power. The Soviet domination of the air was such that transport aircraft like the An-12 and An-26 were used as bombers and as flare-ships for battlefield illumination. The major tasks, support of air assault, close air support and interdiction operations, continued to be performed by the helicopters. The balance of power in the air was, however, slowly tilting in favour of the Mujahideen as they were notching up an increasing number of kills. By 1984 the total Soviet losses were estimated to be 600 and, even if a greater part was due to accidents, weather and human error, it was clear that the Dooshkas and SA-7s were beginning to make a mark.[29] In an incident generally glossed over, an SA-7 achieved the first kill of the Su-25 Frogfoot when an Su-25 piloted by a Soviet lieutenant colonel was struck by an SA-7 missile and downed near Urgun, Afghanistan, on 16 January 1984.[30]

While the war was going on in Afghanistan, back in the Soviet Union a momentous change took place in March 1985 when Mikhail Gorbachev assumed power and one of the first decisions was a shift in the Afghan policy. Keen on ending the war and focusing on his pet idea of *perestroika*, he yielded to the hawks only as much as to give one year more to try the military approach, which had not yet yielded the desired results. As a result 1985 proved to be the bloodiest year of fighting in the war.

With the infusion of new, and more, anti-aircraft weapons, the threat to Soviet aircraft and helicopters was increasing as were the Soviet efforts to neutralise this threat. The Soviets would regularly carry out raids to destroy or capture these weapons. In one such raid, carried out by a mixed group of Mi-24Vs and two Mi-8MTs, the Soviets were able to destroy five DShK and two large-calibre ZGUs and capture as many as four machine guns and three ZGUs. It was important to counter the heavy machine-gun threat as it accounted for almost 65 per cent of all combat damage to aircraft in 1985 and the Soviet General staff realized that, for the most part, the losses were due to the flaws in planning operations and insufficient accounting being taken of enemy air defences.[31]

In 1985, faced with a more offensive approach by the Soviets, the United States proposed to supply a new air defence weapon to the Mujahideen – the British Blowpipe man-portable missile. It was, like the Oerlikon guns, refused by the Mujahids on practical grounds. It was not portable enough over any distance in the mountains and the firer had to remain standing to aim, fire and then guide the missile optically with a thumb control, exposing him to hostile fire all the while. During the weapon demonstration-cum-trials, the missile failed miserably as it could not hit a single target, not even the parachute flares that descended at a very slow rate. The mujahid understandably refused to take the Blowpipes but, the objections notwithstanding, the CIA forced several thousand Blowpipes on to the Mujahideen.[32]

The missile proved to be a disaster. The first time it was used, the missile failed to fire due to technical failure as it would not accept the command guidance. The missiles had to be recalled for repairs, taken to Pakistan and then back to Britain. To help the Mujahid familiarize with the Blowpipes, a small unit armed with the missiles was deployed by the Pakistani Army, but it did not help the situation. During an engagement, not only did the missile fail with at least a dozen fired without a single hit but several Pakistani officers were injured in the Soviet counter-attack.[33] To make matters worse, four of the missiles were captured by the Soviets when a Mujahideen firing party was compelled to withdraw in face of a strong Soviet reaction during an ambush – leaving the missiles behind. During the entire duration of the war, not one confirmed kill was ever credited to the Blowpipe missile.[34]

Meanwhile, the Soviet iron fist policy worked to a large extent, but it was apparent that the policy would not be able to deliver without a massive troop build-up. Unwilling to do so, Gorbachev opted to withdraw Soviet forces from Afghanistan in good order. This was publicly announced by him at the February 1986 Party Congress when he announced plans to 'Afghanize' the conflict and intensify negotiations for a withdrawal.[35] This marked the beginning of the end of Soviet occupation of Afghanistan. Stingers were yet to reach the Mujahideen.

The next year saw the burden of conducting large-scale ground operations shift to the DRA troops and the Soviets scaled down their own involvement. However, the use of air power remained as before, although the number of helicopters decreased due to reduced involvement of Soviet ground troops. The ground operations did not stop altogether, the Zhawar campaign being one of the offensive operations carried out by the Soviets during the year that also saw extensive use of air.

One of the new weapons used during the campaign was the precision-guided bomb. First used by the Su-25s of the 378th OshAP (Independent Shturmovik Aviation Regiment), the Kh-25ML missiles gave the Soviets a stand-off capability to engage targets from up to eight kilometres, greatly reducing the risk posed by anti-aircraft artillery and shoulder-launched surface-to-air missiles.[36] These were especially effective against cave entrances or weapons storage sites.

The Soviets used a similar weapon to deal with ambushes in Afghanistan. Unlike tank and armoured car guns, the Shilka's barrels could be elevated vertically to target Mujahideen fighters on cliff tops. This yielded a special 'Afghan variant' of the ZSU-23-4 that had no radar equipment, so as to increase ammunition storage, and firing capacity to 4,000 rounds per minute.

It was at this juncture that the US supplied the Stingers to the Mujahideen. The missiles were routed through Pakistan and it was the Pakistan Army that trained the Mujahideen at Ojhiri Camp near Rawalpindi. The training capsules were for three weeks each and the Mujahids selected for training were mostly those with experience on SA-7s, preferably who had at least one kill to their credit. The Mujahids achieved 70 to 75 per cent success rate during the training while the Pakistani instructors reportedly achieved a 95 per cent kill rate. These figures may seem impressive, but it needs to be emphasized that this success rate was during the training – without the stress of firing a missile in actual combat, in face of the enemy.

The annual allocation of Stingers for the Mujahideen was 250 grip-stocks with 1,000–1,200 missiles. In addition, the Stingers were provided to Pakistani Army units deployed on the Pakistan-Afghanistan border for use against Soviet 'hot pursuit' incursions. A total of twenty-eight Stingers were reportedly fired by the Pakistan Army, without a single kill. The Stingers were deployed first in areas around Kabul, Jalalabad and Bagram, followed by Faizabad, Kunduz, Mazar-e-Sharif and Maimanah.[37] In the third phase, Stingers were provided to the Mujahid groups in Asbabad, Qalat and Ghazni. Last to receive the Stingers were the groups in Kandhar, Lashkar Gah and Shindand. By August 1987 Mujahideen groups in all but three provinces had been provided with Stinger: 187 Stingers were fired during this period, reportedly achieving a kill rate of 75 per cent.[38]

The first reported kill by the Stingers was in September 1986 when it was used at Jalalabad to down a Mi-24 Hind gunship. The incident is described by Mohammad Yusuf, head of the Afghan department of the Pakistan Inter-Services Intelligence in the book *Bear Trap*.[39]

About thirty-five Mujahideen secretly made their way to the foot of a small high-rise overgrown with shrubs a mile and a half north-east of the runway of Jalalabad airfield, which direction the target could appear in. We organized each calculation in such a way that three people would shoot, and the other two would hold containers with missiles for fast reloading. Through an open sight on the launcher, a system 'friend or foe' intermittent signal signalled that there was in range the enemy target, and 'Stinger' captured head pointing thermal radiation from the helicopter engines. When the lead helicopter was only 200 metres above the ground, Gafar commanded: 'Fire'. One of the three rockets did not work and fell, not exploding, just a few metres from the shooter. Two others crashed into their targets. Two more rockets went into the air, one hit the target as successfully as the two previous ones, and the second went very close, as the helicopter had already landed.

The Mujahideen were grouped in three teams and it was the very first missile fired that had gone dud and landed just ahead of the Mujahid team. By this time the second had locked on to the Mi-24 and fired, scoring a hit. A total of five missiles was fired and scored three hits.[40] The total number of helicopters shot down (as against the number of helicopters hit) is difficult to confirm. Although Soviet accounts mention only one loss,[41] most of the western accounts claim three helicopters to have been downed.[42] The next kill by the Stinger came by the end of November 1986 when the Mujahideen shot down two Mi-24s.

Stinger was a far better missile than the SA-7s and Blowpipes that the Mujahideen had until then and it undoubtedly enhanced the Mujahideen air defence capabilities. The limited numbers – there were only 36 grip-stocks(launchers) and 154 missiles in Afghanistan in 1986 – meant that the overall impact was low, but the Western media and intelligence sources gave an exaggerated account of the kills attributed to the Stingers. As per one report, thirty-seven of these 154 were fired resulting in the shooting down of twenty-six aircraft (including helicopters), a remarkable success rate of 70 per cent.[43]

The Stinger was considered to be equally effective against fixed-wing aircraft with a report claiming the loss of eight Su-25 Frogfoot aircraft to Stingers in 1987 alone, the same as total losses for the Frogfoots in the previous year from both combat and non-combat reasons. Another report mentions 270 Soviet aircraft destroyed by Stingers between October 1986 and September 1987.

While most of the early accounts give flattering details of the Stinger's performance, they did fail occasionally as in the very first incident one missile had malfunctioned, and another missed. The use against aircraft was at times not very encouraging as three missiles fired near Kabul airfield in September 1986 failed to hit the target.

The Stingers were more effective when used offensively. The Mujahideen would present a target for the helicopters to try and lure the helicopters to come low and then engage them with the Stinger. One of the methods used was to move a couple of vehicles into the open, kicking up dust, to depict a convoy movement. Or to raid an Afghan post, forcing them to radio for assistance that would invariably be troops moving in by helicopters, escorted by gunships, to engage the raiding Mujahid party. As the Soviet (or Afghan) quick-reaction team arrived, the Mujahid would be waiting to ambush the gunships from pre-selected positions. Over a period of time the Soviet pilots grew wise to these tricks and would stay away, preferring to land at a distance and then move in with the gunships engaging the Mujahids from a safe distance.

The Soviets upgraded the protective measures in use to cater for the new threat posed by the Stingers. These measures were an enhancement of the measures that they had earlier adopted to counter the SA-7. These included a new flare system which burned at a higher temperature and was more effective in luring away the infra-red (IR) SAMs.[44] There were reports of the Soviets using active IR jammers but they had a serious limitation as they did not work continuously for long. An active IR counter-measures system, the SOEP-V1A IR jammer *Lampa infrakrasnykh pomekh* (infra-red jamming lamp) generally designated as *Lipa* (also called the 'Hot Brick'), was located behind the main rotor, at the root of the tail boom. The *Lipa* had a xenon lamp and a rotating deflector in a thimble-shaped housing. This system produced erratic infra-red signals that disrupted an IR missile-guidance system. The flare dispenser ASO-2V-02 IR flare-launchers was upgraded from the earlier four dispensers to six identical dispensers mounted on the rear of the fuselage sides (three on each side), fixed at an angle of about 15-degrees forward. The flares were launched automatically at a rate of between four to sixteen at one time at two- to six-second intervals. To reduce the helicopter's heat signature, air/exhaust mixers were installed. The fuel tanks were filled with explosion-suppression polyurethane foam to reduce damage in case of a hit; additional armour plating and extra valves were fitted to prevent loss of hydraulic fluid.[45]

The new measures adopted by the Soviets in turn made the Mujahideen review their own tactics. To optimise the Stingers' performance, the Mujahideen did not always follow the American tactics and adapted techniques better suited to their conditions. For example, instead of the regular two-man team to operate the Stingers, they formed three-man teams – one to fire and two to help reload. This ensured that they had a faster re-supply and could engage more targets. Normally they would deploy three such teams in a triangular pattern in case the direction of the arrival of helicopters or aircraft was not known in advance. Ambush near the air bases was a favourite technique and the Mujahid would at times fire rockets at the air base to try to force the helicopters to take off – and then use the Stingers to engage them. Casualties to helicopters and aircraft at the bases, if any, were an added bonus.

The Mujahideen formed roving anti-aircraft (AA) teams with a mix of different types of weapons. Teams consisted of three to four 12.7mm/14.5mm AA machine guns, two RPG-7s, SA-7s or a Blowpipe team and at least two Stinger teams. These roving groups would operate independently, observing the Soviet flightpaths to discern a pattern to select a suitable ambush site. Using surprise, they often succeeding ambushing the unsuspecting Soviet helicopters. The Blowpipes, even though they had never hit any target, were included for psychological impact as their firing put pressure on the pilot and forced him to take evasive action. If nothing else, this was one positive impact of the British SAMs.

The Mujahideen were provided with modified night-sights by mounting PAS-7 Mod I thermal imagers on special brackets.[46] The other method to use the Stingers at night was to rely on the sound of the seeker and, on at least one occasion, the Mujahideen were able to hit an aircraft at night.[47] This method, using the seeker sound, was also used to engage helicopters dropping flares – the Stinger was aimed ahead of the helicopter and, as soon as the tone was heard, the missile would be 'uncaged' and fired on hearing the lock-on sound.[48] This method was practised by the better-trained Mujahids only as it took a very high standard of proficiency to master it.

While the Stingers were being used by the Mujahids for effect, the United States faced some embarrassment when the Stingers were seized by the Soviets in an incident in 1987. A Mujahid team was found to be carrying three Stingers when it was ambushed by the Spetsnaz. The surprised Mujahid could not fire off the Stingers at the helicopters carrying the Spetsnaz and surrendered the missiles to the Soviets. According to a Soviet account, the Mujahideen fired a couple of Stingers but the Soviets managed to overcome them and seize the missiles:

A reconnaissance unit spotted a group of armed men on three motorcycles.

> When they saw our choppers they stopped and started shooting at us and fired two missiles .... The pilots made a manoeuvre and lowered the helicopters .... The Mi-24s were covering us from above and we started fighting after leaving the chopper,

recalled Lieutenant Vladimir Kovtun. He and four other soldiers won the battle against the Mujahideen thanks to the air support. After the skirmish, they searched the enemy and discovered a Stinger and its technical documentation. For years this was believed to be the first time the Soviet came into possession of the missile launcher.

Later, a team of Mujahids, after collecting the Stingers from Quetta, strayed into Iran while returning to their base and were caught by the Iranian Border Guards with fourteen Stinger missiles and three grip-stocks. The Mujahids were later released and allowed to go back but the Iranians refused to return the missiles and the grip-stocks. In all, the Soviets managed to capture eight sets of the Stinger missile system.[49]

The Stingers, and the other anti-aircraft weapons, continued to take a toll of Soviet aircraft and, by the time the Soviets left Afghanistan, over 450 aircraft (and helicopters) had been lost by them, including 118 aircraft and 333 helicopters. The total kills achieved by Stingers alone are hard to confirm as most of these are based on accounts by Mujahideen and are not corroborated by any independent sources. The more commonly attributed figure is 269 total aircraft kills in 340 engagements, giving the Stingers a remarkable 79-per cent kill ratio.[50]

In February 1987 the United States Air Force chief of staff, Larry Welch, testified that 'Stingers have absolutely driven the Russian air force out of the skies in Afghanistan'.[51] Claims that the Soviet losses were one aircraft per day soon became common and the credit for this was directly being attributed to the Stingers. The Pakistani and US intelligence sources revised this figure upwards and estimated that the average loss was 1.3 to 1.4 aircraft per day.[52]

The Soviets lost eighteen of the prized Mi-24 Hind helicopters in the six-month period after the introduction of Stinger with the 335th OVAP alone losing eight of them. All these were not to Stingers alone and if the loss rate of Mi-24s before and after the Stinger is considered there is no remarkable increase in the losses suffered by the Soviets. The maximum losses of Mi-24s were in 1984–85 when the Soviets lost thirty-nine of them. This came down marginally to thirty-eight in 1986–87 but most of the losses in 1986 (seventeen) were before the arrival of Stingers. The loss rate came down drastically to only three per year in 1988 and 1989.[53]

Another perspective which supports the argument that the impact of Stinger was marginal is offered by Selig Harrison who is of the view that about 1,000 Soviet and Afghan aircraft had been destroyed by the end of

1986, mainly by Chinese heavy machine guns and other less sophisticated anti-aircraft weaponry, and only 200 aircraft were destroyed after the Stinger was introduced.[54]

If the later accounts and analyses of the Stinger's impact are considered, the kill rate is just about 10 per cent for Stingers, and even less for Blowpipe. As per one estimate, not more than 200 Blowpipe and 700 Stingers were fired during the period from February 1986 until the Soviet withdrawal, achieving a total of ninety probable kills of which the bulk were helicopters with perhaps twenty Antonov transport aircraft and fifteen to twenty fighter aircraft.[55] Another factor that needs to be considered while evaluating the Stinger's assessment is that all the man-portable air defence systems shot down twenty-seven aircraft in 1987 and only six in 1988. This was due to the improvement in Soviet tactics and better counter-measures, like newer flares and jammers.[56]The losses to heavy anti-aircraft machine guns were more than those from Stinger or other MANPADS; even non-combat losses were higher.[57] In one of the worst losses in a single incident, eight aircraft were destroyed in June 1988 when a rocket struck an Su-25 Frogfoot at Bagram air base.

Much is made of the declining number of Soviet helicopters in Afghanistan in the last three years of the war and relating it to the availability of Stingers from 1986 onwards as if the increased missile threat played a role in the force reduction but, if the numbers over the years are considered, the fallacy of the assumption is revealed. From a high of 600 helicopters in 1982 the number had already come down almost to half in 1986 with only 325 helicopters. The further reduction until 1988 was only from 325 to 275. The reduction in numbers was in line with the declining role played by helicopters over the years and not only due to the threat posed by the Stingers.

It was not that there was no or negligible impact of the Stingers but it was certainly not so serious that it 'brought Soviet tactical forces to a relative standstill, causing an operational stalemate'.[58] Like all new threats, it was taken seriously by the Soviets and counter-measures adopted to mitigate its effectiveness. Use of Chaff had already become a standard operating procedure; flying higher and delivering the weapon loads from greater distances, and restricting the use of helicopter gunships were some of the other measures. The use of helicopters after the introduction of Stingers was limited, especially during daytime, but not given up. The Soviets continued to use air power extensively in support of its ground troops as demonstrated during the re-taking of Kunduz in 1988 and Operation TYPHOON, the Soviet withdrawal in February 1989, when over 1,000 sorties were carried out in support of the ground troops.

The Soviets left Afghanistan in 1989 although they continued to support the Afghan regime. A weekly 600-truck re-supply convoy ran from the Soviet Union to Afghanistan and the USSR maintained its air bridge, providing Afghanistan with supplies ranging from flour to missiles. General Valentin Varennikov, who commanded the Soviet forces in Afghanistan, acknowledged that Stingers forced Moscow to reduce its reliance on air power, but he disputed that they inflicted greater Soviet and Afghan aircraft losses or significantly influenced the decision to disengage. Colonel Alexander Golavanov, regimental commander of the composite aviation regiment at Kabul, echoed these views:[59] 'I would not say that there were a lot more casualties as a result (of Stinger's arrival) but of course Mujahideen morale has gone up.'

Stingers and the SA-7 were a manifestation of a new threat to Soviets but they soon made changes to their tactics and incorporated counter-measures as a result of which, after an initial increase in loss rate, the overall loss rate of aircraft came down to the same level as before the introduction of Stingers. The loss rate of helicopters remained about the same throughout the war, with the Soviet Fortieth Army losing 10 per cent of its helicopter fleet every year.

It was not a game changer as it is made out to be and did not lead to a collapse of Soviet occupation of Afghanistan. In any case the Mujahids had reportedly stopped using the Stingers by 1988 – it could not have had a significant impact if it was not being used for it is unlikely that the mere threat of its possible use would have forced the Soviets to give up use of their air.[60]

After the Soviet withdrawal the Mujahideen made repeated attempts to capture Kabul and Jalalabad but did not succeed, the more serious attempt being the one made in April–June 1990 to capture Jalalabad. The Democratic Republic of Afghanistan (DRA) was not overthrown by the Mujahideen until 1991, when the Soviet Union collapsed and the external support to the DRA stopped.

Ahmad Shah Masood famously once said, 'There are only two things Afghans must have: the Koran and the Stinger.' It was not the most important weapon system in Afghanistan and the psychological impact of the Stinger was of greater value than its physical impact, something similar to the influence of the Patriot missile in the Gulf War but it needs to be remembered that it was not the Stinger, or any other air defence weapon, that led to the Soviet withdrawal, although they all influenced the conduct of war to a large measure.

As Alan J. Kuperman writes in *The Stinger missile and U.S. intervention in Afghanistan*,[61] 'Had Gorbachev not decided autonomously to withdraw, it is unlikely the Stinger could have chased him out of Afghanistan.'

Chapter 4

Falkland Islands (Malvinas) War

On 2 April 1982, Argentina occupied the Falkland Islands (called Malvinas by the Argentinians) in the South Atlantic, off the coast of Argentina. The Falkland Islands, and its territorial dependency, the South Georgia and the South Sandwich Islands, had been a Crown colony since 1841 although Argentina had long claimed sovereign rights over them. Inhabited by fewer than 2,000 people, the islands' occupation by Argentina set in motion a chain of events that would see the United Kingdom send a naval task force 7,000 miles away and re-capture its territories after seventy-four days. The conflict – both sides did not formally declare war – saw two modern armed forces face each other in the windy and desolate terrain of the remote island group, in which the air war played a decisive role in determining the outcome. Argentina, with a mix of modern and vintage equipment, fielded a reasonably capable air force. The *Fuerza Aerea Argentina* (FAA) had twenty Mirage IIIs, thirty Mirage Vs (called the *Dagger* by the FAA), sixty A-4P Skyhawks, sixty IA-58 Pucaras, nine Canberra B.62s, seven C-130s and two KC-130 tankers. The Naval Air Arm, ANA, had ten A-4Q Skyhawks, five Super Étendards and ten Aermacchi MB-339s.[1]

The Royal Navy had despatched its ice patrol vessel HMS *Endurance* to South Georgia on the 25th in response to the raising of Argentine flag at South Georgia Island on 19 March, an act seen as the first offensive action in the war. It was followed by the British submarines HMS *Splendid* and HMS *Spartan* setting sail to the south on 29 March. Argentina, suspecting that the British presence in the South Atlantic might be reinforced, brought forward the invasion of the Falkland Islands, launching Operation ROSARIO on 2 April. It was met by a nominal defence. By late evening of the 2nd, Argentina had pulled back the 1,400-strong invasion force leaving behind 500 troops to hold the islands.[2]

The British Prime Minister announced the decision to recover the islands and, stepping up its response, the United Kingdom despatched the nuclear-powered submarine HMS *Conqueror* on 4 April, whilst the two aircraft carriers, *Invincible* and *Hermes*, left Portsmouth the next day. Twenty-two Sea Harrier V/STOL aircraft onboard the carriers were available to provide air support. The task force also had Westland Sea King HAS Mk5 anti-submarine helicopters and Sea King HC.Mk4 transport helicopters. Another complement of Sea King HC.Mk4 helicopters was abroad the assault ship HMS *Fearless*.

The first Royal Air Force element to arrive were the two BAe Nimrod MR.Mk 1 maritime reconnaissance and anti-submarine aircraft which reached Ascension Island on 6 April and were to perform reconnaissance missions for the task force. In the days to follow, the United Kingdom had not only put together and sent a task force comprising 127 ships including forty-three Royal Navy vessels but had imposed a blockade around the Falkland Islands by 12 April.[3]

By mid-April, the Royal Air Force had also staged forward a sizeable force of Vulcan bombers, Victor refuelling aircraft and F-4 Phantom fighters at its mid-Atlantic air base on Ascension Island. Otherwise, the British were significantly constrained by the disparity in deployable air cover at the Falklands with only forty-two aircraft (twenty-eight Sea Harriers and fourteen Harrier GR.3s) to take on the 122 combat aircraft of the Argentine Air Force. Argentina, on its part, was constrained by the limited numbers and type of aircraft it could deploy on the three airfields on the Islands.

Stanley had the longest and only paved runway on the islands but, even then, it was just 1,250 metres, not allowing the A-4s, Mirages and Daggers to operate. All that Argentina could station at Stanley were the Pucara light aircraft for close support along with the MB-339 light strike jet aircraft and T-45 trainers of Naval Aviation. One squadron of Pucaras was at Goose Green which had a 500-metre airstrip.[4] The bulk of the air force was forced to operate from the mainland, the nearest air base being Rio Grande, 700 kilometres away. The Argentine Naval Aviation operated from the shore bases and its aircraft carrier *Veinticinco de Mayo*.[5] Of the helicopter fleet, Argentina had stationed eleven Bell UH-1 Hueys, six Pumas and four CH-47 Chinooks on the islands; these were used for logistic support and casualty evacuation once the hostilities started.

Argentina stationed a fairly large complement of weapon systems on the islands to build up a formidable air defence. The lack of the required infrastructure at Port Stanley meant that even if the main runway was to be extended, the fighter aircraft for air defence could not be stationed on the islands. The only viable way out to ensure air defence then was by anti-aircraft guns and surface-to-air missiles. These were pooled in from the Argentine Army, Air Force and Marines with the Marines first to deploy their air defence weapons – twelve single-barrel 30mm Hispano Suiza guns, some 20mm AA guns and three triple-launchers of Tiger Cat missiles. The Tiger Cat missile was the mobile land-based version of the subsonic Sea Cat air defence missile, itself developed from the Malkara anti-tank guided missile (ATGM). It had not been used in any combat earlier and was in that sense an unknown factor. The major anti-aircraft component was from the army, of the 601st Anti-Aircraft Regiment, who moved in ten twin 35mm Oerlikon anti-aircraft guns with five Skyguard radars and four triple-launchers of the Tiger Cats, three 20mm Rheinmetall guns and one unit of the Roland missile system. The Skyguard radars gave the AA guns the capability to engage targets in all weather conditions and proved to be an effective deterrent during the war.

The air force complement included fifteen twin 20mm Rheinmetall AA guns with Israeli Elta radars and four twin 35mm Oerlikon AA guns with the *Superfledermaus* radar. In addition, a number of Blowpipe man-portable missiles were also deployed. The most lethal of all the anti-aircraft weapons was the Roland missile with an effective range of over six kilometres. They were sited to defend Port Stanley, the airfield, Moody Brook garrison and the airstrip at Goose Green with two Oerlikon AA guns each deployed at Moody Brook and Goose Green. The remainder of the air defence elements, including the Roland, were deployed at Port Stanley and the airport.[6]

The 601st AA Regiment was responsible for air defence of the airport, with nine twin 20mm guns and a *Superfledermaus* fire-control radar with three Oerlikon 35mm twin guns. One 35mm section was near the east end of the airstrip and the remaining sections with the Roland unit were located in an arc from Moody Brook to the eastern slopes of Sapper Hill. The deployment of its air defences notwithstanding, the Argentines realised that their defences would be vulnerable to heliborne attack and the AA weapons deployed at Port Stanley and the airfield might not be able to counter them. To take on the helicopters likely to be used for dropping British troops, twenty-seven 12.7mm heavy machine guns, some of them with night-vision sights, were deployed by the Argentine Marines at Stanley.

An Anti-Aircraft operations centre was established by Group 2, Air Warning and Control (VYCA Grupo 2) which had moved in the afternoon of 2 April and set up its Westinghouse AN/TPS-43 radar and the supporting Cardion AN/TPS-44 tactical surveillance radar on Sapper Hill, behind Port Stanley. The VYCA 2 was operational by 6 April and controlled the seventy AA guns and the various missile systems. As the radar antenna was damaged in a gale on 10 April, the radar was re-sited nearer to the town which was assessed to be a safer location – from the strong winds as also the raids which were expected once the British task force arrived. However, a dummy antenna and vehicles were erected on the original site and remained there as a deception measure.[7] It was considered a prime target for the British as it not only controlled the air defence weapons but also assisted both the logistic and strike missions operating from the mainland.

As the British had the disadvantage of having to operate away from their bases, several Royal Air Force (RAF) Canberra PR.Mk9 and Nimrod R Mk.1 electronic warfare aircraft were reportedly based in Punta Arenas in Chile for reconnaissance missions and the first British aircraft to begin operations in the area were the same Canberra PR.9s of the RAF's No. 39 Squadron, starting on 10 April or shortly thereafter.[8]

One of the first missions of the British task force was to recapture South Georgia. Codenamed Operation PARAQUAT, it was more of a show of political will and resolve than anything else. Three aerial reconnaissance sorties were carried out to gather intelligence for the operation, the first of which was executed by a Victor K. Mk 2 on the night of 20/21 April. The Argentines reinforced the island but in a short, swift operation, the Royal Marines and Special Forces recaptured South Georgia on 25 April, taking back the island which was the first to be 'liberated'.[9]

With an increased British presence near the Falklands and regular sorties by the Sea Harriers, the Argentines stopped the daytime air transport flights to Falklands on 29 April. The next day, Britain changed the status of the Maritime Exclusion Zone to a Total Exclusion Zone. At this time, it had about seventy ships off the Falklands.

The first round of the air battle was on 30 April/1 May when two Vulcans of the Royal Air Force, supported by eleven Victor tankers, took off from Ascension Island to strike the airfield at Port Stanley. One of the Vulcans turned back after the first aerial refuelling, leaving a solitary Vulcan to carry on. As it approached the target the Vulcan was picked up by the AN/TPS-43 but a delay by the operator meant no warning could be given to the AA defences. The Vulcan's onboard electronic-warfare suite had rendered the fire-control radars of the AA guns ineffective, and it faced minimal AA fire. One bomb fell on the runway, cratering it. The runway was repaired but the crater would continue to cause problems to the Argentinian aircraft.[10]

The Vulcans were followed by twelve Sea Harriers from HMS *Hermes* which attacked targets on East Falklands and at Port Stanley. Nine Sea Harriers attacked Port Stanley but, apart from hitting and setting ablaze a fuel dump, not much damage was caused by them. The Argentine air defences, which had been alerted by the earlier raid by the Vulcan, engaged the Sea Harriers. The 3rd Battery of 601st AA Regiment reported having destroyed two Sea Harriers and seriously damaged one, which was seen 'trailing smoke' as it flew back. The Argentine Coast Guard ship *Islas Malvinas* also engaged the Sea Harriers and claimed to have downed one with its Tiger Cat missiles. Later the Argentines revised the claims to three confirmed kills. According to British sources, only one Sea Harrier was hit by 20mm AA fire – a single shell hit the Sea Harrier in the tail, but it managed to return to *Hermes* and was soon repaired.[11]

The simultaneous air raid on Goose Green by three Sea Harriers managed to destroy one Pucara aircraft on ground and damage two more, without any loss as the anti-aircraft guns had no warning and were taken by surprise. If it was not damaging enough, three British warships stationed themselves six miles from the coast and started shelling. The helicopters assisting the ships in correction of fire were taken on by the Argentine defences with a Lynx hit by machine-gun fire and a Wessex scared off by a Tiger Cat missile fired from Port Stanley. Except for some hits on the Lynx, no damage was caused by the AA fire.[12]

Responding to the shelling by the British ships, Argentinian Southern Air Force (*Fuerza Aerea Sur-FAS*) sent waves of strike aircraft to attack the ships. The controller at Stanley misguided the first wave of twelve aircraft and it failed to find the ships, returning to their base without any success. The next wave attacked the ships off Port Stanley without any major incident but the third wave of four Mirages ran into the Harriers carrying out a combat air patrol (CAP). The Mirages were outmanoeuvred by the Harriers and, in the dogfight, two Mirages were hit. One went down in the sea while the second managed to disengage. Short on fuel, it would not have managed to reach its base on the mainland and instead tried to make an emergency landing at Port Stanley, but in an unfortunate case of *blue-on-blue* was shot down by the Argentine AA gunners.[13] A third Mirage and a Canberra were shot down in separate engagements, bringing the total Argentine aircraft lost to four. The losses notwithstanding, the real import of the first day's strikes by the British was the relegation of Argentina's most modern aircraft, the Mirages IIIEAs, to defence of the mainland.[14]

The next mission by the Vulcan was on 3/4 May but the damage caused, if any, could not be ascertained as the post-strike reconnaissance was not carried out due to bad weather. On 4 May FAA Super Étendards from the 2nd Naval Air Fighter Attack Squadron struck the first major blow against the British task force as they managed to hit HMS *Sheffield*, which had been ordered forward with two other Type 42 destroyers to provide a long-range radar and medium-high altitude missile picket far from the British carriers. Only one of the two AM-39 Exocets launched hit the destroyer but it was enough to cripple the ship. The damaged ship sank a week later.

As the Super Étendards were attacking HMS *Sheffield*, Sea Harriers from HMS *Hermes* were raiding Port Stanley and Goose Green. This time the AA defences at Goose Green were alert and the guns had been re-sited to the north and south of the airstrip. The Skyguard radars picked up the incoming raiders but, as the first aircraft deployed chaff, it could not be engaged. The second Sea Harrier, without a radar warning receiver (RWR), could not deploy the chaff in time and was hit by a salvo from the 35mm AA guns, the first British aircraft to be lost to Argentinian ground-based air defences.[15]

Stunned by the loss of the Sea Harrier, the British decided that the Sea Harriers would concentrate on achieving air supremacy and in case of being used for the ground attack role, would use the high-altitude-loft-bombing techniques for all subsequent air-to-ground operations, to remain well out of the reach of ground fire. It was an inaccurate method of weapon delivery but, in view of the high threat from the air defences, it was the only prudent method. Only after the arrival of the Harrier GR3 did the British resume the low-level missions against the targets on the Falkland Islands.[16]

Argentina withdrew her sole aircraft carrier, the ARA *Vienticinco de Mayo* to port following technical problems with her engine. The next day, two Sea Harriers were lost in an accident, possibly due to a mid-air collision while searching for a contact near the abandoned *Sheffield*. Air operations over the next few days were hampered by bad weather, but the Sea Harriers continued to mount the combat air patrols. A mission to target Port Stanley by Sea Harriers on 9 May had to be abandoned due to heavy cloud cover. The Argentine mission, the first by the mainland-based air units to find and attack British ships, also met the same fate and most of the Skyhawks turned because of the bad weather. However, one group of four A4 Skyhawks pressed on and lost two Skyhawks, presumably to bad weather.[17] Argentina suffered another loss when a Puma helicopter was shot down by a Sea Dart missile fired from HMS *Coventry* over Port Stanley, the first kill by a Sea Dart. *Coventry* was positioned with *Broadsword*, off Stanley, the two ships forming a 'Type 64' deployment to cater for both long range (with the Sea Darts) and short-range (Sea Wolf) air defence. In one of the first engagements, the combination of Type 42 and 24 had worked well.

On 12 May *Glasgow* and *Brilliant* had replaced *Coventry* and *Broadsword* off Stanley and, as they shelled the targets on the island, the Argentine garrison at Stanley asked for help from the air force. Two flights of four Argentine A-4 Skyhawks were sent from the mainland and, as the first wave attacked the waiting ships, they were engaged by the ship-based air defences. The Sea Dart missile system on board *Glasgow* failed to engage but the Sea Wolf missiles from *Brilliant* hit two of the A-4s while a third crashed in the sea trying to evade the missiles. This was the first success for the Sea Wolfs. Meanwhile, the second wave of A-4 Skyhawks was able to attack during a failure of the missile system, hitting *Glasgow* – the second major warship hit by the FAA. The 500lb bomb did not explode and went straight through the ship. The damage was serious enough to put the ship out of action. The Sea Wolf missile was not able to engage any target in the second wave due to technical malfunction. Sea Wolf was very effective in engaging single targets, but its computers became overloaded in case of a raid by four or more aircraft. In this instance, the Sea Wolf was activated but the system 'reset and refused to fire'.[17] Tragedy struck the Argentinians as one of the A-4 Skyhawks, while returning, flew through the prohibited zone at Goose Green. Identified as a hostile, the aircraft was engaged by the AA guns of 601st Anti-Aircraft Regiment and shot down. It was the second instance of fratricide – both at Goose Green and by the AA guns.[18]

After a lull forced by the weather during which the Black Buck 3 raid was cancelled, the British inserted an SAS (Special Air Service) party onto Pebble Island by Sea King helicopters on 14 May. A small air base had been established by the Argentine Navy on the Island, off the north coast of West Falkland, for its Turbo-Mentors. At the time of the raid, six Pucaras were also positioned there, as was a Skyvan transport aircraft. The SAS party raided the *Calderón Naval Air Base* before dawn and destroyed or damaged all the eleven aircraft at the air base.[19] The two grass runways were also disabled by a crater blown at their intersection. The Argentines never used this air base thereafter.

The second wave of the British force arrived on 18 May to join the fleet with more warships, a second infantry brigade and fourteen RAF Harrier GR.3s carried on the *Atlantic Conveyor*. The British now had the desired Harriers to not only carry out ground attack but also support the landing of troops on East Falkland Island. The British landing force set sail for San Carlos on 19 May with the Argentine fleet pushed back to the mainland. The Harrier GR.3s carried out their first sortie against Goose Green on the same day, destroying a fuel dump.

During the night of 21 May, the British amphibious task group mounted Operation SUTTON, the amphibious landing on beaches around San Carlos Water on the north-western coast of East Falkland. The 4,000 men of 3 Commando Brigade landed at San Carlos (Blue Beach), Port San Carlos (Green Beach) and Ajax Bay (Red Beach).

The site had been selected as the surrounding bay masked the landing ships from the Exocet missile radars. As the troops moved in, supported by helicopters bringing in supplies, ground fire hit two of the British helicopters – a Sea King and a Gazelle. Of these, the Gazelle went down into the sea although the crew managed to escape.

By dawn the next day, the weakly held San Carlos site with only a section of the Argentine 25th Infantry Regiment had been overpowered and a secure beachhead established. For air defence, the British had Blowpipe missiles and machine guns in addition to the one unit of Rapier which had been carried as underslung loads by Sea King helicopters.

While the Sea Harriers carried out a CAP, providing air defence cover to the landing force, the Harrier GR.3s attacked an Argentine helicopter base at Mount Kent to prevent any reinforcements from Stanley. The Harriers managed to destroy three of the fourteen helicopters based there.

The British suffered a major setback when a Harrier GR.3 on an armed reconnaissance mission over Port Howard was hit by a Blowpipe missile. It was the only successful engagement by the Argentine AA gunners during the day and the only successful engagement with a Blowpipe for the Argentine forces during the entire war.[20] The Harrier was badly damaged with three-quarters of one wing shot off. With no chance of making it back, the pilot, Squadron Leader Jeffrey Glover, ejected into the sea.[21]

> The plane must have rolled very rapidly to the right, almost through 360 degrees. I looked down, saw my right hand and pulled the ejection seat handle. At that point I blacked out and was unconscious … I had effectively jumped out in a 600mph wind up in the free airstream with my left arm still out.

He was rescued by the Argentine troops and taken prisoner – the only British serviceman to be held as PoW (prisoner of war) during the war. Meanwhile, two Gazelles of 3 Commando Brigade Air Squadron were shot down by ground fire while carrying out a support mission for a Sea King sortie.[22] They were with a reconnaissance party looking for a suitable site for the Rapier missile when the helicopters came under ground fire, hitting the rotor and gearbox of one of the Gazelles. It ditched near the jetty but, as it was without its flotation gear, it sank. Soon enough, another Gazelle was also hit by Argentine ground fire and crashed.

The first flight of the day by the Argentines was made by the local air units. At Goose Green, only one of the six Pucaras of Grupo 3 ordered to take off managed to do so before *Ardent* started shelling to pin down the Argentine aircraft. The pilot, Captain Jorge Benitez, was not aware of the landings and was carrying out a routine patrol of the island when he spotted the British ships and troops at the San Carlos area. As he was lining up to attack a column of troops, he was shot down by a Stinger SAM fired by D Squadron Special Air Service (SAS) pulling back from the Darwin raid.[23] This was the combat debut of the Stinger missile and was more of a lucky shot as the NCO fired five missiles at the Pucara with the fifth and last finally hitting the aircraft.

On the other end, the garrison at Stanley had received the news of the landings late in the morning and a single Pucara was tasked to carry out a reconnaissance and ascertain the details. Lieutenant Guillermo Crippa of 1st Naval Attack Squadron at San Carlos was the first Argentine pilot to reach San Carlos in his Aermacchi MB.339. As he reached the landing zone, Crippa saw the landing fleet and, as he flew closer to the fleet, the ships opened up. Undaunted, he attacked the closest ship, the frigate HMS *Argonaut*, with rockets and 30mm front cannon, damaging a Sea Cat launcher. Crippa was fired at by a mix of missile and gunfire but he managed to turn around and get back to Stanley with only minor damage to his aircraft.[24] None of the Blowpipes and Sea Cats fired by the British hit the aircraft with only the small-arms fire causing whatever little damage the Pucara sustained.

A pair of Pucaras managed to take off from Stanley later in the morning. As they approached San Carlos and overflew the men of 2nd Parachute Regiment (2 Para), they were jumped by Sea Harriers providing air cover to the landings. One Pucara was shot down while the second, finding cover in the clouds, managed to evade. It was now the Argentine air units on the mainland turn to react to the landings as the news had reached them. The Argentines carried out air attacks throughout the day, in three waves, lasting almost five hours. The first wave was of eight Daggers of Grupo 6 and six A-4 Skyhawks of Grupo 5. One of the Skyhawks had to turn back due to technical problems, leaving thirteen aircraft to carry out the attack on the British ships. The incoming aircraft were not picked up by either the radars or visually and managed to get near Falkland Sound undetected but were soon picked up by *Argonaut* and the other ships who let loose a barrage of anti-aircraft fire. The aircraft went low to try and get below the fire in the guns' blind zone. The Skyhawks managed to drop two bombs on *Argonaut* but both failed to explode as the Skyhawks had been flying low, not giving enough time for the fuses to arm themselves. The same problem occurred as the Daggers bombed *Antrim*; the bomb again failed to explode. The Daggers attacked *Brilliant* with their front cannon, injuring several seamen. The ship-based missiles were active now but the ground clutter made it difficult for the missile radar to achieve a lock-on. It was with the help of TV tracking that the Sea Wolf operator on board *Brilliant* managed to guide the missile on to a Dagger, to explode it under the port wing, bringing it down.[25] The Rapier unit of T Battery engaged at least one A-4 Skyhawk but the missile missed.

The next wave of fourteen A-4 Skyhawks was despatched two and a half hours later from the Argentine mainland but, as eight Skyhawks had to turn back, only six carried on. Four Skyhawks, of Grupo 4, were intercepted by Sea Harriers who shot down two A-4s and damaged a third. Only the remaining two Skyhawks, of Grupo 5, managed to reach Falkland Sound. One of them attacked an abandoned Argentine ship in a case of mistaken identity although the second attacked *Ardent*, off Goose Green. The bombs, however, missed the ship and fell in the sea.[26] The second wave had been a disaster for the Argentinians.

The last wave was to see the maximum action. Sixteen of the seventeen aircraft despatched reached Falkland Sound. The leading group of Daggers lost one aircraft to the Sea Harriers but managed to reach *Ardent*. This time the bomb dropped on *Ardent* exploded, damaging the ship. Three more Daggers were shot down by the Sea Harriers although another group managed to attack the British ships with limited damage. The last attacks were by the Skyhawks who again targeted the already damaged *Ardent*. The ship sank later that day. In addition, *Antrim* and *Argonaut* had been damaged with unexploded bombs inside them, and *Brilliant* and *Broadsword* damaged by cannon fire. Argentina had lost twelve aircraft during the day; a rather high price to pay and that, too, without any effective ground-based air defences.[27] By the end of the day, ten Rapier fire units were ashore, but the Rapier could not score any hits. Its detachments found that they were alerting on their own aircraft and the IFF (Interrogation Friend or Foe) interrogation of incoming aircraft was often screened by helicopters operating in the bay.[28] The Rapier shifted to visual acquisition of targets the next day.

Air operations on 22 May were affected by bad weather although the British did carry out a strike by four Harrier GR.3s at Goose Green. The anti-aircraft section at Goose Green tried to engage the Harriers with their 35mm Oerlikon guns but could cause no damage.[29] It was not only the anti-aircraft guns that fired back at the British aircraft but whatever and whoever could do so fired at them, as Captain Pablo Santiago Llanos of 601 Commando Company who was at Goose Green at that time recalls,[30] 'Everyone in Goose Green would leave the houses, they would position themselves behind whatever cover there was, and would fire against the planes.' The Harriers, flying low, managed to deliver their weapon loads and get back safely.

The air strikes at San Carlos resumed on the 23rd when the Argentine aircraft again attacked the British task force and hit HMS *Antelope*. The Argentine losses for the day were three helicopters (two Pumas and one Augusta) shot down by Sea Harriers, four Daggers and two Skyhawks although the British claimed six Mirages and a Skyhawk.[31] Only one of these, an A-4 Skyhawk, was shot down by a ship-based surface-to-air missile with the ground-based air defences failing to hit any targets. The bomb that hit *Antelope* had not exploded and was lodged in its engine room. The next day, during an attempt to disarm it, the bomb exploded, killing one of the bomb disposal team and injuring another. The ship was torn open by the explosion and sank the next day. The other ships were attacked by three waves of Argentine aircraft during the day but except for some damage to two Landing Ships, Tank (LSTs); the damage was not serious. The Argentine losses were four Daggers and two Skyhawks, all to Harriers; except for one Skyhawk that was felled by naval anti-aircraft guns.

The Argentine National Day (25 May) saw the British suffer some of the worst losses during the war, partly due to their own lapses and partly due to Argentine efforts. The first major action was the Argentine aircraft attacking the British ships *Coventry* and *Broadsword*. They had been positioned in a forward position off Pebble Island to serve as advance pickets. The location meant that the ships were visible to the radar on Pebble Island. Argentina decided to attack the ships and launched four A-4 Skyhawks of Grupo 5. The strike mission failed as *Coventry* shot down the leading Seahawk with its Sea Dart missile. The remaining Skyhawks turned back, abandoning the strike mission. The second strike by Skyhawks of Grupo 4 also failed in its mission with the Sea Dart scoring another hit. The third strike package was luckier. The two pairs of Skyhawks approached the ships from two different directions and as *Coventry* launched a Sea Dart, it missed. Carrying on in face of gunfire, the Skyhawks managed to score direct hits on *Coventry*, dropping three 1,000lb bombs, all of which exploded, sinking the ship within an hour.[32] *Broadsword* was also hit but no serious damage was caused. No Argentine aircraft was hit. Again, *Coventry* was lost due to apparent failure of the Sea Wolf missile system. For it to successfully engage the target, the carrier ship must be in position between the attacking aircraft and the other ship it is defending. In this case, *Broadsword* did not get adequate time to position itself between *Coventry* and the A-4 Skyhawks, due to which it could not launch the Sea Wolfs.

The second major success of the day for Argentina was the sinking of the cargo ship *Atlantic Conveyor* although the intended targets were the aircraft carriers. The Super Étendard squadron had been waiting for firm intelligence to launch a major strike against the British fleet. On 25 May, on getting the information about the British fleet's location after an aerial reconnaissance mission, two Super Étendards from *2da Escuadrilla Aeronaval de Casa y Ataque* were launched. They re-fuelled and approached the task force from the north. The British ships were detected by them in the first attempt and the aircraft launched their AM-39 Exocet missiles. One of the Exocets went astray and was reportedly shot down by British AA fire while the second was diverted by chaff and locked onto the cargo ship *Atlantic Conveyor*. The missile hit the ship on the port side, causing a huge fire. The stricken ship was abandoned, the six Wessex and three Chinook helicopters onboard going down with it.[33] Three Argentine aircraft were claimed by Britain during the morning.

The British had been ashore for five days by now, with the landing force beefed up to two brigades. The next phase of the British campaign was to commence the next day as they began their advance to roll up the Argentine defences. The first objective was the isolated position at Darwin. Throughout 27 May Royal Air Force Harriers were active over Goose Green. One of them, responding to a call for help from Captain Paul Farrar's C (Patrols) Company, was lost to 35mm fire while attacking Darwin Ridge.[34] The AA fire reportedly hit other Harriers also but did not cause any serious damage. On 28 May British troops took Darwin Hill and, as they moved down the southern slope of the ridge, were engaged by AA guns in a direct-firing role, causing heavy casualties. The Argentines had a battery of six 20mm Rheinmetall AA guns manned by air force personnel, and two radar-guided 35mm Oerlikon AA guns from the 601st AA Battalion, of which the latter proved to be quite effective in the direct-fire role. The AA gun positions were subjected to mortar fire, forcing them to seek shelter. In addition to the mortar fire, three Harriers made an attack on the Argentine 35mm gun positions; the guns were unable to respond as the fire-control radar had been damaged.[35]

Meanwhile, the Argentine platoon on Goose Green's outskirts continued to resist, supported by Air Force Pucara and Naval Aermacchi aircraft. The Argentine aircraft suffered two losses while providing close support, an Aermacchi 339A shot down by a Blowpipe missile from the Royal Marine air defence troop and a Pucara shot down by small-arms fire.[36] A British Scout helicopter was shot down by another Pucara in what was to be the only air-to-air kill by Argentina. At Goose Green the Argentine troops had been isolated. They surrendered the following day. Unknown to the British, Argentina reinforced Stanley with commandos from 602nd Commando Company and 601st National Gendarmerie Special Forces Squadron in Operation AUTOIMPUESTA (Self-determination initiative). The commandos reportedly had Blowpipe missiles to take on the British aircraft.

With the capture of Goose Green, the British shifted their focus to Port Stanley and, for the next week, the SAS and commandos of 3 Commando Brigade waged intense patrol battles with the Argentine 602nd Commando Company. Both sides used air support during which a FAA Dagger was shot down by Rapier SAMs of T Battery of 12th Air

Defence Regiment on the 29th.[37] The next day, Harriers were active over Mount Kent as part of a preliminary mission and a pair of Harrier GR.3s had been tasked to attack the Argentine gun position at Mount Wall, west of Stanley. The objective was later changed to helicopters about fourteen kilometres to the east. As the aircraft approached from the south, crossing the road to Stanley, one of the Harriers was hit by small-arms fire.[38] The pilot, Squadron Leader Jerry Pook, ejected over the sea and was rescued.

The Argentine Navy used its last Exocet missile on 30 May to try to hit *Invincible* but, although it claimed to have hit the aircraft carrier, the British vessel was safe. Instead, the Super Étendard was shot down by British defences. The same day an SA 330 Puma helicopter was brought down by a shoulder-launched FIM-92 Stinger surface-to-air missile fired by the SAS in the vicinity of Mount Kent. This was to be the second aircraft claimed by the Stingers, and the last of the war.[39]

As the war shifted towards the next and last major objective, neutralizing the air defences at Port Stanley became the prime concern for the British. On 24 May a strike package of four Harrier GR.3s, supported by two Sea Harriers, had attacked the airfield but the damage caused had been minimal. While the Sea Harriers used toss-bombing to drop bombs on the runway, the Harrier GR.3s had approached at low level and used retarded bombs. The runway was repaired and was operational within six hours. The *Superfledermaus* and Roland radars locked on to the Sea Harriers but, as the aircraft remained out of range, they could not be engaged. One Harrier was damaged as the Argentine defences claimed to have hit one Harrier.[40] The British, on their part, claimed that it was debris that had hit the Harrier.

Black Buck missions were revived in an attempt to put down the radars at Port Stanley. Following the failure of previous missions carried out using high-explosive (HE) bombs, the Royal Air Force changed their tactics for the next mission and planned to use the Shrike anti-radiation missiles (ARM). Preceding the Vulcan attack, a Sea Harrier from *Hermes* attacked Port Stanley airfield at 3:20am while a second attacked at 4:10am. These were attempts to lure the AN/TPS-43 radar operators to keep the equipment switched on, but the AA commander was quick to catch on to the ploy and ordered all the radars to be shut down. To bring the approaching aircraft within range of the Roland missiles, the

AA commander decided to gradually reduce the TPS-43's power but the Vulcan remained at a distance and launched the Shrike missile when it was about eight kilometres away.[41] The AA guns opened up but, as the Vulcan was beyond their range, no damage was caused. The Shrike also failed to cause any damage as the first hit ten to fifteen yards from the radar and caused 'repairable damage'. The second missed by eighty yards.[42] The radar remained operational.

By 1 June, with the arrival of a further 5,000 troops, the British had sufficient force to start planning an offensive against Stanley. They continued to target Port Stanley with Harrier GR.3s and Sea Harriers during the day and suffered an avoidable loss of a Sea Harrier to Roland SAM. The Sea Harrier was returning alone from a CAP when the pilot decided to carry out a visual reconnaissance of Port Stanley. The aircraft was, in the pilot's assessment, outside the Roland's engagement envelope when it has hit at about eleven kilometres from the port.[43]

Yet another attempt was made against the Stanley radar with the Black Buck mission on 3 June. This time around four, and not two, anti-radar Shrike missiles were carried – the additional two Shrikes optimised for use against Skyguard radar which had been picked up in the previous mission. The Vulcan loitered over the target for forty minutes in a vain effort to engage the AN/TPS-43, which remained switched off. Not able to get a lock-on to the main AN/TPS-43 radar, the Vulcan fired off two of the four Shrikes, destroying a Skyguard fire-control radar.[44] The AN/TPS-43 radar was not damaged in another failed attempt by the British.

The Argentine air operations had been hampered by bad weather and did not resume till 8 June when four Skyhawks and two Daggers attacked the landing ships *Sir Tristram* and *Sir Galahad*, causing extensive damage. The FAA also attacked British ships in Falkland Sound, hitting HMS *Plymouth*. Ten aircraft were claimed by Britain during the day. On 9 June a Harrier GR.3 was hit by shell splinters over Sapper Hill, defended by a 35mm AA section. The aircraft wings and upper fuselage were hit in several places causing minor hydraulic failure on recovery.

On the night of 11 June, after several days of painstaking reconnaissance and logistic build-up, British forces launched a brigade-sized night attack against the heavily-defended ring of high ground surrounding Stanley. In the last success in the war for the Argentine air defences, a Harrier was hit by 35mm anti-aircraft gun fire and seriously damaged on the 12th while attacking an artillery position near Sapper Hill.[45] Maintaining their momentum, and having cleared the initial objectives, the second phase of attacks began on the night of 13 June. With the defence line at Mount Tumbledown breached, the approach to Stanley was clear. The Argentine garrison commander surrendered the next day and the South Sandwich Islands were taken back by the British on 20 June. It had taken the United Kingdom seventy-four to reclaim the Falkland Islands.

The war had seen a joint operation being undertaken by the British over 7,000 kilometres away from their mainland, in which all services came together to achieve the national objective. Air was an integral part of this effort and it tested both adversaries' resolve in providing support in difficult conditions. Air defence played a major role during the war and not only brought to the fore the need of ensuring for effective air defence cover but also exposed the limitations and drawbacks of some air defence weapons, especially the surface-to-air missiles. The main air defence weapons used during the war were the man-portable and ship-based missile systems, supported by AA guns although the British also deployed the Rapier missile system on the Falklands.

The number of aircraft lost by both sides varies according to different sources. The more commonly accepted figure for British losses is of twenty-two aircraft, of which thirteen were helicopters destroyed aboard ships sunk or damaged by air attack. Argentine ground fire destroyed all but one of the remaining nine, a Scout helicopter downed by a Pucara. The losses included five Harriers – three to 35mm AA guns, one to Blowpipe and one to small-arms fire – and three Gazelle helicopters.[46]

The Argentinians made good use of their limited resources. Keeping their weapons concentrated at Stanley was a wise move as the Roland missile unit, three Tiger Cat missiles, and a good sprinkling of Blowpipe shoulder-launched weapons, as well as a collection of 20mm and 35mm rapid-fire guns, generally kept the British aircraft away. Dispersed, the weapon systems would have been less effective, leaving Stanley open to air attacks. The low number of kills claimed by the Argentine air defences was due to a number of reasons – from the use of electronic warfare (EW) measures like chaff to the low-level flight patterns adopted to avoid detection by the radars. At times the radars picked up the incoming Harriers, but the chaff deployed by them prevented a 'lock-on' and subsequent engagement by the AA guns. The air defences, however, did succeed in acting as a deterrent and made the British adopt more defensive tactics. The Sea Harriers were not used in the ground-attack role after their loss on 12 May and it was only after the arrival of Harrier GR.3s that Britain resumed the ground attacks on Stanley. The presence of Rolands also made the Harriers maintain a safe distance and not venture too close to Stanley for most part of the war. In this, the Argentine anti-aircraft guns and missiles achieved some degree of air denial.[47] The laydown attacks initially favoured by the British were found to expose the aircraft to unacceptable risks to ground fire and were given up for 'toss bombing', safe but with poor accuracy. The ground fire may have shot down only one Sea Harrier at Stanley but the forced change in weapon-delivery tactics had degraded the effectiveness of the air raids.[48] This itself was an achievement of the air defences.

The Westinghouse AN/TPS-43F radar and the supporting Cardion AN/TPS-44 tactical surveillance radar, manned by Argentine Air Force crews at Port Stanley, provided early warning and remained functional throughout, repeatedly foiling attempts made to neutralize it. The radar operators were proficient enough not to be lured by the Vulcans and never presented a target for the Shrike missiles. But the sole radar was not adequate to provide any real-time warning, especially in case of low-flying raids. The change in tactics by the Sea Harriers after their first loss also meant that the aircraft remained outside the effective range of the AA weapons; although the bomb delivery was not very accurate, it was frustrating for the AA gunners to be on high alert and yet not be able to engage the aircraft. The low-level approach by the British aircraft meant that the crews of the man-portable missiles systems did not get the desired response time to engage them effectively.

Argentine losses were estimated to be between forty-four and seventy-two, with the British authorities claiming seventy-two aircraft and the Argentine accounts conceding a loss of forty-four. The British estimate was an obvious exaggeration as most individual claims about the air defence systems turned out to be untrue. More likely, the Argentine losses were forty-four with twenty-one to Harriers, eighteen to SAMs and three to anti-aircraft guns.[49] Argentina lost two aircraft to friendly fire. The losses to Harriers in air-to-air combat are accepted to be twenty-one, although the British accounts credit only twenty aircraft to the Harriers. The main difference is in the claims made for the missile systems.

Rapier was the most advanced and potent air defence missile system deployed by the British in the Falklands with T Battery of 12th Air Defence Regiment Royal Artillery landing at San Carlos on 21 May with 3 Commando Brigade. The initial reports credited the Rapier with as many as fourteen kills and six probables. This figure is contested and most sources credit it with four kills, of which only one is confirmed, a Dagger A of FAA Grupo 6 shot down on 29 May.[50] One reason for deliberate exaggeration of Rapier's capabilities was the apprehension that making public the actual assessment would have an adverse effect on sales.[51] One major reason for Rapier's failure was the lack of appreciation of its technical and logistic requirements. Most of the time the system worked on visual acquisition mode as its radar interfered with the Naval radars. The IFF equipment was blanked by helicopter movement and the lack of a proximity fuse meant that it had to achieve a direct hit; a difficult preposition with manoeuvring, low-flying targets.

Similar exaggerations were made for Blowpipe which achieved only one confirmed kill against the initial claim of nine kills and two probables from ninety-five missiles fired.[52] Similarly, Sea Cat was credited with eight kills and two probables, which was later revised to one kill only. No kills were achieved by the Tiger Cats; the best it could do was achieve a near-miss on 12 June, damaging an RAF Harrier GR.3. Stinger had a satisfactory debut with two kills. As the number of missiles fired to achieve these kills is not known, the performance cannot really be judged.

The shipborne missiles fared equally badly. Initially, only two ships in the invasion fleet carried modern missiles (Sea Wolf) for defence against low-level attacks. The initial claims were of twenty-one aircraft downed by the Royal Navy SAMs, including between five to eight aircraft by both Sea Wolf and Sea Dart and eight by Sea Cat. Of these, Sea Dart proved ineffective in countering a multi-aircraft raid as it could handle only one aircraft at a time. This proved to be a serious limitation in the case of HMS *Coventry* when the failure of Sea Darts presented a window of opportunity to the four A-4 Skyhawks to strike the ship.

Whatever may be the actual number of aircraft shot down, the presence of surface-to-air missiles forced Argentine aircraft into low-level tactics and releasing their ordnance from very low altitude, not giving the bomb fuses sufficient time to arm before impact. Thirteen bombs hit British ships without detonating.[53] The Argentine air force sank seven ships. Had they not been forced to follow the low-level delivery tactics the overall results may well have been different.

Surface-to-air missiles had been seen as an effective counter to the air threat and a large number of these were deployed during the war by both sides. Their performance, however, was mixed and was clearly overrated in the initial assessments. It was not the number of kills achieved but the indirect impact of these weapon systems, keeping the aircraft away and forcing them to change tactics that was of greater import and their real impact on the conduct of the war.

Chapter 5

Lebanon

Bekaa Valley Air Battle, June 1982

The circumstances that determined the outcome of the Bekaa Valley battle can be traced back to 1967 when the Israelis launched a devastating surprise air attack on Egyptian airfields to begin the Six Day War. The Arab states, particularly Egypt and Syria, responded by establishing a system of surface-to-air missiles (SAMs) to deal with any future Israel incursions into their airspace.

During the War of Attrition from 1967 to 1970 the Israeli Air Force (IAF) admitted losing at least twenty-two aircraft to the new Arab missile defences, although Egypt claimed twenty-one in July 1970 alone. Even so, it was not until the three-week-long October War in 1973 that SAM warfare came of age in the Middle East. Egyptian SAMs, along with 23mm ZSU-23-4 anti-aircraft cannon, destroyed some forty Israeli aircraft in the first forty-eight hours of the war, or 14 per cent of the front-line strength of the IAF. In contrast, only five Israeli aircraft were destroyed in air-to-air combat during the entire conflict.

In the end Israel prevailed over the Arabs, but the cost of the October War made it clear that the Israeli Air Force's tactics would have to change. Having wrested back a semblance of control over the skies by the end of the war, Israel was still struggling to find a solution to the SAM problem, losing five Phantoms in a single raid. The Israeli Air Force's loss of effectiveness was devastating. 'At the end of the war,' said David Ivry, Deputy Chief of the Israeli Air Force,[1] 'we managed to come up with quite an impressive victory' but Israel's military leaders had 'a very bad feeling' about the fact that the F-4 was 'not successful against SAM batteries'. SAM belts had restricted the ability of the Israeli Air Force to interdict the invading armies. Surface-to-air missiles could also shelter batteries of short-range surface-to-surface missiles like the SS-21, which would be capable of holding Israeli territory at risk of attack.

Coupled with the high number of aircraft lost to ground-based air defences in Vietnam, the results of the October War prompted some analysts to ask whether tactical aircraft had outlived their usefulness on the modern battlefield. In Ivry's view, the main lesson of 1973 was simple: 'We have to find an answer to the SAM batteries.'[2]

In time the Israelis did develop a coherent SAM-suppression doctrine[3] and, during spring 1981, came close to putting their new doctrine and capability to the test. On 28 April the Israeli F-16A fighters from 117 squadron in Ramat David air base shot down two Syrian helicopters while providing air cover for Christian militiamen in Zahle, Lebanon. Syria reacted by deploying three SA-6 batteries to Lebanon's Bekaa Valley the next day.[4] The missile batteries were not a direct strategic threat to Israel as Syria had already deployed several SAM batteries in east Lebanon, across the border, but Israel regarded the newly-emplaced SAMs as a violation of a tacit Syrian-Israeli agreement regarding the Syrian presence in Lebanon and as a threat to vital air reconnaissance, putting it in a dilemma: to accept the deployment would damage Israel's deterrence credibility but a strike might lead to an unnecessary clash with Syria. Faced with Hobson's choice, Israel decided to attack with the strikes to be launched on 30 April, but the operation was called off due to bad weather conditions.[5]

Although the Israelis had threatened to remove the missile batteries by force, the crisis was defused by diplomatic means; Syrian missiles and troops, however, remained in Lebanon.[6] For the next year the IAF continued to carry out extensive air reconnaissance over the Bekaa valley and trained in the Negev Desert against mock SAM sites identical to those in Lebanon to prepare for the contingency if the need to execute strikes against the SAM sites came up again.[7]

A year later, in 1982, however, the elimination of the Bekaa Valley SAM sites became an urgent priority as Israel faced an escalating cross-border conflict with Palestine Liberation Organization (PLO) forces in southern Lebanon. Aimed at Israeli settlements, the PLO regularly fired artillery and rockets against Israeli civilian areas in Galilee. Meanwhile, Defence Minister Ariel Sharon and Lieutenant General Rafael Eitan, chief of staff of the Israeli Defence Forces (IDF), developed the plans for an invasion to rid northern Israel of Palestine Liberation Organization (PLO) raids and shelling from southern Lebanon, which had killed twenty-five Israelis and wounded 250 more between July 1981 and June 1982.[8]

After three years of frenzied shelling and counter-shelling, the situation took a turn for the worse when an assassination attempt was made against the Israeli ambassador in London on 3 June 1982. Convinced that the attack was orchestrated by the PLO, the IDF decided to launch the long-planned, often-delayed invasion Operation PEACE FOR GALILEE.[9] Its goal was to destroy the infrastructure and bases of the PLO in southern Lebanon and remove the artillery threat to northern Israel. Although Israel proclaimed a desire to avoid any direct confrontation with Syrian forces in Lebanon, Damascus decided to reinforce its Lebanon contingent, including the Syrian SAM batteries deployed in the Bekaa.[10] Although Syria intended this action as an act of deterrence, the Israelis decided that the batteries must be destroyed, for by now hostilities had erupted between Syrian and Israeli forces.

On 6 June Israeli ground forces began an advance into the PLO settlements in Lebanon with the Israeli Air Force fighters and attack helicopters providing close support. The Israeli advance, after an initial push to Jazzin, stalled. To break the impasse, the ground troops needed continued air support, but aircraft and helicopters would be in the range of the SAMs deployed in the Bekaa Valley. The Israeli Air Force decided to execute their operational plans to take out these SAM sites and the initial plans called for attacks on the fourteen known SAM sites, but intelligence reported on 8 June that Syria had moved an additional five SA-6s from the Golan Heights into the Bekaa Valley. This movement had been picked up by Israeli remotely-piloted vehicles (RPVs) which had been active over the area for the past year.

The Israeli plans had to be changed to factor in the reinforcement of the SAM belt and the new plan was ready by the morning of 8 June. The go-ahead by Israel's cabinet, however, was not given until 10:00am. and the attack was accordingly pushed back to 2:00pm on the 9th.[11] Assuming that the SAMs would be adequate to take on the Israeli Air Force, and to avoid any fratricide incident, Syria withdrew her combat air patrols when the Israeli aircraft were picked up. As a result, when Israel launched the strike force, with the Syrian CAP no longer over the area, the Israelis had a free run to take on the SAMs and the AAA.[12]

It is generally accepted that, in the course of the first attack against the Bekaa on 9 June, the Israelis destroyed seventeen of the nineteen Syrian SAM batteries and their radar sites, as well as twenty-nine Syrian Air Force (SAF) fighters, without loss.[13] The following day the Israeli Air Force destroyed the remaining two missile batteries. The destruction of nineteen SAM batteries was carried out in less than forty-eight hours but the planning and preparation for this had gone on for over a year. As per the initial plans, Israel had three options – a ground offensive, a heliborne assault and a joint air/missile attack.[14] Of these, the air/missile attack was considered to have the best option of success with least casualties. The option as assessed by the Central Intelligence Agency (CIA) was, first, the use of Lance surface-to-surface missiles, to be followed by an attack by F-4s and A-4s using Shrike and/or Standard anti-radiation missiles (ARMs) with the Walleye and Maverick laser-guided bombs (LGBs). Even this option, as assessed by the CIA, could not be exercised by Israel as it did not have the Lance missiles and thus had to work out a viable option using the resources it had and beginning to develop what it felt it needed to carry out its plan successfully. This was done over a period of almost thirteen months, during which Israel developed and refined not only the tactics but also the required weapon and support systems.

The first step was to get maximum possible intelligence about the SAMs in the valley. For a long time, Israeli UAVs, namely the Mastiff and the Scout, overflew the area defended by the Syrian SAMs, gathering intelligence about the missiles. Drawing on the experiences of the Yom Kippur War, Israel had wanted a system that could give its field commanders the ability to look 'over the hill' and, with this in mind, had gone in for the unmanned aerial vehicles (UAVs). One of the first UAVs to be acquired was the Tadiran Mastiff, which could carry a 10kg payload and had a range of thirty to fifty kilometres. It could stay aloft for over seven hours, giving an unprecedented depth of coverage, speed of information delivery, and on-station surveillance time. Scout, on the other hand, was an indigenously developed UAV.

While the Mastiffs contained a gyro-stabilized television and a high-resolution panoramic camera which was used for photo-reconnaissance, the Scouts were configured for electronic intelligence and picked up the radar emissions which enabled the fingerprinting of the SAM radars.

Both were capable of relaying their information to ground and airborne command posts for immediate analysis. The Scout UAV was first used in 1981 when one of the UAVs was sent over Lebanon and had successfully broadcast real-time pictures of the Syrian anti-aircraft systems deployed in the area.

In 1982 Israel had one squadron of UAVs, enough to keep at least two UAVs in the air all the time, which provided constant locations of the Syrian SAM batteries.[15] Using the information now available, Israel got on with preparing the plan for taking out the SAMs. This was facilitated by two mistakes made by the Syrians which proved to be their undoing. The first was the lack of movement by the SA-6 missiles which remained dug in for over a year in the Bekaa at the same locations, allowing the Israelis to pinpoint the precise location of each target. The second mistake was the lack of emission control by the Syrian SAM operators who turned on their radars frequently, often using more radars than required when practising engagements. This allowed the Israelis to fingerprint or identify the exact radar frequencies used by the Syrians.

The next stage was the training and rehearsals for executing the plan for which it set up simulated SA-6 sites in the Negev Desert and carried out simulation attacks, refining the drills and procedures for over thirteen months. An important part of the plan was the weapons to be used to attack the missile sites. Though Lance tactical missiles had been identified as suitable to attack the SA-6 sites, the US refused to supply them, forcing Israel to develop its own weapons and support systems.

One aspect that required development of a new support system was to deceive the Syrian SAM operators about the exact nature of the air strikes. Without putting the aircraft at risk, Israel wanted a system that would make the Syrians believe that a massed air attack was being carried out against them. Israel hoped that it would force the Syrians to switch on their radars, facilitating kinetic attacks against them. While the UAVs were useful in gaining information about the SAMs, they were too slow to be taken as attack aircraft and were not suitable for the deception role. To overcome this problem, Israel developed two decoys – Samson and Delilah. Samson was a 300-pound unpowered decoy with a cylindrical fuselage having a top speed of Mach 0.8 to 0.9 launched from a F-4 Phantom while Delilah was an indigenous air-launched cruise missile

(ALCM) that was used to simulate a combat aircraft and act as a decoy. It also had the ability to both loiter and carry out repeated passes that made it the ideal weapon for attacking mobile sites.[16]

To destroy the SAM sites, Israel had the Shrike and Standard anti-radiation missiles (ARMs) but they were not considered very reliable. Shrike had been used in the Yom Kippur War and its performance had not been satisfactory. The Standard AGM-78 that came into service with the Israeli Defence Force after the 1973 Yom Kippur War was a more advanced ARM, but even this was not found to be effective enough – primarily because its warhead was not lethal enough to destroy the radar installations. The Israel Military Industries (IMI) was then contracted to develop a new warhead with controlled fragmentation to meet the air force's request. Some reports indicate that development was carried out with help from General Dynamics.[17]

Using the basic AGM-78, Israel developed Keres, a surface-to-surface anti-radiation missile under the new designation RGM-66D/2 with a range of several dozen kilometres. Unlike Shrike and Standard ARMs, Keres was launched from a modified M4 Sherman tank, called the Kilshon.[18] Another weapon system developed was the Ze'ev (Wolf), a short-range missile system, a 216mm 'flying bomb' capable of delivering a 90kg warhead over short ranges, approximately less than four kilometres. Reportedly, one version was fired from a 'pipe-frame' launcher, something akin to the famous Soviet *Katusha* rockets.

On 6 June Syria had deployed fourteen SAM batteries in the valley – two SA-2, two SA-3 and eleven SA-6. The S-75, S-125, and 2K12 sites had serious limitation in that they could only engage one target per site, leaving them susceptible to saturation. Moreover, these had been used extensively during the previous wars and were not a novelty for the Israelis, unlike the SA-6 which was faced for the first time in 1973 and had proved to be the most lethal of all SAMs since the Israelis had no countermeasure against it. This time around the Syrian reliance on aging and well-known Soviet SAM systems was to prove a serious defensive liability.

The plan to destroy the Syrian SAMs was put into action on 9 June. Just prior to the air attack, a commando raid destroyed/neutralized a control centre, paralysing the Syrian Command and Control system.

Simultaneously, an EC-135 (a modified Boeing 707), E2C Hawkeye and a CH-53 helicopter carrying radar-jamming devices approached the battle area, not only picking up radar transmissions but also disrupting the communication networks. These aircraft carried a variety of electronic sensors and palletized jammers for use against the Syrian communication nets and missile site radars. To further cripple the Syrian defences, the first air strike was against the Syrian radar at the top of Jebel Baruk that covered most of the target area.[19]

Next was the deception phase. Waves of decoy drones simulating strike aircraft were sent over the Syrian batteries who reacted by turning on their radars to track them. The Mastiffs were the first to go in. Once they were tracked by Syrian radar, the tracking signals were relayed to another Scout outside the missiles' range. The Scout then relayed the signal to an E2C Hawkeye aircraft orbiting off the coast. The data gathered was analysed by the E2Cs and Boeing 707 ECM aircraft in real time. As the decoys came overhead, the Syrians ordered their combat air patrols to return to base and land, assuming their SAM belt to be capable enough to take on the Israeli air attack. Some of the SAM batteries, assuming this to be a real air raid, engaged the drones, expending valuable, ready-to-fire missiles.[20] As had been anticipated, the Syrians continued to radiate long after the need for tracking information was over. To add to the confusion and deception, the Israelis dropped chaff, using rockets and aircrafts.

Following this, the Israelis began the SAM attack phase. The first wave was made up of ninety-six F-15s and F-16s to provide interception and air defence capability, followed by a second wave of ninety-two F-4 Phantoms armed with anti-radiation missiles attacking the SAM batteries. To destroy the SAM sites, Israel also used the Keres, launched from the Kilshon mounts, and Ze'ev (Wolf) short-range missiles.[21] The Syrians reportedly fired fifty-seven SA-6s, but to no effect.[22]

As the fighters were striking known locations, the attacking aircraft moved fast, minimizing their exposure to the SAMs. The rapid flight time of the missiles also furnished just enough stand off to maximize the F-4s' chances of getting away. All it took was ten minutes to destroy ten of the Syrian SAM batteries. Facilitating the accurate targeting were the laser-guided bombs, with laser designators mounted on the RPVs illuminating the targets to guide the bombs.[23] Once the attack on the

Syrian missile battery radars with ARMs had been completed, the missile sites were attacked by cluster munitions and regular bombs launched by the Kfir C-2 aircraft. By the time the operation was called off for the day, Israel had destroyed fourteen of the sixteen SAM batteries.[24]

Syria moved four more SA-6 batteries into the area on the night 9/10 June. All six, in a repeat performance, were destroyed the next day. The Syrian fighters that rose to defend the SAMs and ZSUs were badly mauled, with eighty aircraft reportedly shot down without the loss of a single Israeli aircraft.[25]

Wiping out the Bekaa Valley SAMs cleared the way for the IAF to give full support to the Israeli ground forces. However, the Syrians did not give up moving SAM batteries into the region. Just two weeks after the first operation, a F-4 Phantom loitering in the area was shot down by a Syrian SAM which the Israelis believed came from Syria and not from inside Lebanon.[26] The Israeli Air Force again attacked the SAM sites, destroying three more batteries. By the end of July Syria had lost at least eighty-seven aircraft, while Israeli losses amounted to a few helicopters, one RF-4E, and an A-4 Skyhawk downed by a PLO SA-7.[27] Of the UAVs used by Israel, two Firebees and one Scout were lost to ground fire.[28]

Understandably, Arab claims differ from Israeli accounts. While not mentioning the destruction of SAMs, Syria claimed that it shot down nineteen Israeli aircraft on 9 June for the loss of fourteen and that six more Israeli aircraft were shot down the next day.[29]

The success in achieving almost a complete destruction of the SAMs in the Bekaa Valley was an unprecedented event, and something which has not been truly repeated, even by Israel. Never again has an air defence network been disabled so badly. A number of factors enabled the Israelis to be successful in June 1982. First was the familiarity with the terrain. The Israeli Air Force had been flying virtually unopposed over Lebanon and the Bekaa Valley for years, giving it a familiarity with the target area and the deployment of enemy forces unprecedented in modern warfare. Secondly, not only had its pilots carried out extensive training, including simulated attacks on SAM sites, practising their tactics for months together, but most of them had combat experience which is the most realistic training of all.

The weapons and support systems, including Ze'ev, Keres, Samson, Delilah, Mastiff and Scout, were almost 'made to order' systems which made all the difference, effectively targeting and destroying the SAMs while keeping the aircraft away at stand-off ranges. An added advantage was that South Africa had shared the experience gained during Operation PROTEA against Angola in which the Scout UAVs had been employed for the first time in combat. This helped Israel refine its plans of using the UAVs.[30] The use of drones to fingerprint the SAM radars was invaluable in providing information vital to Israeli countermeasures.[31]

The major factor which contributed to Israeli success and helped them was in fact the Syrians' handling of their air defence network. Although the Syrian air defence system was based on the Soviet air defence model, the basic Soviet PVO-Strany doctrine of manoeuvre and camouflage was not followed by the Syrians: the Soviets advocated regular re-positioning of mobile SAMs to confuse enemy intelligence, use of alternative firing positions, defensive ambushes and the emplacement of dummy SAM sites as the fundamental considerations for the effective deployment and survivability of ground-based air defences.[32] The static deployment of Syria's missiles, exposing them for years, gave a tactical advantage to the Israelis, providing valuable intelligence so very critical for accurate targeting of the missile sites.[33] Not only that, some measures taken by the Syrians to protect the missile sites, like using smoke to hide them, in fact made it easier to locate them.[34]

The Israeli air strikes had left the Syrian air defences crippled, but not totally beaten. Just two weeks later, Israel suffered the loss of an F-4 Phantom in the same area to a Syrian SAM. An air defence system is made up of multiple layers of intertwined elements – interdependent and yet capable of operating independently. It has a resilience that allows it to continue inflicting attrition even if it is in a degraded state.

Chapter 6

Lebanon 1983

In September 1982 President Ronald Reagan authorized the deployment of US marines to Lebanon as part of a Multinational Force (MNF) consisting of US, French and Italian troops 'with the mission of enabling the Lebanese Government to resume full sovereignty over its capital, the essential precondition for extending its control over the entire country'.[1] While the United States was supposed to have been a neutral entity in Lebanon as part of the MNF, by summer 1983 it had openly sided with the pro-Israeli Lebanese government. By late August the marines of the MNF were getting caught up in firefights with armed elements outside their perimeter in the predominantly Shia suburbs of south Beirut. The marines also received occasional fire from nearby mountain slopes, largely held by Druze fighters, supplied by Syria. On at least two occasions, the fighting spilled over to the marine positions to which the marines responded with artillery, small-arms, and a helicopter gunship.

As the fighting between Lebanese Armed Forces and the militia groups intensified and the battle lines blurred, it was directly threatening the Americans in Lebanon. Realizing the changing ground situation, the United States changed its stance and the marines were authorized to fire in support of the Lebanese Army. It was now a direct intervention on the side of the Christians and the government. To add to the available firepower, the United States despatched the battleship *New Jersey* to Lebanese waters.

The multinational force, as part of its regular operations, had carried out regular reconnaissance missions from September without any untoward incident or opposition. The local militia were reported to have limited anti-aircraft capability as they had some heavy machine guns and man-portable surface-to-air missiles, including the Soviet SA-7, in the hills ringing Beirut, but it was believed that their employment was tightly controlled and that they did not pose a significant threat to the reconnaissance flights.

The situation changed on 20 September as two US Navy carrier-based reconnaissance aircraft were attacked for the first time by an SA-7 surface-to-air missile. Fired from an unknown location, the missile never acquired the lead aircraft and missed it by more than two kilometres. Two weeks later, a United States Marine Corps CH-46 helicopter on a routine logistic mission drew hostile ground fire, sustaining minor damage.[2] The skies over Lebanon were no longer safe and free of hostile fire.

On 23 October two truck bombs struck buildings in Beirut, housing American and French service members of the Multinational Force. The first was detonated at the building serving as a barracks for the United States' 1st Battalion 8th Marines, while the second was at the nine-storey Drakkar building, a few kilometres away, where the French paratrooper contingent was stationed. The attacks killed 241 US and fifty-eight French peacekeepers. As a retaliation to the truck bombing, France launched airstrikes in the Bekaa Valley against alleged Islamic Revolutionary Guard Corps (IRGC) positions.

Fourteen French Super Étendard fighter jets from the aircraft carrier *Clemenceau*, off the Lebanese coast, flew at least two raids against pro-Iranian Shi'ite militia bases east of Baalbek in central Lebanon, which was under the control of Syrian troops. The air strikes began at 4:20pm and were a pre-emptive action designed to 'prevent fresh terrorist actions against French forces in Lebanon'.[3]

The Israeli Air Force had carried out a raid against a nearby training camp that belonged to the same pro-Iranian Shi'ite militia although there was no suggestion that the two air strikes, by France and Israel, were linked. There was no loss of any aircraft during the air strikes.

The air strikes by France seemed to be an act of revenge but, after the strike, French defence ministry officials insisted its purpose was not revenge but was 'to prevent further attacks against French forces in Lebanon'.[4] The International Peacekeeping Mission continued to serve in Lebanon and the reconnaissance missions carried on as before.

Except from shelling by naval guns, no retaliatory action was taken by the United States.[5] On 3 December two F-14 Tomcats on a routine tactical-reconnaissance mission encountered anti-aircraft fire and at least ten SAMs were fired at them. No damage was caused, but it was an unprecedented incident in sheer volume of fire and use of multiple SAMs while attacking the US fighters.[6] It was then that the United States decided to carry out a retaliatory air strike against Syrian air defence emplacements.

At this time the Syrian air defences were a mix of anti-aircraft guns, including the radar-controlled ZSU-23-4B Schilkas, and the man-portable SAMs with no serious SAM presence since most of the Soviet SA-6 SAM batteries had been destroyed by the Israeli Air Force during the Bekaa Valley campaign just a year before and were not reported to be operational at this stage. As the experience of the past few months had also shown, it was not a serious air defence threat that the United States faced at this stage. The low level of air defence notwithstanding, the air strikes ended up as a misadventure with the first loss of combat aircraft since the Vietnam War.

The strike was carried out by twelve A-7 Corsairs and sixteen A-6E Intruder light bombers from the USS *Independence* and the USS *John F. Kennedy*, escorted by an E-2 Hawkeye, two EA-6 Prowlers, and two F-14s.[7] Right from the beginning, the planning for the attack was marked by confusion. When the strikes had been cleared by the US president, one of the Navy aircraft carriers, the *Kennedy*, was about to leave for the Suez Canal and had already stored its bombs. The aircraft of the other carrier, *Independence*, were armed with heavy bombs in anticipation of orders to attack a different target. Those bombs had to be replaced with a type more suitable for use against anti-aircraft emplacements. Even the time of the attack was moved from 11:00am to 6:30am, over the objections of the US fleet commander, which did not leave enough time to re-arm all twenty-eight aircraft taking part in the strike.

A-7 Corsairs and A-6 Intruders are subsonic attack aircraft that carry a heavy payload of bombs, but do not have the speed of the Navy's F-14 Tomcats. They were tasked to strike a string of three sites south-east of Beirut in areas near the Beirut-Damascus highway containing Syrian, Druze and Palestinian fighters, which were suspected to include an ammunition depot, air-defence radars, anti-aircraft guns, and SAMs.

The early morning haze obscured the targets and the pilots were forced to fly low into the intense fire of the anti-aircraft guns in an attempt to spot the targets. Compounding the lapse was the fact that all the aircraft in the strike package were following the same route, making it easy for gunners to train their weapons.[8]

A few Syrian guns were destroyed, but the intensity of the Syrian fire forced many of the planes to drop their bombs away from the targeted positions. An A-7 Corsair was hit by the ground fire, severely damaging it and forcing the pilot to eject. The A-7 smashed into a house just north of Beirut. The other downed jet was an A-6 Intruder, the pilot of which was killed although the navigator managed to eject safely and was taken prisoner.[9] The Pentagon declared that the raid was a success although in hindsight it was an abject failure with the Syrian air defence threat remaining as lethal as before.

The Syrian air defences survived and continued to harass the US aircraft. Days after the air strike, Syrian anti-aircraft guns were once again active but failed to shoot down any aircraft. In response, the battleship USS *New Jersey* fired 1,900-pound shells at Syrian positions east of Beirut. No air raids were carried out by the United States.

The erratic and sporadic nature of the attacks was dramatized again on 28 January 1984, when an SA-7 missile was fired at a United States Marine CH-46 approaching a landing zone which had been used extensively since November the previous year.[10] Fortunately, the SA-7 missed the aircraft.

The only good to come out of the failure was the establishment of the Naval Strike and Air Warfare Center (Strike University) at the air station in Fallon, Nevada, to study better ways of getting bombs on target while surviving intense SAM environments, and their research yielded more thorough mission planning processes, off-axis attack profiles, and the improved use of jammers to better suppress the SAM threat.

Chapter 7

Libya

The relationship between the United States and Libya has been marred since the 1960s with the US accusing Libya of supporting terrorist activities and carrying out weapons smuggling and espionage. The relationship took a turn for the worse when the TWA Flight 847 was hijacked on 14 June 1985, followed by the terrorist attacks on the Rome and Vienna airports on 27 December. The United States accused Libya of being implicit in the hijacking and the terrorist attacks.

Operation ELDORADO CANYON

A major cause of tension between the two nations had been the assertion by Libya over control of the entire Gulf of Sidra and claiming a 115-kilometre fishing zone, drawing the so-called 'Line of Death'. The United States had continued to challenge Libya's claim to the Gulf of Sidra and repeatedly crossed the self-proclaimed 'Line of Death' at 32 degrees 30 minutes north latitude, conducting several 'Freedom of Navigation' missions under Operation ATTAIN DOCUMENT in the area around Libya. US warships would carry out operations up to and then southward across the 'Line of Death'.[1]

The United States Navy stepped up its activities following the incidents in December 1985. The first two parts of the operation were held in January-February, without incident: the United States Navy repeatedly intercepted Libyan fighters over the Gulf of Sidra in excess of 150 sorties, but neither side opened fire. The US Navy task force, however, gathered valuable intelligence on the Libyan air defence system.[2]

Matters came to head during the third 'Freedom of Navigation' mission in March 1986. On 23 March US aircraft from three aircraft carriers crossed the 'Line of Death' and were operating in the Gulf of Sidra. The next day a three-ship surface action group, covered by a CAP, moved across the line into the disputed waters.

A Libyan MiG-25 that had come a bit too close to a US Navy battlegroup was intercepted by the F-14 Tomcats. In response, a Libyan missile installation near Surt (Sirte) launched two Soviet-made SA-5 'Gammon' SAMs against the F-14A Tomcats on the southern CAP. Libya had begun the installation of Soviet SA-5 surface-to-air missile batteries and radars only in December 1985 and this was the combat debut of the long-range SAM.[3]

As the Tomcats took evasive action, the missiles missed their target and fell harmlessly into the sea.[4] The Libyans on the other hand claimed that both Tomcats were destroyed by the SA-5s. Later in the day, the Libyans fired two additional SA-5s, but both were reportedly jammed by an EA-6B that was operating in the area. The Libyans, however, claimed that a second group of two aircraft was detected in the evening at about 6:00pm and was engaged by the SA-5 at a range of seventy-five kilometres, bringing the total kills achieved to three. The United States denied having lost any aircraft during the day.[5]

A Soviet account of the incident by Colonel Alexander Marchenko, a former adviser to the commander of the Libyan SA-5 anti-aircraft missile brigade, claims that the SA-5s did indeed destroy three U.S. aircraft, although it mentions the aircraft to be A-6E Intruders and not the F-14 Tomcats that were fired at in the first incident.[6]

> As soon as two deck attack aircraft, presumably the A-6E Intruder, appeared over the bay, at 13 hours 50 minutes at a distance of 115 km both Vega battalions fired one rocket at them. Violators, moving away from Soviet missiles, tried to manoeuvre in height (from 4.5 to 2.5 km) and speed, to carry out anti-missile manoeuvres, but everything turned out to be ineffective. On the screens of indicators there were signs of destruction of targets – loss of height and speed. After 3 hours, the first duty division, by launching another missile at a distance of 100 to 75 km knocks down another single American attack aircraft.

As the action was unfolding in the air, several Libyan patrol boats were headed out towards the US battlegroup, of which a La Combattante-class patrol boat was taken out by two air-launched RGM-84 Harpoon cruise missiles fired by an A-7 Corsair, setting it ablaze. The patrol boat was subsequently towed back to Benghazi. This was the first air-to-surface firing of a Harpoon missile in combat.[7]

Two Harpoon missiles were launched from the cruiser USS *Yorktown* also but hit no targets. Forty minutes later, F-14s, F/A-18s, A-7Es and EA-6Bs headed towards the SA-5 site, which was attacked by the A-7Es, launching several HARM missiles. It was not clear if any of the US missiles struck their intended targets.[8]

The statement by the United States Secretary of Defence, Caspar W. Weinberger, is, however, explicit in claiming that the HARM missiles hit the SA-5s:[9]

At about three o'clock this afternoon, Eastern time, we fired, it was 3:06 actually, we launched the response in the form of HARM missiles fired by an A-7 from the *Saratoga*. It hit the square pair of radars that service the SA-5 site. It hit another radar. The SA-5 site is out of action.

The Soviet accounts also acknowledge that the HARM guided missiles launched on the positions of the Surt (Sirte) city missile base resulted in damage to the Vega transceiver cabin.[10] Another Soviet account is more detailed and mentions that one of the missiles exploded eight metres from the S-200 complex, disabling the antenna systems and waveguides, and the second missile went flying past the SA-5 site, missing the target.[11]

During the course of the night, two Nanuchka-class missile boats were attacked by A-6s as they approached the task force. Both boats were hit, and it was initially claimed that the A-6s had sunk them but later the claim was revised to only one. A total of five attacks was carried out on Libyan ships, destroying two patrol boats. The SA-5 site was not attacked again as the 'Libyans had not turned on the radar'. Other air defence radars were detected but were not attacked.[12] The US surface action group withdrew north of the 'Line of Death' after two days, on 27 March.[13]

The next phase of the events unfolded in April when a bomb exploded on TWA flight 840 over Argos, Greece, on the 2nd. The United States government blamed Libya for the deaths of four people killed in the incident. Three days later, terrorists bombed the La Belle Discotheque in West Berlin on 5 April, killing two American servicemen, and injuring seventy-nine others. Three terrorist groups claimed responsibility for the bombing, but the United States and West Germany independently announced 'incontrovertible' evidence that Libyans were responsible for the bombing.[14]

In retaliation for the Berlin bombing, the United States president ordered air strikes against Libya – Operation EL DORADO CANYON. It was a long-range strike at 'terrorist centres' in Libya and had been developed by the 48th Tactical Fighter Wing (TFW) of the United States Air Force. Five targets were selected, the first four because the US believed them to be associated with Libyan terrorist operations, and the last for force protection. These were the Aziziyh Barracks and the military facilities in Tripoli, Side Bilal Base, Jamahirayah Military Barracks, Benghazi, and the Benina Air Base, south-east of Benghazi.[15] All except one of these targets were chosen because of their purported direct connection to terrorist activity. The single exception was the Benina military airfield which housed the MiG-23 Flogger E interceptor aircraft. This target was hit to pre-empt Libyan interceptors from taking off and attacking the raiding aircraft.

The operation was launched on 14 April 1986 when twenty-four US Air Force F-111 Aardvarks, supported by five EF-111 Ravens, took off from their bases in England. The F-111s had to be re-fuelled four times during the 3,500-mile flight due to flight restrictions. After the first refuelling, six F-111s and one EF-111A airborne spare returned to their bases, leaving eighteen Aardvarks and five Ravens whose targeting, weapons delivery, and terrain-following radar were all fully functional at that point.

At about the same time that the USAF task force had taken off from its bases, the United States Navy's battlegroups began their high-speed dash toward Libya. At 12:45am the two US Navy aircraft carriers, the *Coral Sea* and *America*, launched fourteen A-6E strike aircraft and twelve F/A-18 and A-7 strike support aircraft. After the F-111s finished their last re-fuelling, they left their mother tankers in three attack groups, nine for Bab al-Aziziyah barracks, six for the Tripoli airport; and three for Sidi Bilal.[16]

Defending the Libyan airspace was a well-developed air defence network comprising of four long-range S-200 Vega/Dubna Vega anti-aircraft missile units with twenty-four launchers and eighty-six S-75 Dvina/SA-3 Neva anti-aircraft missile units with 276 launchers. Covering Tripoli alone were seven S-75 Dvina Volkhov missile units with six missile-launchers each, twelve S-125 Neva missile units with four missile-launchers each, three 2K12 Kub missile units with forty-eight launchers, one 9K33 Osa Osa-AK regiment with sixteen launch vehicles and two Crotale II units with sixty launch pads. The capital city was well protected by a number of anti-aircraft guns which included the radar-controlled ZSU-23-4 Schilkas.

At ten minutes before the strike was to be carried out, the EF-111As and the Navy's EA-6Bs commenced electronic jamming against Libyan radar and communications. The six A-7Es from the USS *America* and six F-18As from the USS *Coral Sea* approached the coastline as the F-111s and A-6s neared their targets and popped up to allow the Libyan air defence radars to detect them. As the radars tried to lock on, they fired over a dozen Shrikes and about thirty HARMs to suppress the missile systems.

At approximately midnight, the Libyans launched several SA-2s and SA-5s at the American A-6Es and A-7Es, which responded by heading towards the coast. A-7Es from VA-83 launched HARM missiles, disabling several Libyan radars. Three more SA-5s were launched from Sirte with a single SA-2 launched near Benghazi. Corsairs and Intruders responded in force: A-7Es of VA-83 closed to only twenty-five kilometres of the Libyan coast, and a whole bunch of AGM-88s was fired, disabling several Libyan radars, including at least two Square Pairs, used for the guidance of SA-5s and several other SAM-fire-control systems, foremost Fansongs, used for SA-2 guidance.[17] The Americans suffered no losses, although at least three more SA-5s were fired by the site near Sirte, and one SA-2 from another site, stationed near Benghazi.

According to a Soviet source, the United States used decoys to deceive the Libyan radars although this is not mentioned in any other accounts while some mention that the air defence radars did not activate until four minutes prior to the planned Time Over Target (TOT) and were immediately suppressed when they came on.[18] The Flat Face, Low Blow,

Straight Flush, Fansong and possibly Land Roll acquisition radars associated with the SA-3, SA-6, SA-2 and SA-8 Gecko surface-to-air missile systems were now effectively suppressed.

The coast was clear for the strike aircraft. Although joint in nature, the actual execution of the strike had been operationally and geographically divided between the Navy and Air Force. Navy A-6s were assigned the two targets in the Benghazi area, and the other three targets in the vicinity of Tripoli were to be attacked by the Air Force F-111s. As the strike aircraft approached the target areas, one of the F-111s assigned the Bab al-Aziziyah target in Tripoli, Karma 52, crashed in the sea.[19] No reason was given by the United States for this but it was almost certainly due to a hit from a Libyan SAM as it was reported to be on fire in flight.

Of the remaining eight F-111s assigned for the Bab al-Aziziyah, one had flown in the wrong direction after the final re-fuelling, one aborted while still over the water, and three aborted their attacks in the target area due to equipment malfunctions. Only three F-111s remained to drop their laser-guided bombs. Two of these caused considerable damage to the compound, but the third F-111 crew misidentified its 'offset-aim point' on the radar screen and dropped its bomb load near the French embassy, one-and-a-half miles north-east of the intended target.[20]

All three F-111s assigned the Sidi Bilal naval commando training complex about fifteen miles west of Tripoli managed to hit the target with laser-guided bombs but, of the last six Aardvarks, one F-111 lost its terrain-following radar and aborted the mission before reaching the Tripoli Airport.

The Navy strikes to the east in Benghazi were more successful. Six of eight A-6s allocated to Benina airfield reached their targets, destroying several MiGs, helicopters, and transport planes, and six of seven A-6s planned for the Jamahiriyah Barracks missed most of the complex, but fortuitously destroyed four MiGs in a nearby warehouse. Two of the Intruders aborted their bombing runs. The A-7s and F/A-18s assigned the SAM suppression mission severely damaged the Libyan air defence network with HARM and SHRIKE missiles.[21] By 2:13am all strike aircraft, except Karma 52, had safely crossed back over the Libyan coast, the A-6s heading toward the carriers and the F-111s toward the tankers waiting for them over the Mediterranean.

The raids were met by intense anti-aircraft fire by both SAMs and guns but, as the Libyans fired their missiles and anti-aircraft guns reportedly without radar assistance, it was all rather ineffective. The large number of SA-2, SA-3, SA-6 and SA-8 SAMs continued to fire blindly into the sky for hours after the American aircraft had departed.

By 7:53pm, all Navy aircraft had returned to their carriers. When the F-111s linked up with the tankers for their first return aerial re-fuelling, they confirmed that one F-111 had been lost. En route back to England, one F-111 diverted to Rota, Spain, because of an overheated engine. Search and rescue efforts for the missing F-111 lasted throughout 15 April but were terminated later that evening.

The United States declared the raid to be a success, having met all its objectives, but it was not without controversy. The Navy later claimed that the entire operation could have been accomplished using only the Navy assets. Even though all three US Air Force targets had been hit, only four of the eighteen F-111s dropped their bombs successfully. Six were forced to abort due to aircraft difficulties or stringencies of the rules of engagement. Seven missed their targets and one was lost.[22]

Libyan air defences performed poorly, particularly in view of the warning time involved. Intense but unco-ordinated AAA fire was encountered, and the Libyans fired a large number of SA-2, SA-3, SA-6 and SA-8 SAMs, most of which were not correctly guided in the absence of radar and full communications. The heaviest SAM activity was reported over Tripoli and the city of Benghazi. Of the gun systems, the vintage ZSU-23-4B was reportedly the most effective, especially in the area around the el Aziziya Barracks.[23] Soviet accounts, published in the state newspaper *Red Star*, state that it was the ZSU-23-4B deployed around el Aziziya Barracks that shot down one F-111 and damaged another.[24]

Libya's MiG-25 Foxbats, MiG-23 Floggers and Mirages remained on the ground throughout the strikes. A total of five Libyan national air defence anti-aircraft missile units were destroyed, specifically two SA-2 missile units and one each of SA-3, SA-6 and Crotale II.

The failure of Libyan air defences was analysed and studied by the Soviets and, as in all other cases, the study found that it was not the missile systems that had failed but poor command and control over the air defences, coupled with insufficient level of training, that led to the failure in countering the US air strike. Amongst other reasons were inadequate radar coverage over the Mediterranean which catered for a minimum acquisition altitude of 250 to 300 metres, allowing the strike aircraft to approach undetected at low level. The gap between the kill zones of the neighbouring SA-2 and SA-3 sites above the Tripoli airfield was also exploited by the strike aircraft to approach the targets undetected.

The Soviet report further claims that the SAMs deployed around Benghazi destroyed five to six targets and the HARMs launched by the A-6 aircraft destroyed at least one guidance unit of the SA-6 missile system.[25] Interestingly, the report mentions that some weapon crews ran away in panic once the raids started.

Following the US raid, Libya added a second SA5 missile site at Benghazi on the Gulf of Sidra. The original SA-5 site at Sirte, which US Navy bombers had knocked out of action, was also put back in service with all twelve launchers being made functional. The second site at Benghazi was to provide wide coverage of the Gulf of Sidra.[26]

The air strikes were among the shortest operations in recent times and were executed with precision but, apart from the political and ethical issues raised, militarily they also raised questions about the front-line strike aircraft F-111's ability to strike targets in a dense air defence environment as fourteen F-111s were supported by about 100 aircraft. Secondly, the failure, technical or otherwise, of almost half the aircraft while delivering their weapon loads raised serious questions about their capability to operate in a more hostile environment.

The anti-radar missiles did not live up to the promise and the destruction they caused was hard to ascertain – it was never known what damage was really caused by the numerous missiles launched. Lastly, the operation again brought to the fore the resilience of the air defence systems. Not only was the destroyed SA-5 site at Sirte back in action but Libya had added another site, at Benghazi.

The debate of the success, or otherwise, of the air strikes and performance of the (then) Soviet missile systems will go on. Adding to the same is a more recent Russian article that is more critical of the performance of the (then) Soviet missile systems:[27]

For the Soviet military it is time to think. Despite the 20 Libyan air defence brigades and Gaddafi's personal warning from the Italian

Prime Minister, the overwhelming majority of American aircraft flew calmly, bombed and departed without loss. The air defence system revealed a lot of deficiencies. The anti-aircraft systems practically did not change positions, and half were not even equipped in engineering terms. The radars did not unite into a single system, and when repelling the raid they worked for several minutes in a row, facilitating the guidance of the missiles. Conversely, some of the anti-aircraft missile guidance stations simply did not turn on because of the fear of defeat by anti-radar missiles.

The failure of Libyan Air Defences cannot only be attributed to the vintage of the equipment; more than fair blame lies with the poor training standards and operational readiness of the Libyan air defenders.

Libyan Civil War 2011–2018

In February 2011, as part of the Arab Spring protests, mass unrest against the Gaddafi regime broke out in Libya leading to armed clashes between the government forces and the rebels. Beginning with protests in Zawiya and Benghazi, the protests spread all over the country.

A National Transitional Council was formed by the anti-Gaddafi forces on 27 February to act as an interim authority in the rebel-controlled areas. A large number of Libyan armed forces personnel defected to join the rebels by March. The rebel air force, called the Free Libyan Air Force, had been operating against the Gaddafi regime since February; the first time it operated was on 15 February when a MiG-23 and a helicopter attacked some loyalist tanks near Brega and Ajdabiya. Later, they attacked and sank two pro-Gaddafi warships off the eastern coast.[28]

The armed clashes intensified with Gaddafi's forces, supported by the Libyan Air Force, rolling back the rebels and reaching Benghazi as they re-took several coastal cities. A number of Libyan aircraft were reportedly shot down by the rebels including a Mirage F-1 at Berga[29] and a Sukhoi Su-24 bomber and a Mi-24 at Ra's Lanuf. However, the exact number of aircraft cannot be verified due to conflicting claims, with the rebels giving a figure of fifteen, the majority of which were by ZPU-4 AA guns.[30] Syrian pilots were reportedly helping the Libyan Air Force and at least one MiG piloted by a Syrian Air Force pilot was shot down by the rebels.[31]

The clashes saw widespread atrocities by both sides taking a heavy toll of the civilian populace. Both sides even used the anti-aircraft guns in a direct-firing role, especially the 14.5mm ZPU-1 and 23mm ZU-23 guns with telling effect.[32]

The United Nations intervened on 17 March, authorizing member states to establish and enforce a no-fly zone over Libya, and to use 'all necessary measures' to prevent attacks on civilians.[33] Meanwhile the fighting between the pro-Gaddafi and rebel groups continued, including the use of air forces by both sides. During the battle for Benghazi, a free Libyan Air Force MiG-23 was shot down by rebel anti-aircraft guns on 19 March.[34]

With a complete breakdown of command and control channels, such fratricidal incidents were expected, and it was only a miracle that they did not occur more often. The United States started its air operations on 19 March 19, codenamed Operation ODYSSEY DAWN.[35] The first main strike was by 110 Tomahawk cruise missiles launched from United States and British ships against shore-line air defences,[36] including sites in the capital, Tripoli, and Misrata, while French and US Marine aircraft struck at pro-Gaddafi forces attacking rebel-held Benghazi[37] with the aim of dismantling Libya's ability to hinder the enforcement of the UN no-fly zone. Following bomb damage assessments, an additional twelve cruise missiles were launched against remaining IADS targets.

The Libyan Arab air force (LARAF) at this time was a marginalised force and, with the exception of a so-called 'Guard Squadron' of MiG-23s based at Sirte, distrusted by Gaddafi. The United Nations' sanctions and falling revenue had resulted in a rundown air force with antiquated aircraft, poor training and operational standards, and inadequate infrastructural support. The large-scale defections added to the problems, making the Libyan Air Force hardly a threat to the coalition forces.

The air defence forces were viewed as a 'formidable threat'[38] and had been accordingly targeted as a priority target. Libya reportedly possessed one of the more robust air defence networks in Africa, although made up of vintage, obsolete missile and radar systems, the last of which was introduced in the 1980s and had all been faced by the US and other air forces. It did not have any of the newer air defence systems. The air defence forces were subordinate to the Libyan Air Force, divided into five separate regional commands and included the strategic SAMs, tactical SAMs and the anti-aircraft guns.

The strategic SAMs operated by Libya were the S-75 (SA-2 Guideline), S-125 (SA-3 Goa), and S-200 (SA-5 Gammon), deployed at a total of thirty-one sites primarily arrayed along the coast line and at Tripoli. These included eleven S-75 Dvina and sixteen active S-125 sites deployed predominately along the coastal region; these were arrayed around Ibn Nafa air base, Tripoli, Misratah, Benghazi, Bombah, and Adam. At places the S-75 and S-125 batteries were located in close proximity to provide both redundancy and mutual support. The long-range S-200 SAM system was operated by four SA-5 brigades deployed at Tripoli, Misratah, Sirte, and Benghazi with two battalions each of six launchers (forty-eight in total), four air defence gun batteries, and a radar company.[39]

The proximity of these four locations to the coast allowed them to range far out into the Mediterranean, theoretically providing a significant stand-off engagement capability but with only SA-5 deployed at Sirte, the coastline along the Gulf of Sidra was relatively undefended.

The tactical SAMs operated by the Libyan army included the 2K12 Kvadrat (SA-6 Gainful), 9K33 Osa (SA-8 Gecko), 9K31 Strela-1 (SA-9 Gaskin), 9K35 Strela-10 (SA-13 Gopher), and Crotale, of which the SA-6 could be used to fill gaps in the overall air defence network, but the others were primarily point defence systems only. Early warning (EW) coverage was provided by a mix of radars – predominately Soviet-era systems located primarily at seventeen sites along the western and eastern coastal regions, monitoring the airspace around Tripoli and Benghazi.

Libya's strategic surface-to-air missiles had been under an Air Defence Command, formed in 1973, which was re-organized after the US air strikes in 1986 with a central command centre linked to five regional sector operations centres using high-capacity communications systems. The system was over-centralized with relatively slow data process and high vulnerability to electronic warfare and anti-radiation missiles.[40]

The United States' assessment of the Libyan air defence was that it was 'an integrated air and missile defence system much like the one that Iraq had and has surrounded Baghdad, built on older Soviet technology, but still good capability'.[41] The large numbers of the air defence systems and the US assessment notwithstanding, the following was a truer reflection of the capabilities of the Libyan air defences:[42] 'The Libyan air defence network was not capable of repelling an attack over 20 years ago and there is no reason to suspect that it will be capable of such action today.'

The air strikes by United States and Denmark were first carried out on the second day of the operation, 20 March, using B-2 Spirit stealth bombers, EA-18s, AV-8A Harriers, F-15s and F-16s and was met by intense but ineffective anti-aircraft fire[43] and all the strategic SAMs were claimed to have been destroyed or neutralized by the third day.[44]

The United States Air Force lost a F-15 on the 22nd as the aircraft crashed near Benghazi. This was the first loss of a coalition aircraft, reportedly due to technical reasons.[45]

An arms embargo imposed on 23 March, and the enforcement of the no-fly zone, had virtually grounded the Libyan Air Force and the only time it tried to defy the no-fly zone the single-engine military G-2/ Galeb was shot down by French aircraft over the city of Mistara. It was also claimed that the Tomahawk missile strikes had effectively degraded Libyan air defences to the point that no Libyan radar activity was being recorded and 'Libya's air force no longer existed as a fighting force'.[46]

On 31 March a multinational coalition led by NATO forces took control of all military operations, including the protection of civilians from attack or threat of attack. The air strikes continued till 31 October, leading to the defeat and removal of the regime of Colonel Muammar Gaddafi.[47]

April 2011 saw the arrival of drones as part of the air campaign with the US Predator armed drones making sorties over Libya, but the first strike was carried out only on the 23rd, targeting a multi-barrel rocket launcher near Misrata.[48] The drones conducted a total of 145 armed sorties between then and 20 October, and continued with patrols over Libya during the following years, occasionally launching attacks.[49]

The nature of air operations underwent another change with the British Apache and French Tigre and Gazelle helicopters in June 2011 operating against 'military vehicles, military equipment and fielded forces'. One of the sites targeted by the Apaches was a Libyan air defence radar station near the town of Brega.[50]

The helicopters repeatedly faced ground fire during their operations, including the occasional SA-7 man-portable missile launched at them, the first of which was fired on 9 June at a British Apache carrying out a mission against a Libyan command and control node near Misrata.[51] For the helicopters, the bigger danger, however, was the numerous twin-barrel ZU-23-2 guns, most of them mounted on the body of a flatbed truck. The AAA mounted on flatbeds were called 'Technical' by the coalition pilots and these were found on both sides of the divide. With no control over ground weapons, it was these guns that posed a major threat; they were routinely encountered by the Apaches and the Gazelles while engaging ground targets.[52]

The common method of defeating the MANPADS was to deploy flares and they worked well as no helicopter was lost during the entire air campaign although Libya claimed to have shot down an Apache helicopter; however, it was an MQ-8B Fire Scout helicopter drone that had been brought down by ground fire.[53] Apaches completed their last attacks on 6 August. A total of twenty-five strike missions were carried out as against the forty planned. Insufficient intelligence information and the threat posed by anti-aircraft systems were the reasons for the remainder of the missions being aborted.[54]

The missions by fixed-wing aircraft continued until October but were not without problems. Although no aircraft was lost, the lack of intelligence and surveillance resources seriously undermined the coalition air operations. At times air strikes were carried out at targets that may have already been neutralized. A large part of the effort was mounted against the Libyan air defences although it was hardly a threat even at the start of the campaign.

The SA-2, SA-3 and SA-6 missile systems were not encountered by the coalition forces during their air campaign and it is more likely that they were not even operational in March 2011. The lack of spares and technical support had made most of the SAM systems non-operational, with the SA-5 being the sole effective system in service with only 10 per cent readiness.[55]

Libya's strategic SAM network had many flaws, the main being its over-reliance on ageing Soviet technology which was by then obsolete in a modern air combat environment which had already proved its ineffectiveness during the mid-1980s. The poor command and control, inadequate radar coverage, and a lack of appreciation for American anti-radar weapons and tactics had been the reasons for failure of the Libyan air defences earlier in 1986 and there had been no improvement since then – with the situation only worsening as the vintage equipment got more difficult to maintain and operate. Also, no strategic SAM system operated by Libya possessed a multi-target engagement capability. The only SAM representing a threat to multiple aircraft was the S-200, but the relatively small number of sites hardly represented a real threat to a well-co-ordinated air strike using SEAD support mission. The layout of the strategic SAM network had a significant number of gaps that were exploited by the coalition aircraft while carrying out the strikes.

All the fixed air-defence sites and radars of the Integrated Air Defence System (IADS) were destroyed within a fortnight of the start of the campaign, leaving only the 14.5mm and 23mm anti-aircraft guns and man-portable air defence systems, including the SA-7 Strela and SA-24 (Igla), to offer a semblance of resistance to the coalition aircraft. Without any radar cover, these weapons were blind and could hardly oppose a well-co-ordinated air campaign.[56]

With such major limitations, the Libyan air defence network was not capable of repelling an attack in 1986 and was not so in 2011. The air operations carried out by fourteen NATO nations were against a poorly-equipped, obsolete air defence system. What is of interest is not the failure of the Libyan air defence system but the fact that, even when facing such an ineffective IADS, the NATO nations struggled to carry out the air operations: 26,500 sorties were launched during the campaign, much less than the 38,000 sorties flown during the seventy-eight days of Allied Force. The air operations were designed for an effort of 300 sorties a day but barely managed 150. Even so, these were carried out only with massive support from the United States that included nearly all the suppression of enemy air defence missions and the majority of support missions for Intelligence, Surveillance and Reconnaissance (ISR).

Libya's IADS was demonstrably the least challenging that Western air power has confronted since the defeat of Saddam's IADS in 1991, bringing out a simple lesson – even the most antiquated air defence is deterrent enough and cannot be taken lightly at any stage.

Chapter 8

Iraq

Desert Storm

Iraq had one of the largest standing armies in the Middle East with almost 800,000 troops, over 4,700 tanks and 3,700 artillery guns. It was a battle-hardened army, having fought a decade-long war with Iran, but this did not hide the fact that Iraq was reeling under debt which stood at $37 billion in 1990. With falling oil revenues, Iraq had no means to repay the war debt and had demanded an increase in its oil exports quota and an immediate loan of $30 billion to help tide over grim economic times. His demands not met, Saddam Hussein, the Iraqi strongman, threatened to attack Kuwait but did not elicit any favourable response. The threat was supported by a justification that Kuwait was drilling from Rumaila oil fields, across its border with Iraq, and should decrease its oil production so that Iraq could have a larger exports share.

Kuwait, in 1990, had a much smaller army with about 20,000 troops organized mainly in two armoured and one mechanized brigade, supported by about 165 tanks and 200 armoured vehicles. Facing a formidable Iraqi Air Force of over 950 combat aircraft, Kuwait could muster only four squadrons, two each of Mirage F.1 and A-4KU Skyhawk fighters. For air defence Kuwait had the improved HAWK missiles, the Soviet SA-8 and SA-7 as also 35mm Oerlikon anti-aircraft guns.[1]

After mobilizing four of its elite Republican Guard Divisions equipped with the new Soviet T-72 tanks along the border, Iraq invaded Kuwait on 2 August. Supporting the ground forces were the Army Air Corps with a squadron of Mil Mi-25 helicopter gunships, Gazelle attack helicopters, several units of Mi-8 and Mi-17 transport helicopters and a squadron of Bell 412 helicopters, while the Iraqi Air Force supported the invading force with two squadrons of Sukhoi Su-22s, one of Su-25s, one of Mirage F.1s and two of MiG-23 fighter-bombers.[2]

Caught unawares, Kuwaiti forces could only offer token resistance as the Iraqi forces rapidly took control over Kuwait City and the adjoining areas although the HAWK batteries reportedly shot down at least fifteen Iraqi aircraft.[3] Of these, only two kills could be verified later, a MiG-23BN and a Su-22. In response, an Iraqi Su-22 from No. 109 Squadron is reported to have fired a single Kh–25MP anti–radar missile against a HAWK missile battery at the Failaka Island battery, forcing the associated radar to shut down.[4] Iraqi forces captured four or five Kuwaiti Hawk batteries.

Kuwait was able to move out almost four-fifths of its aircraft to Saudi Arabia and Bahrain to prevent their falling into Iraqi hands as Iraq completed the occupation by the next day, 3 August, declaring Kuwait to be Iraq's '19th province'.

This brought immediate condemnation by the international community. The United Nations Security Council adopted a resolution on 3 August asking for an immediate withdrawal from Kuwait. Further economic sanctions were imposed on Iraq. Alarmed by the Iraqi actions, Saudi Arabia asked the United States for military assistance, responding to which the first US Air Force fighter aircraft began arriving on the 8th. This was followed by a massive military build-up codenamed Operation DESERT SHIELD.

Other nations also joined Saudi Arabia and United States in the build up, initially designed to guard against a possible Iraqi attack on Saudi Arabia. The United States and Saudi Arabia assembled a coalition of thirty-four nations in the days that followed while Iraq increased its occupation forces in Kuwait to approximately 300,000 troops and, in an effort to garner support from the Muslim world, Hussein declared a jihad, or holy war, against the coalition.

With no sign of withdrawal by Iraq, the UN Security Council on 29 November authorized the use of 'all necessary means' of force against Iraq if it did not withdraw from Kuwait by the following 15 January. By January, the coalition forces prepared to face off against Iraq numbered some 750,000. It was to be the largest military alliance since the Second World War with the majority of military forces being from the United States.

After Iraq failed to withdraw from Kuwait, the coalition forces launched the military offensive on 17 January 1991, beginning with an aerial and naval bombardment that continued for five weeks, followed by a ground assault on 24 February that led to the liberation of Kuwait. The coalition forces advanced into Iraqi territory but, soon thereafter, declared a ceasefire just 100 hours after the ground campaign started. During the war the air and ground operations were confined to Iraq, Kuwait, and areas on Saudi Arabia's border. More than the ground campaign, it was the war in the air that saw most action and defined the war. Even though Iraq had the sixth largest air force in the world, with about 915 aircraft,[5] it hardly put up a fight and it was only the ground-based air defences that offered any real opposition to the coalition air forces which were a formidable strike force with over 2,250 combat aircraft from ten nations, including 1,800 from the United States alone.[6]

Facing them was an Integrated Air Defence System made up with a mix of Soviet and Western air defence systems. While the surface-to-air missiles were predominantly of Soviet origin, the heart of the system called KARI,[7] was built by the French defence contractor, Thomson-CSF. Designed primarily to provide air defence against Israel and Iran, it could handle twenty to forty hostile aircraft and not the massive air campaign that it was subjected to during Operation DESERT STORM. The system operated at three levels:

- National/strategic, operated by the Iraqi Air Force,
- Key point defence, operated by the Republican Guard, and
- Mobile air defences, operated by the Iraqi Army

The Iraqi air defence system was highly centralized, the hub of which was the Air Defence Operations Centre (ADOC) in Baghdad linked to four sector operations centres (SOCs) controlling the air and air defence assets in respective sectors. Under each SOC, intercept operation centres (IOCs), a total of seventeen of them, ran ground-control intercepts and SAM defences and co-ordinated the flow of information from individual radar stations and visual reporting sites to the SOCs. Information collated at the centre then flowed back down to anti-aircraft units, air bases and SAM sites with all crucial decisions being made at the central

In 1979, the Soviets invaded Afghanistan to protect its new socialist puppet government. The Mujahedin were ill-equipped to defeat the far superior Soviet forces and were given only limited support by the United States. In a major shift, in 1986, United States decided to supply the Mujahedin with heat-seeking, shoulder-launched Stinger antiaircraft missiles. These man-portable missiles are often credited, wrongly though, with turning the tide and forcing the Soviets to withdraw from Afghanistan.

'First Sting' depicts the first of many shoot-downs of Soviet helicopter gunships by Mujahedin fighters armed with Stinger missiles. (*Public Domain*)

A Terminal High Altitude Area Defence interceptor missile launches during a flight test at the Ronald Reagan Ballistic Missile Defence Test Site in the Marshall Islands, Aug., 30, 2019. The Missile Defence Agency, Ballistic Missile Defence System Operational Test Agency and soldiers assigned to the 11th Air Defence Artillery Brigade conducted the intercept test. (*Public Domain*)

Stinger Missile was used by British Army's Special Air Service (SAS) in the Falklands, where it made its combat debut. On 21 May 1982 an SAS soldier engaged and shot down an Argentine Pucará ground attack aircraft with a Stinger. Shown here is United States Marine Corps Pfc. Joshua English firing a FIM-92 Stinger missile during training at the Marine Corps Air Ground Combat Centre in Twenty-nine Palms, California. (*Public Domain*)

Avenger Surface to Air Missile. An AN/TWQ-1 Avenger air defence system fires a missile over the Black Sea at Capu Midia Training Area in Romania, July 19, 2017. The drill was part of Tobruq Legacy, an air defence exercise with the U.S. and its NATO allies and partners. Photo by Army Pfc. Nicholas Vidro. (*United States DOD Images/Public Domain*)

A U.S. Marine Corps Sikorsky CH-53D *Sea Stallion* helicopter hovers above the ground near a Soviet ZU-23 anti-aircraft weapon prior to picking it up during "Operation Urgent Fury", the U.S. invasion of Grenada in October 1983. The *Sea Stallion* was from Marine medium helicopter squadron HMM-261 *Raging Bulls*, which was deployed aboard the helicopter carrier *USS Guam* (LPH-9). (*Public Domain*)

An Israeli Mirage shot down on the west bank of the Suez Canal during the Yom Kippur War during the battle of Ismailyia. (*Public domain*)

US military personnel look at a Soviet-made SA-2 surface-to-air missile launcher demolished in an Allied attack during Operation Desert Storm. A section of the missile is in the foreground. (*Public domain*)

A C-130 Hercules deploying flares, sometimes referred to as *Angel Flares* due to the characteristic shape. These are commonly used to deflect and confuse the heat seeking air defence missiles and are standard fitment on most modern aircraft. (*By TidusTia, public domain*)

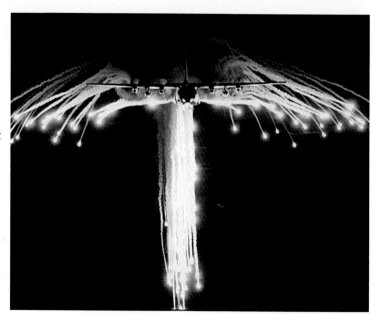

U.S Patriot Missiles were the mainstay against the Scud missile sduring the Gulf War and were also used by Israel. The main import of the missile was the psychological impact it had with its performance coming under cloud with a couple of fratricide incidents and failures. The Patriot missile remains deployed in the idle East, including Saudi Arabia.

This image shows U.S. Soldiers with a Patriot missile battery of 3rd Battalion, 2nd Air Defense Artillery Regiment when it was deployed at a Turkish military base in Gaziantep, Turkey in 2013. (*DoD photo by Master Sgt. Sean M. Worrell, US Air Force / Released, Public domain*)

A view of an Iraqi radar site destroyed by the French 6th Light Armoured Division during Operation Desert Storm. (*Photograph by Staff Sgt. Dean Wagner, US Air Force VIRIN: DF-ST-92-09371 United States DOD Images, Public Domain*)

S-125 Neva air defence system from 250th Air Defence Brigade of Serbian Army on display at Batajnica airbase. A similar S-125 missile was used to shoot down a United States Air Force F-117 Nighthawk Stealth fighter, serial number 82-0806, call sign 'Vega 31' over Yugoslavia on 27 March 1999 making it the first stealth aircraft to have been shot down by a SAM. (*By Srđan Popović, CC BY-SA 3.0.*)

Remains of F–16C #87-0257 from the 614th Tactical Fighter Squadron 'Lucky Devils', shot down over Iraq during Operation Desert Storm. With no viable Iraqi Air Force, it was the ground based air defences that was responsible for almost all the US Air Force losses.

The wreckage was discovered by US forces during Desert Storm and the canopy was found by US forces during Operation Iraqi Freedom. The canopy and photos are now part of a display at the Pima Air and Space Museum. (*Public domain*)

Romanian S-75 Dvina (NATO designation: SA-2 Volhov) missile launch at Capu Midia firing range in 2007, during 'ŞOIMUL 2007' military exercise. (*By Petrică Mihalache, CC BY-SA 3.0.*)

The Rapier Missile System was deployed in the Falklands War but did not prove to be much of a success, primarily due to technical limitations. The missile system is more suited to use in plains of Europe rather than in the rough countryside.

Shown here is a Rapier missile as it speeds towards its target during a live firing exercise by 20 Commando Battery Royal Artillery at Benbecula in Scotland. 20 Battery provides air defence to 3 Commando Brigade Royal Marines that had participated in the Falklands War. (*Contains public sector information licensed under the Open Government Licence v3.0.*)

A Chinook comes into land firing flares on its approach in Helmand, Afghanistan. The decoys are designed to give a greater heat signature than the engines of the aircraft thus confusing any heat seeking missiles fired from the ground. (*Contains public sector information licensed under the Open Government Licence v3.0.*)

An Air Force F-15 Eagle aircraft deploys flares while flying away from a KC-135 Stratotanker after an aerial refuelling in the skies over Iraq, March 16, 2018. Even after years of occupation the threat of Heat-Seeking Missiles force the United States Air Force to continue taking defensive measures to safeguard its assets. (*Air Force photo by Tech. Sgt. Paul Labbe (VIRIN: 180316-F-MQ799-0096C.JPG, United States DOD Images. Public Domain*))

Post-strike bomb damage assessment photograph of the Kragujevac SAM Site, Serbia, used by Joint Staff Vice Director for Strategic Plans and Policy Maj. Gen. Charles F. Wald, U.S. Air Force, during a press briefing on NATO Operation Allied Force in the Pentagon on May 17, 1999. (*Public domain*)

Canopy, ejection seat and wing of F-117, serial number 82-0806, shot down over Serbia in 1999; Belgrade Aviation Museum, Serbia. (*By Petar Milošević – Own work, CC BY-SA 4.0*)

ADOC in Baghdad. The communications were based on land line and/ or microwave with inbuilt redundancy. The intercept centres were placed near existing telecommunication trunks capable of carrying both voice and data communications with the system modems so designed that each node could easily switch from one form of communication to another. The communication and control nodes were housed in hardened shelters to provide them protection from any air attack. With multiple and redundant communication modes, the system could, in theory, rapidly detect attacking aircraft and direct anti-aircraft defences against them.[8]

The ground-based air defences included both surface-to-air missiles and anti-aircraft guns. The missiles included the Soviet SA-2, SA-3, SA-6 and SA-8 and the Franco-German Roland I/II missiles. Of these, SA-2s and SA-3s made up the strategic air defence while the SA-8s and the Rolands were the tactical SAM systems. The SA-6 was used for both the tactical role and to fill up gaps in the strategic SAM layout. While the SAMs were linked to the KARI, the 8,000 or so anti-aircraft guns were reportedly not integrated in the overall air defence system and were designed to operate independently.[9]

The air defence network was backed by over 500 radars located at about 100 sites providing early warning. While the majority of the radars were of Soviet origin with almost no capability to detect the stealth aircraft, the P-12 and P-18 radars had a limited capability to detect stealth aircraft as did the six Chinese (Nanjing) low-frequency radars.[10] The air defence network was optimized for threats from two axes: from Iran to the east or from Israel to the west. The entire network was not catering for any major threat from the south or the north.[11] Nor was it designed to work against a massive air assault as it was subjected to during the Gulf War. An assessment made by the US Navy's Strike Projection Evaluation and Anti-Air Research (SPEAR) Department said as much:[12]

the command elements of the Iraqi air defence organization (the ... interceptor force, the IADF [Iraqi Air Defence Force], as well as Army air defence) are unlikely to function well under the stress of a concerted air campaign.

Since the country's material assets were so widely dispersed, and the available resources did not allow the entire country to be covered, no attempt was made to defend all assets; instead, the SAMs and AA guns were concentrated to defend selected areas or sectors like Baghdad, Basra, the Scud-launching sites in western Iraq, and the northern oil fields only, with the defence of the capital given the foremost priority. With concentration of the SAMs and AA guns at select areas, it was in fact a point defence layout that Iraq had adopted.

The strategic SAM systems, the SA-2s and SA-3s, which formed part of the Iraqi Air and Air Defence Forces were organized into battalions and regiments with fifty-eight SAM batteries with fifty-five missiles, almost half of the total 120 batteries, deployed to defend Baghdad alone along with 1,300 AA guns.[13] The other areas with these missile systems were Basra with fifteen and Mosul/Kirkuk with sixteen batteries. The airfield complex of H-2/H-3 had thirteen SAM batteries and the Talil/Jlaibah complex had three.[14]

The SA-2s and SA-3s, being vintage missiles, were supplemented by the newer SA-6s with a battery deployed at important sites. These were used to defend airfields, key logistics centres, and command and control positions, the heaviest concentration being around Baghdad and the H3 areas. Although this made defence at these sites more potent, it had an unintended effect that with the SA-6s moved back from the front-line units, the forward army units were left devoid of the most effective SAM in the inventory.[15] HAWK, with comparable range, would have been an effective deterrent but they did not have the technical expertise to operate it, the HAWK was never used by the Iraqis.[16] The SA-8 and Roland missile systems were used to defend high value targets.[17]

With most of the radar-operated SAMs deployed for defence of assets in the rear, the field army was left with infra-red (IR) SAMs, the mounted SA-9s and SA-13s with the man-portable SA-7 and SA-14 missiles. Although vulnerable to countermeasures like flares, the IR SAMs were deployed only with the field army units and proved to be more effective than radar missiles. Supplementing these missiles in the field army were the radar-guided ZSU-23-4B Schilka gun mounts. In fact, it was the 8,000 anti-aircraft guns that proved to be more effective than any other anti-aircraft weapon during the war.

Even with such a large inventory of SAMs and AA guns, the Iraqi air defence system had serious limitations. The layout of the SAMs and AA guns was concentrated to defend selected areas in the west and the central sectors, the sectoral bias leaving large areas undefended and offering an open approach towards Baghdad from Saudi Arabia. The IADS had a principal deficiency in target-handling capacity and could effectively handle only twenty to forty targets at a time while the radar systems had limitations in detecting aircraft with low radar cross section. A second design deficiency was the ease with which its nodes could be targeted and disrupted. The variety and vintage of the SAM inventory made integration of all systems difficult, downgrading the overall capability of the system. Moreover, not only was the AAA, the most numerous of the anti-aircraft resources, not integrated with the IADS, the Iraqi Air Force hardly played any role during the conflict, which effectively degraded the IADS, although this was not known at the time the coalition air forces launched their air campaign.[18]

The Kuwaiti Theatre of Operations (KTO) was again a neglected area and although some radar SAMs were deployed in the KTO they were far from adequate and the combined SAM resources for all the forty-three Iraqi divisions in the KTO were less than would be generally allocated to a single Soviet division. There was, however, a heavy concentration of anti-aircraft artillery all throughout Kuwait with a few IR-guided SAMs. These were effective only at lower altitudes and could be easily defeated by flying above the effective range. This, however, did have an adverse effect as it forced the pilots to fly high which degraded the effectiveness of air strikes. The AAA was especially concentrated in a belt extending thirty kilometres west of Kuwait City and was referred to as 'Flak Alley'.

The coalition forces fielded a mix of air defence weapon systems with the United States deploying the full range of its air defence weaponry, including the Patriot and HAWK missiles although the main air defence system deployed by the US Army was the Patriot missile system, of which twenty-one batteries were deployed in the Gulf, all operated by the 11th Air Defence Artillery (ADA) Brigade.[19]

The 11th ADA Brigade was responsible for the air defence of Saudi ports and airfields. Each corps had its own organic air defence units and these were co-ordinated and integrated with the Coalition air and air defence forces by the commander of 11th ADA Brigade. The first US ADA unit deployed in Saudi Arabia were the Stinger teams of 2nd Battalion, 52nd Air Defence Artillery, touching down with the XVIII Airborne Corps headquarters within twenty-four hours of the decision to deploy US forces. Among the first to deploy was the 4th Battalion, 5th Air Defence Artillery with a total of six Avenger platoons – the first three with the battalion's Vulcan crews and Stinger teams in early October. As the ADA units had to be pooled from different brigades, two Avenger fire units from 6th ADA Brigade were grouped with the first Patriot fire units from 11th ADA Brigade, amongst the first to reach the Persian Gulf.[20]

The other air defence systems fielded by the different nations were the Vulcan air defence gun system, M48 Chaparral, Avenger, Improved HAWK and Stinger surface-to-air missiles by the United States, Rapier (both tracked and stationary versions) and Javelin man-portable SAMs by the United Kingdom, and Mistral SAMs with 20mm 53T2 towed AA guns by France. Saudi Arabia had multiple air defence systems, including the Vulcan, Shahine and the Improved HAWK missile systems, backed by AMX-30SA self-propelled AA guns, Bofors 40mm L/70 and Oerlikon-Bührle twin 35mm AA gun systems.

The air defence artillery (ADA) units were grouped with the field army, as per tactical requirements and the progress of battle but, as the Iraqi Air Force generally kept away, most ADA units never got the opportunity to engage any hostile targets with the exception of the Patriot batteries which remained active throughout.

Unlike the United States Army which deployed only part of its ADA units, the United States Marines deployed almost all their available air defence units in the Gulf. The marines were equipped with the shoulder-fired FIM-92 Stinger heat-seeking missiles and radar-guided, semi-active homing MIM-23 Improved HAWK missiles, and also some Avenger systems.[21] The 2nd and 3rd Light Anti-Aircraft Missile (LAAM) Battalions were equipped with HAWK missiles and 4th LAAM Battalion with a mix of Vulcans and Stingers. When the deployment orders were issued on 7 August 4th LAAM Battalion was in the midst of the re-organization to the Avenger system. Since the availability of Avenger systems prior to deployment was uncertain, the battalion quickly re-organized back to its original configuration with Vulcans and Stingers.[22]

The Marine LAAM Battalions were deployed to cover the Jubayl Airport, Jubayl Port Complex, King Abdul Aziz Naval Base, and Shiek Isa Airfield, Bahrain. The 2nd and 3rd LAAM Battalions were affiliated with 1st and 2nd Marine Divisions and later during the ground operations covered them at the breach point where they entered Kuwait

The ADA units of other nations remained with their respective field army components, with T Battery and 58 Battery of 12th Air Defence Regiment, Royal Artillery, with its tracked Rapier missile system serving with 1st (UK) Armoured Division. Both armoured brigades of the division had an air defence missile battery with thirty-six Javelins each.[23] In addition, No. 20 Squadron RAF Regiment, with Rapier Field Standard B1 (M), was deployed for air defence of the air bases, first RAF Akrotiri and then at the Muharraq airfield, Bahrain. The other squadron of the RAF Regiment deployed during the war was No. 26 Squadron at Dharan, Muharraq, and Tabuk.

The French air defence component was drawn from the *35e Régiment d'Artillerie Parachutiste* equipped with Mistral surface-to-air missiles. It served with the *Division Daguet*, an ad hoc formation created for the Gulf War, drawing the basic resources from 6th Light Armoured Division with additional units from 2nd Armoured Division, and the French Foreign Legion. The French operated on the left flank of the ground offensive and, initially, did so independently although they were later placed under the tactical control of the US XVIII Airborne Corps

Developed as the successor to HAWK and Nike-Hercules missiles, Patriot (Phased-Array TRacking to Intercept Of Target) was initially meant to be a mobile air defence system with anti-missile capability. Designed as a point defence weapon against low flying aircraft, it had no capability against the ballistic missiles and as a cost cutting exercise, the anti-ballistic missile requirement was taken off by the United States Army, though it was added back in 1980 to enable the Patriot to counter the Soviet ballistic missile threat. The first upgraded version with the anti-ballistic capability, PAC-1 (Patriot ATM Capability), was completed by December 1988 and a second upgrade, PAC-2, added the anti-ballistic missile capability. The anti-ballistic missile capability was first demonstrated in September 1986 when a Patriot missile intercepted a Lance ballistic missile and later in November 1987.

The functional centre of the battery is the engagement control station, which receives target information and controls the missile launch. Each battery has a multifunction phased-array radar and eight launcher stations containing four missiles each. Though the Patriot can track up to fifty targets, and simultaneously engage five of them, it has certain design limitations that restrict its capabilities as it can engage targets in an area extending twenty kilometres forward but only five kilometres to its right and left. Also, it carries a conventional warhead which makes intercepting and destroying a missile difficult. In the automatic mode, the Patriot fires two missiles at each target, ten seconds apart.

The Patriot batteries deployed during Desert Shield were often equipped with a mixed load of PAC-1 and PAC-2 missiles, the first of which was Bravo Battery, 2nd Battalion, 7th Air Defence Artillery, which reached Saudi Arabia around midnight on 11 August 1990. At its peak, a total of thirty-two Patriot batteries were deployed – twenty-one in Saudi Arabia, seven in Israel and four in Turkey.[24]

In Saudi Arabia five 2-7 ADA Patriot batteries were deployed into the coastal area from Al Jubayl to just south of Dhahran, and three 3-43 ADA Patriot batteries at the air base complexes at Riyadh. The deployments were completed by 27 September. To shore up the air defence capability, an additional task force, 8-43 ADA, was created using four batteries from 8-43 ADA (Patriot) and two HAWK batteries from 6-52 ADA (HAWK), deploying with VII Corps. For the King Khalid Military city, a HAWK battalion, with its three HAWK Phase III batteries (2-52 ADA), and a Patriot battalion (2-43 ADA,) were earmarked but as the Patriot battery was late in arriving, a provisional battery was created from personnel and equipment taken from 2-7 ADA and 3-43 ADA; that provided the only air defence for the massive logistics base. As 2-43 ADA equipment arrived, the KKMC anti-missile defence grew into an integrated four-battery defence and the provisional battery was disbanded.

During the build-up and expansion phase of DESERT SHIELD, the 11th ADA Brigade forward command post split in two, with a tactical operations centre at KKMC and the forward command post at Dhahran, the brigade logistics base. The brigade also established a forward support battalion with a transportation company, break-bulk point, Class M warehouse and postal detachment. On the eve of the air campaign, 11th

ADA Brigade units were spread 1,250 kilometres east to west and 900 kilometres north to south.

During the ground offensive phase, two mixed HAWK-Patriot Battalions supported the United States Army formations. XVIII Airborne Corps was supported by Task Force SCORPION while Task Force 8/43 supported VII Corps.[25]

Task Force SCORPION and elements of Task Force 8/43, as well as air defence units positioned along the main supply route DODGE, or Tapline Road, provided air defence for the advance of XVIII Airborne Corps to its jumping-off points. While none of the Patriot missiles of Task Force SCORPION advanced into Iraq, Task Force 8/43 provided air defence to elements of VII Corps during breaching of the Iraqi defensive berm in their front and its further advance to the east.[26]

One of the main reasons for the success of the Coalition air forces during the Gulf War was the detailed and exhaustive preparations carried out to counter the Iraqi Air Defences. The Coalition forces monitored the Iraqi IADS closely during the period of DESERT SHIELD, using a range of ELINT (Electronic Intelligence) resources to map the Iraqi electronic order of battle, building up a detailed layout of the deployment and composition of Iraq's air defences. Not only were the radar systems mapped but so were the stations and frequencies used for command and control of the network.

The main systems used for this were the EC/RC-135 Rivet Joint, TR-1 (U-2), the US Navy's EP-3 and EKA-3B aircraft and the Royal Air Force's Nimrod R.1. One common tactic employed was to penetrate Iraqi airspace, making the Iraqi radars 'illuminate' the targets thereby reveal not only the location and identity of the radars but the composition of the air defence batteries also. One major lapse by Iraq that helped the coalition forces was the uncontrolled switching on of radars and the almost static deployment patterns. Once the radars were switched on, the air defence battery should shift its location to an alternative location so that its targeting is made that much more difficult. However, Iraqi forces, like Syrian air defence earlier in the Bekaa valley, did not move and made it much easier for the coalition forces to take them on. The fact that the command and control system for the Iraqi air defences, the KARI, was made and installed by the French also helped as they provided valuable technical data about it.

Using the intelligence gained, the Coalition planners prepared an elaborate plan to attack the air defences simultaneously with the strategic targets.[27] The plan called for targeting fifty-six strategic air defence targets and thirty-one airfields.[28]

While the Iraqi electronic order of battle was being built up and the target list updated, the Coalition air forces carried out extensive training, routinely flying low as it was considered it to be the only way to survive the 'formidable' Iraqi air defence network. A training deck of 500 feet was imposed after a RF-4C crashed near Abu Dhabi on 8 October while practising low level tactics.[29] The British, however, continued to fly as low as 200 feet even after they lost a Jaguar on 13 November.

Training also was a joint Army-Air Force team to take out Iraqi radars using AH-64 Apaches and MH-53 Pave Low helicopters made up of the 20th Special Operations Squadron and the 1st Battalion, 101st Aviation Regiment of 101st Airborne Division. The plan called for Apaches to target and destroy Iraqi radars with Hellfire missiles and, during the training for the mission, no fewer than six live-fire drills were practised to evaluate the Apache's ability to take out the targets and the Pave Low's ability to get them there. In the end, it all went off as planned.[30]

The six-month preparatory period had permitted identifying and studying important strategic targets in Iraq and accumulating intelligence on the nature of Iraqi defences. In one of the lesser known operations, a combined team of US and British Special Forces raided an Iraqi missile site on 7 January and got away with a Soviet-made radar.[31] The technical details obtained from captured radar were to pay rich dividends when the war started in January 1991.

When Saddam Hussein did not withdraw from Kuwait by 15 January 1991, the deadline set by the United Nations Security Council, the stage was set for the military operations to start. The opening round was to be against the Iraqi air defences. With the aim of achieving tactical deception, Coalition air forces had started carrying out regular sorties in September 1990 with a consistent mix of aircraft flying the same flight tracks. When the air operations started on 17 January, the airborne warning and control system (AWACS), Rivet Joint, CAPs, high-value airborne assets and tankers, were all in their familiar tracks, presenting the same routine activity to the Iraqi radar operators. But these were not the first to strike.

The opening round against the Iraqi air defences was by 101st Airborne Division. Task Force Normandy took out two Iraqi radar codenamed Nebraska and Oklahoma, about seventy kilometres apart, in the western desert. The Task Force consisted of eight Apache helicopters, split into two teams – Team Red and Team White. Guiding each team was a US Air Force special operations MH-53J Pave Low helicopter. Additionally, a UH-60 Black Hawk was available for contingency search and rescue operations, and one spare Apache was to cater for any of the prime force of eight Apaches developing a problem before the infiltration into Iraqi airspace began.[32]

The task force took off from Al Jouf Air Base, a small airfield in western Saudi Arabia at about 1:00am on 17 January and crossed over into Iraqi airspace at 2:12am, just forty-eight minutes before the scheduled H-hour. The Apaches, guided by the Pave Low helicopters, reached their objective and, exactly at 2:38, the first Hellfire missiles struck the targets that had been laser-painted by special forces teams and commandos. In all, the Apaches fired twenty-seven Hellfires, 100 rockets and 4,000 rounds of 30mm ammunition, destroying the radar stations and blowing open a corridor, about thirty kilometres wide, in Iraq's early-warning radar network.[33] The attack on the radars had succeeded, but it also alerted the Iraqi defences who picked up the Apaches on their way back and fired several SA-7s, although no damage was caused to the task force.

The strike by the Apaches was followed by eight United States Air Force F-15 Strike Eagles attacking the local air defence command and control centre, further degrading the network and facilitating the strike by the F-117s. The path for the Nighthawks was clear.[34] The F-117 stealth aircraft were preceded by three EF-111 Ravens. In all, seventeen F-117s were tasked to deliver twenty-seven LGBs on fifteen Iraqi air defence system related targets.

As the Ravens reached their targets, they switched on the jamming equipment in an attempt to jam the Iraqi radar network, but the massive jamming gave away the surprise and cost the Nighthawks 'one free pass over Baghdad' as the Iraqi air defences opened up. In this, a GBU-27 Paveway III hit the International Communications Centre at 3:00am, the first bomb to hit Baghdad. In addition, 167 other aircraft also struck eighteen air defence-related targets (IOCs, SOCs, and radars) on the first night.

Although the initial reports claimed that all the F–117s successfully attacked the given targets, only nine of the fifteen targets were hit and eight remained operational even after the air strikes. One of the main targets, the Air Defence Operations Centre in Baghdad was not damaged and remained operational.[35]

As part of the suppression of enemy air defences (SEAD) mission, thirty-seven BQM-74C target drones were launched at Baghdad, in flights of threes to draw out the SAM defences. This was to facilitate the targeting by the anti–radar missiles (ARMs). One trio of drones was intercepted and shot down by Iraqi fighters but the rest managed to reach their target. Following the drones were F/A-18 Hornets armed with AGM-88 high-speed anti-radar missiles (HARMs). Once the drones had taken on an orbit over Baghdad, making the Iraqi radars open up, the Hornets and Weasels fired seventy-five HARMs, of which about half hit their targets.[36] Simultaneous with the attack by the F–117s, Tomahawks hit Baghdad. The first of these were launched by the United States Navy destroyer *Paul F. Forster*. The joint SEAD effort also used ten long-range army tactical missile system (ATACMS) missiles to attack an Iraqi air defence site. With all the effort against Iraqi air defences, the Coalition air forces did not go unscathed as the Iraqis fought back, firing several SAMs and putting up a heavy AAA barrage against the Coalition aircraft. By the end of day one, Coalition air forces had lost six aircraft, all except one to ground-based air defences. The AAA shot down two aircraft (one F-15 and a Tornado GR.1) while the R-SAM claimed three. One F/A-18 was shot down by an Iraqi MiG-25.[37] Ground-based air defences damaged a dozen more aircraft.

The first use of Scuds was on 17 January when Iraq reportedly fired two at targets at Dhahran in Saudi Arabia. The United States claimed that the 2nd Battalion (Patriot), 7th Air Defence Artillery, 11th Air Defence Artillery Brigade successfully intercepted the Scuds, making it the first successful interception of a ballistic missile by an air defence missile in combat.[38] One report noted that Patriot units fired five missiles at three (rather than the actual two) Scuds indicating a failure – a false target being picked up and fired at. This was to continue throughout the war and the details of Scuds fired, and engaged, remains a matter of contention.

The second day saw the Coalition air forces continue their strikes against Iraqi targets, including air defence sites, as they lost three aircraft to ground fire over 2,250 sorties. One aircraft each was claimed by AAA (a US Navy A-6) and IR-SAM (US Marine Corps OV-10) while the cause of loss of an Italian Tornado GR.1 could not be ascertained.[39] Iraq launched the first of the Scuds at Israel, three at Tel Aviv, one at Haifa, three in largely unpopulated areas in remote regions, and one in an unknown district, with one more at Dahran in Saudi Arabia. These were reportedly not engaged by the Patriots.[40]

The next day, a number of missions were called off due to bad weather although the strikes against Scud launchers continued during the day. The Iraqi SAMs shot down two United States F-16s over Baghdad and an additional F-15. Four Tornados were lost, two each by the Royal Air Force and Royal Saudi Air Force, while a USAF F-4 crashed after being hit by AAA.[41] Three Scuds hit Israel during the day and the United States moved Patriot batteries from Germany to Israel and deployed them over the greater Tel Aviv and Haifa areas.[42] These were all manned and operated by US personnel.

The air operations on 20 January were scaled down due to continued bad weather and, with losses mounting, especially to AAA, the United States Air Force imposed a minimum altitude to reduce attrition. The next day Iraq launched ten Scuds at targets in Israel and Saudi Arabia while the strikes against Scud launchers continued. Patriot missiles reportedly intercepted two of the Scuds. The Iraqi air defences, on their part, shot down two Coalition aircraft: a United States Navy F-14, downed by an SA-2 and an RAF Tornado, besides damaging three more. Iraqi air defences shot down one more RAF Tornado to ground fire with a USAF F-15 also being hit by an IR-SAM. The Patriot missiles failed to intercept the Scuds launched against Israel, leaving three dead and ninety-six injured in one of the more serious Scud attacks to that date.[43]

On 23 January Coalition forces claimed to have destroyed nineteen Iraqi aircraft thus far and achieved air superiority over Iraq. Coalition losses to Iraqi air defences were fifteen, including one more Tornado shot down and an A-10 damaged by ground fire. At the end of the first week of the air campaign, all except one of the Coalition losses were inflicted by ground-based air defences (anti-aircraft fire or SAMs). The unexpected intensity of ground fire by AAA and hand-held SAMs was forcing Coalition aircraft to adopt higher-altitude delivery tactics. Although the radar-guided SAMs had been neutralized to a large extent and a virtual sanctuary existed for Coalition aircraft above 10,000 feet, the threat from the SAMs remained.

The second week saw a marked decrease in air losses by the Coalition forces with the Iraqi air defences not being able to cause any worthwhile attrition. The Iraqis were relying more on Scuds and the Patriot missiles were having a difficult time intercepting them. On 25 January seven Scuds were launched at Israel and only two of these were reportedly intercepted.[44] An Iraqi air defence missile site was targeted by a US ATACMS (Army Tactical Missile System) on the 26th, making this the successful combat debut of the ATACMS.[45]

The next loss to Iraqi air defences was on the 28th when a US Marine AV-8B was shot down by an IR-SAM although a number of Coalition aircraft were hit by AAA fire. The Iraqi air defence system, KARI, was badly fragmented by the end of week two and only three of sixteen IOCs were reported to be fully operational.[46] Coalition losses during week three were again quite low, with only three aircraft (an A-10, an AC-130 and an A-6E) lost to Iraqi air defences. The following week, also, Iraqi air defences managed to shoot down only three Coalition aircraft – two AV-8Bs and a Saudi F-5E.

The radar-guided SAMs had been targeted repeatedly, but the Iraqis continued to launch them, although sparingly. In one such instance, an SA-3 shot down an RAF Tornado GR.1 on 14 February. The Iraqis managed to shoot down five aircraft during week five, including two A-10s on the same day (15 February) by SA-13s. This forced the Coalition air forces to restrict the use of A-10s in high threat areas. As the war entered its final phase with the Coalition aircraft attacking from lower altitudes,, the losses went up with Iraqi air defences shooting down eight aircraft during this final week of the war: three AV-8Bs, one OV-10, one OA-10, one A-10, and two F-16s. This marked the second highest weekly loss rate since the beginning of the war.[47]

The Ground Offensive

On the eve of the ground battle, 11th ADA Brigade began moving Patriot fire units farther north to provide air defence for staging areas nearer the Kuwaiti and Iraqi borders. On 20 January Bravo Battery of Task Force SCORPION moved 600 kilometres to its new location, Rafha. The two HAWK fire platoons were operational by the end of the day. As the location was about twenty kilometres from the Iraqi border, the greater danger at the site was more from artillery shelling than anything else. For local protection, Bravo Battery was assigned a platoon of infantry on 11 February.[48]

More than the Patriot fire units, it was the Avengers that provided close air defence to the field army. The Avenger crews moved with the lead elements of the 1st Cavalry Division during its 500-kilometre move to defensive positions north of King Khalid Military City and later during its offensive across the Iraqi frontier. On 18 February, when the division launched probing attacks, the Avenger platoons provided an effective day and night umbrella as they accompanied multiple-launch rocket systems and 155mm self-propelled howitzers. Later on, Avengers defended critical trains and command posts while providing air defence of the probing forces from overwatch positions on the Saudi side of the berm.

On G-Day Avengers continued to support division deception operations as the 1st Cavalry Division's 2nd Brigade conducted a limited attack forty kilometres into Iraq to fix the enemy forces in place as part of the deception plan. Subsequently, the Avengers protected not only the division's manoeuvre elements during the move west through the breach opened by 1st Infantry Division, but also the vital division command posts and brigade tactical operations centres, critical Class IV and V logistics trains and logistics support trains as they moved forward to sustain the momentum of the attack.[49]

On 24 February, G-Day, Bravo Battery was to re-locate itself to a site about twenty kilometres inside Iraq to cover the advance of XVIII Airborne Corps. The battery was to move at 2:00pm although it was delayed to 4:00pm.[50] As the HIMAD Battery with associated HAWK fire units was spread over a large area, an infantry platoon was attached with

Task Force SCORPION. At times, they even made use of abandoned Iraqi weapons, including a ZU-23 AA gun at a site inside Iraq. When the ceasefire came into effect, only two HIMAD Batteries were inside Iraq: Bravo Battery and TF 4-43 ADA, serving with VII Corps in the centre.

The Scud versus the Patriot

Iraq had fired two Scuds during Operation DESERT SHIELD on 2 December 1990, at targets within Iraq, signalling its intent to use the Scuds if an offensive was ever launched against it. The Patriot batteries went into 'Scud Alert' but, as the Scuds landed in Western Iraq, no engagement took place. A second Scud alert was sounded on 15 December but this time no Scuds were fired; it turned out to be a false alarm. The first use of Scud was on 17 January when Iraq reportedly fired two Scuds at targets in the Dhahran area in Saudi Arabia.[51] This was reportedly the first time a ballistic missile had been engaged successfully by an air defence missile in combat. One report noted that Patriot units detected three Scuds (rather than the actual two launched by Iraq) and fired a total of five Patriot missiles at these *'three'* targets thus indicating a failure in the Patriot missile system – a false target being picked up and fired at. This was to continue all throughout the war and the details of Scuds fired and engaged remains an issue of contention.

False alarms were generated even before the start of DESERT STORM as the United States Space Command raised five such alarms between 25 and 30 December 1990, three the result of live ballistic missile test firings by Iraq. The problem was more profound in the initial days of Operation DESERT STORM although the incidents declined in frequency after the first eight days of the war, possibly because of refined drills and procedures or software changes. In all, a total of twenty false target detections were carried out by the Patriot batteries, but not all were fired at. The Patriot batteries, however, did fire a total of twenty-two missiles at false targets, but none were fired at false targets after 23 January.[52]

The most controversial incident involving the Patriot was its failure to intercept a Scud missile on 25 February which killed twenty-eight people although it was not the only time it failed to intercept the Scud(s).[53]

An Iraqi Scud fired on February 25 hit the barracks in Al Khobar near Dhahran killing 28 people, the war's single worst casualty toll for Americans. Two Patriot batteries were deployed at Dhahran that night – Alpha and Bravo batteries of the Second Battalion, Seventh Air Defense Artillery Regiment. Just four hours before the Scud attack, Bravo Battery was shut down to repair a radar malfunction while the second, Alpha, battery shut down at the time of attack due to multiple computer problems, including four days of continuous operation. The Scud was picked up by the Patriot batteries north of Dhahran but did not engage it, assuming that Alpha Battery in Dhahran would attack. In this confusion, no Patriot was fired and the Scud hit the barracks, killing 28 people and wounding 97 others.

Not all failures to intercept the Scuds ended in such tragedy as the Scuds for the most part fell harmlessly in open areas in the desert, or in the sea as happened on 16 February when a Scud was fired at Al Jubayl. The total number of Scuds fired is generally accepted as eighty-seven,[54] with forty-six fired at the Kuwaiti theatre of operations and forty-one at Israel although these figures vary in different sources. While carrying out interception, the first requirement was to detect the Scud launches. In this it is accepted that all Scuds launched were picked up by the United States Space Command and information on the launches was available to the Patriot batteries[55] but not all ended with a successful interception. While the actual number of Scuds launched and detected may be of academic interest, what is of greater interest is the number of Patriots fired and the number of Scuds intercepted and destroyed. It is generally accepted that a total of 158 Patriot missiles were fired but what is not clear is the number of Scuds destroyed. One United States Army report mentions that, at the onset of ground operations, Patriots were tentatively credited with knocking down sixty-four of the sixty-five Scuds that entered their engagement zone.[56]

Another report mentions that, of the eighty-seven Scuds launched, thirty-three were outside the area of coverage of the Patriot and were accordingly not engaged, while Theodore Postal of the Massachusetts Institute of Technology claims that Patriot was 'a near total failure in terms of its ability to destroy, damage, or divert Scud warheads'.[57] The truth lies somewhere in between. In December 1991 the United States Army claimed a success rate of 80 per cent over Saudi Arabia and 50 per cent over Israel. These were later revised to 70 and 40 per cent respectively. Raytheon claimed an 89 per cent success over Saudi Arabia and 44 per cent over Israel. Israel, on its part, was not impressed with the Patriot and downplayed its performance as the following report suggests:[58]

> They indicate that the Patriots destroyed fewer than 44 per cent of the Iraqi Scud missile warheads, the figure both the Israeli Government and the missile's manufacturer, the Raytheon Corporation, had offered immediately after the war. Under the new analysis, the estimate ranges between zero and 20 per cent of the warheads. An Israeli official acknowledged today that there is 'strong evidence to suggest' that the number of Scud warheads destroyed 'may be lower' than the Government's official estimate.

The Patriots were supplied to Israel after the first Scud attack on 22 January, in an apparent attempt by Saddam Hussein to draw Israel into the war – and cause rifts in the Coalition. Four Patriot batteries arrived first and while two were staffed by Israeli crews the other two were staffed by US Army personnel under IAF operational command. Two more batteries arrived later, again staffed by US personnel under the command of Israeli officers. Four of these batteries were deployed in the metropolitan Tel Aviv area and two in the Haifa region. The seventh battery arrived much later from The Netherlands but was not used operationally in interception of the Scuds. According to a testimony made on behalf of Israel's Chief of Air Staff, to the Committee on Government Operations of the US House of Representatives, the Patriots destroyed one, at best three, Scud warheads only.[59] The poor performance is borne out by the details of the incident on 25 January 1991 when seven al-Hussein missiles were fired at Israel -- six at metropolitan Tel Aviv and one at Haifa. A total of twenty-seven Patriots were launched that night against the seven al-Husseins, but not a single al-Hussein warhead was hit. Moreover, several Patriot missiles hit the ground and caused property damage.[60] The testimony, however, mentions the claim that in some cases Patriot missiles deflected al-Husseins from their course. This was based on the presumption that in cases where the al-Hussein was supposed to hit a point close to a Patriot battery, it was slightly deflected and landed a few kilometres away. However, these claims of deflecting the Scuds are without any corroborative evidence.

The actual figures of Scuds destroyed may never be known but what is of interest is that, in spite of its failures and limitations, the Patriot served its purpose in having an impact on the morale of the soldiers and decision-makers, and kept the Coalition together by keeping Israel out of the war. That was its success.

A total of thirty-eight aircraft were lost to Iraqi action, and forty-eight others were damaged in combat, making a total of eighty-six combat casualties. The majority of losses were to IR SAM which claimed thirteen aircraft and damaged fifteen more while the radar-guided SAMs shot down ten aircraft and damaged four. The least number i.e. nine, were shot down by AAA although it damaged twenty-four more aircraft. The remaining losses were due to accidents/technical reasons. Considering the 'lost' and 'damaged' aircraft together, the maximum casualties were due to AAA, claiming 333 aircraft (38 per cent of the total losses) with the IR SAMs accounting for twenty-eight aircraft (31 per cent). Only 16 per cent of the casualties were attributed to radar-guided SAMs.

The low kill rate by the radar SAMs is attributable to a number of factors, the primary one being the SEAD missions carried out by Coalition air forces which forced the radar SAMs to shut down for most part of the operations. All the radar SAMs held by Iraq were vintage Soviet-era missiles which had been used in combat earlier – there were no new weapons, like the SA-6s in the Yom Kippur War, which could have posed difficulties for the Coalition air forces. Moreover, the six-month preparatory period available was used by US and others to identify and map the SAM threat in detail – and this was used to target the SAM sites from the first day itself. The initial focus was always on the degradation and neutralization of the Iraqi air defences. Every time the radar opened up, it was targeted using an anti-radar missile. As a result, the losses to radar SAMs dropped significantly after the initial operations. While nine aircraft were claimed by the radar SAMs in the first five days, only five more were lost in the remaining thirty-eight days. Iraqi air defences shot down two, possibly six, Tomahawk cruise missiles also.

An extract from a blog by an ADA officer who served with Task Force SCORPION is illustrative:[61]

> Our equipment was worn out. Most of the vehicles and HAWK equipment we had brought to the Gulf was either old or refurbished. Vehicles were missing windows, rear-view mirrors, and other bits and pieces. The missile system was becoming a nightmare to work with because of the high failure rate of our generators and the war weariness of the components. Knowing that we were the only battery in sector, we did our best to remain operation, but (not) one eight-hour shift went by with hardly an hour straight of fully operational, or Green, time, due simply to minor failures.

Accidents did happen. On 2 March 1991 a HAWK fire unit of Bravo Battery deployed in Iraq accidently fired a missile, luckily without causing any damage. With no Iraqi air operating against them, the Coalition air defences did not have much to their credit, and any assessment can only be in the realm of speculation.

Seventeen coalition aircraft casualties or nearly 20 per cent of the war's entire aircraft casualties occurred within the first twenty-four hours. It was during this time that Iraqi defences were at their strongest and the Coalition pilots at their lowest levels of DESERT STORM combat experience. Similarly, there was a significantly higher overall daily casualty rate in the first five days of the war, during which thirty-one aircraft casualties occurred (36 per cent of the total and an average of 6.2 per day), compared to the following thirty-eight days, with a total of fifty-five more casualties (an average of 1.45 per day). Losses to radar-guided SAMs fell to nearly zero after day five, having accounted for 29 per cent (nine out of thirty-one) of total casualties by then. They accounted for just 9 per cent (five out of fifty-five) of all aircraft casualties in the remainder of the war. It is apparent, therefore, that by the end of day five of the air campaign, radar SAMs had been largely eliminated as an effective threat to coalition aircraft.

Moreover, in the first three days of the war, some aircraft (B-52s, A-6Es, GR-1s, and F-111Fs) attacked at very low altitude, where they were more vulnerable to low-altitude defences. As a result, on day two all

Coalition aircraft were asked to observe a minimum attack level of about 12,000 feet. This restriction was reinforced when two A-10s were lost on one day to IR-SAMs. While probably improving overall survivability, this tactic also resulted in much less accuracy with unguided weapons. Looking at the data on the altitude at which thirty-two US Air Force aircraft casualties occurred (data is not available for other aircraft), twenty-one, or about two-thirds, of these were hit at or below 12,000 feet, implying that restrictions imposed on minimum altitude to be maintained did serve to reduce losses.[62] The losses suffered by British Tornado GR.1s at low level also illustrate the efficacy of low-level air defences against Coalition aircraft. Of the seven British Tornados that were lost, four were shot down during the first week of the campaign at very low altitude while conducting strikes against airfields. After the change to medium-altitude deliveries, only three more British Tornados were lost in the remaining five weeks of the air campaign.

The Coalition subjected the Iraqi air defence network to a heavy and pointed air assault to suppress and degrade it, and its efforts were largely effective, but the Iraqis, contrary to earlier appreciation, managed to maintain a fair degree of air defence capability throughout the war. The primary role in this was of KARI which expanded the responsibilities of various nodes and developed local *back-up* air-defence networks using different communication networks, over combat phone lines and wire between various stations. These back-up networks could control local air defences, even when the communication to the central network was down. For information on Coalition aircraft, these back-up systems used ground observers passing information over voice and data channels. Radars associated with the Roland or SA-8 would be used to gain information about the altitude of inbound aircraft. The radars would be brought online for short fifteen-second bursts to ensure survivability in a hostile environment. The SAMs were fired at times without using the target-tracking radars, again to prevent being targeted by the anti-radar missiles. Optical tracking mode was also used while firing the SAMs.

The major weakness of air defences was in the use of its most numerous asset, the AA guns. There was an apparent lack of co-ordination between AAA sites and most of the firing was random or indiscriminate. The large number of guns, however, still made the random and indiscriminate firing a serious threat for Coalition aircraft. The large number of aircraft shot down by the AA guns, all through the war, was a testimony to the threat posed by them, and that the air defences remained effective in spite of the all-out efforts to suppress them.

> At the end of the war, Iraqi air defences were far from finished. According to Anthony Cordesman of Washington's Center for Strategic and International Studies, Iraq retained at least 380 Soviet-made surface-to-air missile launchers, about eighty French-made Roland units and 'large numbers' of portable Soviet-made anti-aircraft systems,[63] not counting the hundreds of AA guns. After having claimed almost complete destruction of the Iraqi air defence network, the claims were revised with new goalposts established. As United States Air Force Colonel David Deptula, one of the architects of the air campaign, put it, 'We didn't go in there to eviscerate the whole network. The aim was to suppress their defences.'[64]

The Soviet reaction to the Gulf War was important as the entire IADS was made up of Soviet SAMs. In an understatement, Marshal Dmitri Yazov, the Soviet Minister of Defence admitted that Iraq's air defences 'failed in most cases'.[65] Commenting on the initial attack on the IADS, Lieutenant General V. Gorbachev, dean of the faculty at the General Staff Academy opined that 'The Iraqi air defence system was paralyzed by powerful electronic warfare devices. Command and control of troops was overwhelmed in the first few minutes' but also added that 'As far as Soviet equipment is concerned, it is not so much a problem, I think, as the people operating it. Iraqi military professionalism is not, as we can see, up to the mark.'[66] Reinforcing this view, the Soviets believed that, as the air defence systems employed by the Iraqis were able to down every type of Coalition aircraft used, including a Stealth fighter, it suggested that the problem was more one of manpower than technology and that modern wars demand well-trained professional soldiers to man and maintain it, and not a large conscript army.[67]

After DESERT STORM, Iraqi air defences continued to harass the Coalition aircraft, defying the restrictions imposed by the no-fly zone. During Operation DESERT FOX, over a three-year period, Iraq engaged Coalition aircraft more than 1,000 times and fired nearly sixty surface-to-air missiles.[68] The Iraqis would even fire unguided rockets at the aircraft to harass them.

The IADS remained operational throughout and was never 'put down'.

Iraq 1991–2003

Following Operation DESERT STORM, the United Nations (UN) imposed severe sanctions against Iraq and restricted its military operations. Resolution 668 by the UN Security council established no-fly zones, further limiting the Iraqi Air Force's ability to carry out any operations against the Kurds while the United States and other Coalition nations of the Gulf War launched Operation PROVIDE COMFORT to defend Kurds fleeing their homes in northern Iraq in the aftermath of the Gulf War and deliver humanitarian aid to them. Except for an occasional incident, the Iraqi Air Force and air defences did not oppose the Coalition air effort in the region. The air defence radars occasionally 'painted' Coalition aircraft, but there were no incidents involving actual firing of SAMs or anti-aircraft guns until things changed in 1993. The first serious incident occurred on 15 January 1993, when Iraqi air defences guns opened fire on USAF F-111 bombers in two separate incidents.[69]

On 17 January a US F-4 Phantom destroyed an Iraqi radar which had been targeting French reconnaissance aircraft. The next day F-4 Phantoms attacked Iraqi air defence sites. During the year more Iraqi sites fired on the American patrols, with United States and Coalition aircraft retaliating by attacking Iraqi anti-aircraft and radar sites in northern and southern Iraq on at least five occasions.[70] The repeated 'painting' of Coalition aircraft continued although no aircraft was lost to Iraqi air defences.

In August 1996 Iraqi troops intervened in the Kurdish regions of Iraq and the United States responded with Operation DESERT STRIKE against targets in southern Iraq, launching twenty-seven cruise missiles against Iraqi air defence targets in southern Iraq, followed by a second wave of seventeen missiles. The missiles hit targets in and around Kut, Iskandariyah, Nasiriyah, and Tallil.[71] It is debatable whether the attacks had a substantial effect on Iraq's northern campaign as, having installed the Kurdistan Democratic Party (KDP) in control of Irbil, Iraqi troops withdrew from the Kurdish region back to their initial positions. Operation PROVIDE COMFORT II ended on 31 December 1996 and was followed by Operation NORTHERN WATCH with the mission of enforcing the northern no-fly zone. The coalition partners of the United States, United Kingdom, and Turkey provided approximately forty-five aircraft. For most of the mission, northern Iraq was quiet, with no major incidents. In 1998 the United States carried out Operation DESERT FOX, a four-day air campaign against targets all over Iraq, citing Iraq's failure to comply with UNSC Resolutions. The operation had an unintended result in that it led to an increased level of combat in the no-fly zones which lasted until 2003.

After DESERT FOX, Iraq announced they would no longer recognize the no-fly zones and urged their troops to attack Coalition aircraft. On 28 December 1998 Iraq fired SA-3 surface-to-air missiles against Coalition aircraft patrolling the northern no-fly zone. In retaliation, US Air Force and US Marine Corps aircraft targeted the SAM site with anti-radiation missiles and precision guided munitions (PGMs), destroying it.[72] From December 1998 to March 1999, U.S. aircraft over northern Iraq came under almost daily fire from Iraqi surface-to-air missile sites and anti-aircraft guns with US aircraft responding by bombing Iraqi air-defence sites, using laser-guided bombs as well as AGM-88 HARM missiles and AGM-130 long-range air-to-surface missiles. The Iraqi air defences failed to shoot down any US aircraft during the entire operation with over 36,000 sorties flown by the Coalition aircraft.

While Operation NORTHERN WATCH was being conducted in the north, Operation SOUTHERN WATCH was in place to enforce the no-fly zone south of the 32nd Parallel (extended to the 33rd Parallel in 1996) in southern and south-central Iraq during the period following the end of the 1991 Gulf War until the 2003 invasion of Iraq. It began on 27 August 1992. Military engagements in SOUTHERN WATCH occurred with regularity, with Coalition aircraft routinely being shot at by Iraqi air defence forces with SAMs and anti-aircraft artillery (AAA).

In August 1996, when Iraqi forces invaded the Kurdish regions of northern Iraq and American forces responded with Operation DESERT STRIKE, the no-fly zone was extended north to the 33rd parallel. This marked renewed conflict with Iraqi air defences and several more radars were destroyed by F-16s. That did not prevent the firing of SAMs at the Coalition aircraft with over 470 separate incidents of AAA or surface-to-air missile firings after Operation DESERT FOX until May 2000, even as US aircraft attacked Iraqi targets on seventy-three occasions.

The air operations against Iraqi air defences were scaled up in 2002 with Operation SOUTHERN FOCUS targeting 391 sites. The operation began as a response to the Iraqis' deployment of additional surface-to-air missiles and anti-aircraft artillery south of Baghdad which had thickened the defence of the Iraqi capital. It was carried out from June 2002 until the beginning of the invasion in March 2003 to 'soften up' Iraq's air defence and communications. The operations peaked in September 2002, including a 100-aircraft attack on the main air defence site in western Iraq on 5 September.[73]

Chapter 9

Operation Iraqi Freedom 2003

The invasion of Iraq had been preceded by Operation SOUTHERN FOCUS, which had been carried out with the explicit purpose of softening up Iraqi air defences. The years of isolation and sanctions had left the Iraqi air defences weakened and they were in no position to offer any serious opposition though they were always assessed as 'formidable'. It was more to do with political signalling rather than being a pure military assessment. It was true that attacks on coalition aircraft had continued throughout the period of Northern/Southern Watch due to the 'heroic missile forces and brave ground-to-air defences'[1] but these were sporadic firings in an un-aimed manner, more to harass than to attrite. The only time the Iraqis came close to destroying a coalition aircraft was in July 2001 when a surface-to-air missile exploded near an American U-2 spy plane flying over southern Iraq.[2] The only other success was by the Iraqi air defences shooting down a US Predator drone.

The estimates of Iraqi air defence systems at the beginning of the war vary from 380 to 850 SAM systems.[3] In an assessment reported by the BBC, Iraq's air defences were thought to have some 12,000 operational air defence launchers with about 1,200 long-range missiles and 6,000 anti-aircraft artillery (AAA) guns of 23mm or larger and some 6,000 short-range and shoulder-fired SAMs.[4] These numbers were an obvious exaggeration – if the claims made during Operation DESERT FOX in December 1998, and in later operations, are considered. The United States had claimed that it had destroyed about 30 per cent of Iraqi air defence capability in the south and 15 per cent in the north. With regular firing of SAMs, it was appreciated that Iraq would have expended a large number of its holdings in attacking US and British forces in the no-fly zones by the time the war started – at the rate of about 140 to 160 missiles every year.[5]

The aircraft holding was about 300 aircraft of which only 135 were combat aircraft including the French Mirage F-1 and the Russian-built MiG-23, 21, and 29, although no Iraqi combat aircraft flew during the war. Iraq was reported to have some 350 helicopters, about eighty of which were armed.[6]

The Iraqi command and control structure had been targeted during SOUTHERN FOCUS, leaving a large part of it non-operational. Over 4,000 sorties between 1 and 20 March left the Iraqi radars, air defence guns, and fibre-optic links badly bruised and battered.[7] Of the four air defence sectors, only the central sector around the capital remained somewhat operational, with the major air defence effort concentrated around Baghdad. The majority of the air defence systems were composed of the older SA-2s, SA-3s, SA-6s and SA-8s which posed no major threat. It was again the AAA and hand-held missile systems that would pose a threat to the Coalition aircraft.

The United States air, on the other hand, were spearheaded by the Patriot missile system that had been tried out during DESERT STORM. The experience of the Gulf War had led to the creation of a single command for theatre air and missile defence (TAMD) – the 32nd Army Air and Missile Defence Command (AAMDC), created in 1998.

In preparation for Operation IRAQI FREEDOM, the 32nd AAMDC participated in various exercises to focus on developing co-ordination, tactics, techniques, and procedures for the air defence missions. The first component of 32nd AAMDC reached the theatre of operations on 15 November 2002, with the major build-up beginning in mid-January 2003. When Operation IRAQI FREEDOM started, Patriot was deployed at a number of sites in Kuwait, Saudi Arabia, Jordan, Qatar, Bahrain, and Israel. The Patriot missile radars faced teething problems before the start of the operation as they were regularly malfunctioning due to the harsh environmental conditions. These malfunctions were observed until two days before the start of the operation.[8] The missile system faced another problem – 'cluttered cyberspace', causing electronic interference between various systems, creating confusion for radars and communication systems.

The main concern of the Patriot units was the type of Scud likely to be used by Iraq; the shorter-range Ababil 100 and Al Samoud ballistic missiles gave a smaller response window of thirty to ninety seconds.[9] This put additional pressure on the Patriot crew during an intercept – and was to prove a major factor during later operations.

At the start of the operations, on 19 March 2003 at 9:00pm air strikes were carried out against Iraqi visual observation posts along the southern and western borders of Iraq. Unlike DESERT STORM, no lengthy air campaign was carried out as SOUTHERN FOCUS had already been in place. The only dedicated attacks against air defences were by the Royal Air Force Tornados targeting the radar defence systems protecting Baghdad. The Iraqi air defences did fire a few SAMs but most of them were in un-guided mode, without switching on the radars. The main resistance was by the AAA guns which did put up a stiff fight but failed to score any kills.

A modified Seersucker cruise missile was launched by Iraq on 19 March which struck just outside a United States Marine Corps camp. It was not intercepted by the Patriots. The next day the Iraqis fired an Ababil 100 at an area assigned to 101st Airborne Division but it was successfully intercepted by PAC-2 and guidance-enhanced missiles (GEM). A second Ababil 100 was intercepted by a PAC-3 hit-to-kill missile, the first combat kill for PAC-3.[10]

Two days later, on 22 March, the Patriot was involved in a fratricide incident resulting in the first loss of a coalition aircraft when an RAF Tornado was shot down by an American Patriot missile as it returned to its air base in Kuwait.[11] An E-3 Sentry AWACS aircraft had successfully interrogated the. Tornado in all interrogation-friend-or-foe (IFF) modes and had tracked it as a friendly flight, but the Patriot battery had no access to this air picture. As the Tornado overflew the Patriot battery, it descended steeply to land at Ali Al Salem Air Base and, as the flight profile momentarily matched the Patriot's parameters for an anti-radiation missile, the Patriot crew decided to exercise self-defence under the rules of engagement and engaged the aircraft, assuming it to be an incoming anti-radiation missile.

The Iraqi air defences achieved one of their first successes on 24 March during the Battle of Najaf when the Iraqis, in a well-planned operation, took on the AH-64 Apaches called in to support the US airborne and armoured units, bringing down well co-ordinated, heavy anti-aircraft, small-arms, and RPG fire. One Apache was shot down with thirty-two more severely damaged. Frustrated, the Apaches had to be withdrawn in face of the intense ground fire.[12]

Though there was no SAM used, it brought to the fore the vulnerability of attack helicopters to ground fire. This was again experienced on 26 March during an assault by the US Rangers at an objective codenamed Objective Beaver when the MH-60Ks helicopters used to insert the Rangers came under ground fire, hitting two of the four machines. They could be extracted only after the aircraft providing close support took on the Iraqi positions.

Patriots were involved in another fratricide incident; only this time a Patriot battery was targeted by a friendly aircraft as an F-16CJ aircraft fired an AGM-88 high-speed anti-radiation missile at a Patriot PAC-3 battery deployed about thirty miles south of An Najaf. The F-16CJ pilot believed, incorrectly, that he was being tracked for engagement by the Patriot radar. He was not aware of the presence of Patriot in the area. The missile damaged a Patriot radar but caused no casualties.[13]

On 27 March Iraqi forces fired a Scud missile at the American Battlefield Update Assessment Centre in Camp Doha, Kuwait. The missile was intercepted and shot down by a Patriot missile before it could hit its target.[14]

Iraq launched two Seersuckers on 29 March against the harbour of Kuwait City. The Seersucker attack was repeated on 31 March. These were not intercepted by the Patriots. During the operation, Iraq launched at least twenty-three ballistic and cruise missiles. Of these, nine were engaged and shot down by the Patriot missile system. Of the fourteen Iraqi missiles not engaged by Patriots, four were reported as outside the range of any Patriot system and one exploded shortly after launch.[15]

As Coalition forces advanced into Iraq, Patriot batteries deployed forward to provide continuous coverage. As this was the first operation in which Patriot provided coverage for land forces while they were manoeuvring, Patriot batteries were rotated to ensure that the more experienced units moved forward to provide continuous cover to the ground forces. Moving together with land forces presented operational challenges. The bigger challenge was to ensure security to the logistics tail. On 1 Apri Iraqi forces fired an Al Samoud missile at a logistics support area which was intercepted by two PAC-3 missiles.[16]

The next day, 2 April, a Patriot battery deployed near Karbala was involved in the third fratricide incident, this time engaging a US Navy F/A-18 aircraft. The Patriot crew mistook a 'ghost track' (a spurious radar return) for an incoming ballistic missile and engaged the F/A-18 with two PAC-3 missiles.[17] Iraqi air defences, on the other hand, had had no fixed-wing kills as yet. There had been incidents of the anti-aircraft guns hitting Coalition aircraft but without any losses.

On 3 April Iraqi air defences managed to score two kills – US Navy F/A-18 Hornet and a UH-60 Blackhawk helicopter.[18] This was the first loss of a fixed-wing aircraft to Iraqi air defences. On 7 April an A-10 piloted by Captain Kim Campbell was hit repeatedly by anti-aircraft fire over Baghdad. An IR-SAM hit the Warthog and got stuck in the plane's tail, damaging the hydraulics and horizontal stabilizers. Campbell managed to bring back her aircraft safely to its base.[19]

In one of the last incidents of Scud launches, a ballistic missile hit the tactical operations centre of 3rd Infantry Division near Baghdad. The missile was not intercepted by the Patriot. The next day, 8 April, an A-10 was hit and shot down by an IR-Sam over Baghdad, making it the last Coalition aircraft to be claimed by the Iraqi air defences.[20]

The 'formidable' Iraqi air defences had crumbled without offering any resistance to the Coalition air forces. The assessment of the strengthening of air defences around Baghdad, thought to be 'stiffer' than in 1991, was mere exaggeration. Iraq was thought to be in possession of 'thousands of SA-8b, SA-11, and SA-13 short- and medium-range missiles' as late as 1 April.[21] These assessments obviously played safe in over-estimating the Iraqi capabilities and did not take into account the intelligence available – or ignored it. Until 22 March there were sporadic instances of anti-aircraft fire and SAM launches but these declined sharply after the 23rd. The only resistance being offered was by smaller calibre AA guns and small arms with occasional use of IR-SAMs. One possible reason for the absence of Iraqi resistance was that Iraqi commanders were conserving their resources, and the second was that the Iraqi air defences were so badly beaten that they were in no position to fight back. Later events indicate that it was more likely the latter.[22]

However, the absence of radar-SAM firings should not be taken as absence of air defence capability since a tactically sound adversary can use ad hoc resources and innovate to continue resisting and denying a 'free pass' to the air forces. Iraq was a good example of this tactic.

After Operation IRAQI FREEDOM

After the end of Operation IRAQI FREEDOM, as Iraq descended into a civil war and insurgency, US forces stayed on until 2011. The deployment saw extensive use of air power to quell opposition and restore order during which US and Coalition aircraft regularly used to be targeted by the insurgents. Over the hundreds of missions carried out each day, the aircraft were shot at about 100 times a month, with seventeen of them being hit. Mostly, the losses were of rotary-wing aircraft with only two fixed-wing machine losses attributed to hostile action – a Royal Air Force C-130 Hercules shot down in 2005 and a USAF F-16 shot down by insurgents on 7 November 2006 near Fallujah.[23] While this shooting down was suspected to have been carried out using a MANPADS, most of the aircraft shot down were hit by heavy machine guns and small arms; there was a paucity of dedicated anti-aircraft weapons. At times, even rocket-propelled grenades (RPGs) were used to hit and force down low-flying helicopters as during the incident in December 2003 when an OH-58 Kiowa helicopter crash-landed after being hit by an RPG.[24]

In 2006, faced with a shortage of anti-aircraft weapons, insurgents tried improvised explosives to target Coalition helicopters. The new home-made weapons, called the 'aerial improvised explosive devices' were fired into the air from the ground and made to explode close to passing aircraft. They were placed along known flightpaths and triggered when a low-flying helicopter approached, fired to a height of about fifty feet before a proximity fuse detonated the explosive, filling the air with thousands of metal shards. These 'aerial improvised explosive devices' were used on numerous occasions. As these devices were based on old anti-aircraft or artillery shells, the bombs would have a devastating effect if detonated close to a thin-skinned helicopter; 'more than one' helicopter was lost to these devices.[25]

As the insurgency continued and insurgents got hold of more weapons from caches captured or supplied by outside agencies, the use of MANPADS like the SA-7 was observed. To make up for their limited numbers of dedicated AA weapons, the insurgents made co-ordinated use of multiple weapons systems, including heavy machine guns, from several different directions, akin to the tactics adopted in Afghanistan. The positioning of the weapons was based on the regular flight patterns taken by the US aircraft, after observing these over several days.[26]

2007 saw a spurt in incidents of anti-aircraft fire on US aircraft with seven aircraft shot down in the first two months alone. On 20 January an Army Black Hawk helicopter was shot down north-east of Baghdad, followed by the downing of an AH-64 Apache attack helicopter north of Baghdad on 2 February. What was more worrisome for the US was the first use of SA-14/ -16 missiles against US aircraft, also on 7 February, when a CH-46E Sea Knight was shot down outside Fallujah, killing all seven on board.[27] Another innovative use of technology was the employment of geotags to destroy target aircraft. As the newly-arrived airmen and soldiers' choppers uploaded to the Internet, the insurgents used the geotags to determine the exact location of the helicopters. At least four AH-64 Apache helicopters were targeted and destroyed by mortar fire using this technique.[28]

The shootings, however, reduced considerably after February 2007, further reducing losses in Iraq.[29] Over 150 coalition aircraft were lost until the withdrawal of US forces in 2011, of which forty-six were to hostile fire.

Chapter 10

The Balkans

After the death of Marshal Tito, the Yugoslav strongman, the authority of the central government waned, resulting in a period of political turmoil. Fuelled by economic problems and the rise of nationalism, a civil war broke out amongst the six constituents of the erstwhile Yugoslavia, namely Bosnia and Herzegovina, Croatia, Macedonia, Montenegro, Serbia, and Slovenia, leading to its break up. Croatia and Slovenia were the first to declare independence in June 1991, followed by Macedonia in September of the same year. The disintegration of Yugoslavia was greatly enhanced by the promotion of Greater Serbia with Slobodan Milosevic at its head who opposed the Slovenian declaration of independence – the first to secede, with the Yugoslav People's Army (YPA) invading Slovenia in June 1991.

Yugoslavia had large, well-equipped armed forces with its air force operating over 400 fixed-wing and 200 rotary-wing aircraft that included one squadron of MiG-29s and nine squadrons of MiG-21s. The air force also had the indigenously produced J-22 Orao and G-4 Super Galeb fighter-bombers. Eight battalions of the SA-2, six of SA-3, one of SA-5 and four battalions of SA-6 surface to air missiles, backed by fifteen regiments of anti-aircraft guns and over 100 radars, gave the air defence forces a reasonable capability to deter any air force.[1] Comparable Slovenia had a small Territorial Defence Force with only infantry weapons, and a few 20mm anti-aircraft guns and 82mm mortars, but no tanks, aircraft or artillery. Portable grenade launchers were all that Slovenia had for use as anti-tank weapons while the man-portable SA-7 Strela rockets were the only air defence capability against low-flying aircraft.[2]

The war for Slovenia started with a Yugoslav armoured column, led by an anti-aircraft battery, entering the Slovenian border near Metlika. It was a short war, lasting all of ten days, after which the Yugoslav forces withdrew and the secession of Slovenia was accepted. The war hardly saw any air action with only two reported instances of Yugoslav aircraft attacking the Slovenian positions; first, on 28 June and later on 2 July, when they attacked Slovenian barricades. In the absence of concentrated artillery and air interdiction, the Slovenians were able to mount an effective defence against the Yugoslav Army; bringing the war to an end in just ten days. The only aircraft shot down during the war were two helicopters, one over Ig and the other over Ljubljana.[3] Reportedly, it was the SA-7 missiles that were used to bring them down.

After Slovenia, Croatia faced an invasion by the Yugoslav armed forces but with a much larger force that included a bigger presence of the erstwhile Yugoslav Air Force resources. The aircraft were used to strafe Croatian positions, causing extensive damage, including the MiG-29 attack on the presidential palace with Maverick missiles on 7 October 1991.[4] Croatia had a fledgling air force made up of An-2s and the Yugoslav UTVA-75s that were modified to carry armament. An An-2 was shot down by the Yugoslav air defences, using SA-6s, in December 1991 over Vinkovci in eastern Slavonia.[5].

Before this, small-arms fire was the only real threat to the Croat aircraft with two HRZ UTVA-75s sustaining damage while on a reconnaissance mission near Petrinja. One Mi-8 of the Yugoslav Air Force was also damaged by small-arms fire and forced to land near Slavonski Brod on 4 October. This was captured by the Croats who thus acquired the first real military aircraft for their air force.

About forty-six Croat and Yugoslav aircraft and helicopters were shot down during the war although, according to the Croatian sources, the number of aircraft lost by Yugoslavia alone was nearer 100.[6]

In November 1991 the warring forces agreed to a Yugoslav withdrawal from Croatia. Unlike the Slovenes, the Croatians allowed the Yugoslav National Army (JNA) to take its equipment with it. In return the JNA agreed to return the weapons seized from the Croats in spring 1991 but the ceasefire was shortlived with fighting breaking out again. The 2 January 1992 UN-sponsored ceasefire, the fifteenth in just six months, came into force next day and became a lasting ceasefire. Croatia was officially recognized by the European Community on 15 January 1992.

The fighting in Croatia had not even stopped when the next flashpoint ignited in Bosnia.

Bosnia 1992–1995

The multi-ethnic Socialist Republic of Bosnia and Herzegovina – which was inhabited by mainly Muslim Bosniaks (44 per cent), as well as Orthodox Serbs (32.5 per cent) and Catholic Croats (17 per cent) – passed a referendum for independence on 29 February 1992 but this was opposed by the Bosnian Serbs who had boycotted the referendum. Although the declaration of independence by Bosnia and Herzegovina gained international recognition, the Bosnian Serbs, supported by the Serbian government and the Yugoslav People's Army, tried to secure ethnic Serb territory as part of a greater Serbia, leading to a fullscale war spread across the country, accompanied by ethnic cleansing. The Serbian offensive was supported by a small but effective air force with about fifty fighter-bombers and thirty helicopters.

In March 1992 a United Nations Peacekeeping Force (UNPROFOR) was sent to Bosnia and Croatia. In May, despite all diplomatic efforts to negotiate a lasting ceasefire, the conflict – between the Bosnian Muslims and the Bosnian Croats on the one side and the Bosnian Serbs on the other – intensified. By May Serbians had overrun almost half of Bosnia and laid siege to Sarajevo, the capital. As the war threatened food deliveries in Sarajevo, the United Nations responded with a humanitarian airlift called Operation PROVIDE PROMISE.[7] It was the longest-running humanitarian airlift in history, from 2 July 1992 to 9 January 1996, with aircraft from twenty-one countries flying 12,886 sorties into Sarajevo, delivering 159,622 tons of food, medicine, and supplies and evacuating over 1,300 wounded people.

As the warring sides were reasonably well equipped with air defence weapons but with poor command and control arrangements, there was always a possibility of the relief aircraft coming under fire. The most significant threats in Bosnia were the radar-guided SA-2s and SA-6s. The only way to ensure security while carrying out the relief operations was by avoidance (flying above or outside their threat envelope) or by diplomatic assurance that they would not be used. During PROVIDE PROMISE the relief aircraft avoided known SA-2 and SA-6 sites and the air-drop crews were instructed to abort their missions and exit the area at the first sign of SAM radar activity. An additional precaution taken was to vary the air-drop routes as much as possible. In mid–August a British C-130 Hercules was locked-on by a Serbian radar as it took off from Sarajevo airport although it was not fired at. The major threat was from the IR-SAMs, namely the SA-7s and SA-16/18s, due to their unpredictable deployment and use. To counter these, night-time, medium-altitude air-drop tactics were adopted although it did not prevent the shooting down of an Italian Air Force G.222 by an IR-SAM on 3 September 1992 while approaching Sarajevo airfield.[8] The rescue mission could not be carried through due to ground fire. The location of the crash site indicated that it was the Croatian forces that had shot down the aircraft, and not the Serbs.

The ground fire, from anti-aircraft guns and small arms, was quite prevalent with small calibre anti-aircraft artillery (AAA) fire reported by the relief aircraft on several occasions but, as these threats were most likely reliant on optical acquisition and tracking, they failed to score any hits.

The United Nations airlift was resumed after a month, with all aircraft now fitted with flare and chaff dispensers for self-protection. Further, the United Nations Security Council passed a resolution prohibiting unauthorized military flights in Bosnian airspace. During the course of the eighteen-month operation, crews reported instances of radar illuminations and possible targeting by AAA fire but, except for the loss of the Italian G.222 aircraft, no other aircraft were shot down.[9] The experience during most of the relief operations was of being 'locked-on' by radars with occasional firing by the ground troops although United States Air Force Colonel Thomas P. Witt, the overall operation commander, remarked, 'We were looking for something (anti-aircraft activity), but we didn't see anything at all.'

However, the claim made by Colonel Witt that 'we did not see anything' needs to be taken with caution as the NATO aircraft were subjected to repeated attacks; well over 270 aircraft were attacked during the operation with over fifty aircraft sustaining hits from ground fire.[10]

Although Operation SKY MONITOR was carried out by North Atlantic Treaty Organization (NATO) member states to monitor violations, and by April 1993 over 500 violations had been observed, no military action was taken against the offenders. Stepping up the restrictions, a total no-fly zone was enforced in April 1993 with NATO launching Operation DENY FLIGHT on 12 April 1993 with the purpose of preventing interference with the humanitarian airlift and an escalation of the conflict. By April 1993 NATO planes were told that they 'may fire warning shots' but would not be authorized to bomb anti-aircraft positions or surface-to-air-missile sites unless attacked and were told to fire on violators only as a last resort.[11] This was a retrograde step as the Serbs had a viable anti-aircraft capability to interfere with the NATO operations. While it was easy to identify and neutralize the fixed-site SA-3s, the more mobile SA-6s and the infra-red SAMs were always going to pose a threat to air operations. There was no answer to them, as yet.

The mandate for NATO was expanded further to include provision of close support to UNPROFOR. The first combat air mission by NATO was, however, the shooting down of four Serbian J-21 Jastreb light-attack jets on 28 February 1994, south-west of Banja Luka, Bosnia and Herzegovina. It was the first instance of active combat in NATO's history.[12] The NATO aircraft were first used in close support mission on 10 April when two USAF F-16s attacked a Serbian position with 500lb bombs, making it the first air strike by NATO in its forty-five-year history. The air situation changed dramatically after this incident. A French naval Étendard aircraft was hit by a surface-to-air missile on 15 April while on a photo run over Gorazde. The pilot managed to return to his ship, the French carrier *Clemenceau*, despite the plane being very badly damaged.[13]

A British Sea Harrier was hit by a SAM the next day in the same area was not so lucky. Part of a two-ship mission, the Harrier was guided on to engage Bosnian-Serb armour on the outskirts of Gorazde. By the rules of engagement the aircraft were required to first make a low-level pass over the armour to try to stop it from advancing on the city. As the Sea Harriers were executing the pass, SA-16 Igla missiles were fired by the Serbs. The Sea Harriers deployed flares to distract them but, as they were on the second pass, one of the SA-16s scored a hit on the Sea Harrier. The pilot managed to eject as the Sea Harrier crashed in the woods. This was the first loss of a NATO aircraft during Operation DENY FLIGHT.[13] Neither of the Sea Harriers managed to drop bombs and engage the Serb armour.

Operation DENY FLIGHT was meeting with mixed success. While it had largely stopped air operations over Bosnia by aircraft of the *Republika Srpska*, its own operational limitations had prevented the same from being achieved regarding aircraft of the Republic of Serbian Krajina whose main base was the former Yugoslavian air base at Udbina, located in what was recognized as Croatian territory. DENY FLIGHT was restricted by the UN to Bosnian airspace only and, given Udbina's proximity to Bihać, its aircraft could make raids across the lines in support of the Bosnian-Serbs and retreat back into Croatia before NATO could respond.

The situation in Bihac, Velika Kladusa and other parts of the safe areas deteriorated when aircraft belonging to the so-called Krajina Serb forces flying from Udbina airstrip dropped napalm and cluster bombs in south-west Bihac, endangering not only the civilian population but also the UNPROFOR personnel. The act of aggression by the Krajina Serb forces was repeated when its aircraft bombed the town of Cazin, about ten miles north of Bihac. In an effort to enforce the no-fly zone aggressively and prevent such air raids, thirty-nine NATO aircraft attacked the Serb air base at Udbina on 21 November 1994, targeting not only the airfield but also the nearby anti-aircraft batteries and a surface-to-air-missile site in the largest air strike by NATO to date.[14] Initially, only the radars associated with anti-aircraft batteries and the SAMs were planned to be jammed as the UN feared that a direct attack might invite retaliatory attacks against UNPROFOR personnel but later the go-ahead was given by the UN, permitting NATO to attack the surface-to-air-missile and anti-aircraft-artillery sites in order to protect the strike aircraft.[15]

The mission was under the overall command of the Dutch contingent who, along with the British, were primarily tasked with attacking the runway. The strike force was protected by US and French fighters while USAF EF-111A Ravens provided electronic warfare support for jamming of the Krajina Serb radars. As the strike force, under the guidance of a Sentry AWACS, approached the objective, United States Marine Corps F/A-18s fired AGM-88 HARM anti-radar missiles at the air defence radars, shutting them down and facilitating the strike by USAF F-15Es and F-16Cs on the surface-to-air-missile batteries and anti-aircraft gun emplacements, followed by British Jaguars and Dutch F-16s attacking the runway using unguided conventional bombs.

The Serbs fired back IR-SAMs but no damage was inflicted as the strike force exited after a successful raid that put down the air base for a month. The Serbs' reaction was as expected. They continued harassing the NATO forces with repeated 'illumination' and lock-on of aircraft by SAM radars with the occasional launch of SAMs. The very day after the strike, two Sea Harriers from HMS *Invincible* were fired upon by a surface-to-air missile just fifteen miles from Bihać. Fortunately, the flares deployed by the Sea Harriers succeeded in decoying the missiles away.

In retaliation for attacks launched from a surface-to-air missile site south of Otoka (north-west Bosnia and Herzegovina) on two NATO aircraft, air strikes by more than fifty aircraft were conducted against three Serbian missile sites in that area on 23 November.[16] It did not put an end to the Serb activity and the Bosnian Serb air defence radar locked-on to a NATO reconnaissance aircraft, prompting NATO to again conduct air strikes against surface-to-air missile sites in the Bihać area. As a retaliatory act, the Bosnian Serbs took a number of United Nations personnel hostage, restricting their movement.[17]

There was a pull back of the NATO air operations after that but NATO aircraft continued to provide close support to UNPROFOR and carry out combat air patrols as required and were subjected to hostile ground fire during these missions but did not suffer any further loss until mid-1995 when the USAF lost its first aircraft in Bosnia.

The aircraft shot down was an F-16, part of a routine combat air patrol over north-west Bosnia when it was picked up and locked-on by a Serb SA-6. According to some reports, the radar lock-on was detected by the two aircraft but they did not take any action and continued with the mission. The Serbs reportedly launched two SA-6 missiles, without radar guidance, using optical guidance and only in the terminal stage was the guidance radar switched on. The first missile burst between the two F-16s while the second hit one of the F-16s, piloted by Scott O'Grady who manged to eject.[18] The pilot was eventually rescued by two Sea Stallions and two Cobra attack helicopters on 8 June. As the pilot was picked up, the Bosnian Serbs opened fire at the departing helicopters but failed to cause any damage.

In May 1995 over 400 UNPROFOR soldiers were taken hostage and used as human shields by the Serbs. This, and the previous instances, had an effect on NATO air operations, with permission to provide air support to the Dutch contingent in the UN-declared Safe Area of Srebrenica being withheld in July 1995. The failure to do so allowed the Serbs to capture the area, leading to the worst genocide in Europe since the Second World War. The nearby Safe Area of Zepa was overrun by Bosnian Serb forces shortly after.

If this was not bad enough, the Serbs threatened another UN safe area, this time in Goražde. NATO responded with the threat of use of air power, aimed at deterring an attack.

In a repeat, the Croatian Serb air defence radars near Udbina airfield and Knin in Croatia were again targeted by NATO air strikes on 4 August. In order to undermine the capability of the Army of *Republika Srpska* (VRS), NATO had prepared a contingency plan for a direct military intervention to prevent any further attacks on the safe-zones and prevent genocides or massacres. The Markale massacres triggered the plan to be put into place which was Operation DELIBERATE FORCE.[19]

Meanwhile, the Croats took back the Serb-held Krajina region of Croatia in a swift five-day campaign against the Bosnian Serbs. The Serb use of aircraft, attacking the Croat targets with cluster munitions, did not help and, to make matters worse, the Croat air defences shot down two Serb aircraft.[20]

The Serb action that precipitated DELIBERATE FORCE was the attack on Sarajevo. On 28 August 1995 a Serb mortar fell upon a marketplace in Sarajevo, killing thirty-eight civilians and injuring eighty-five others. This was yet another violation of a United Nations Security Council resolution and, this time, NATO responded with force. Operation DELIBERATE FORCE was launched as soon as the last UNPROFOR troops left Bosnian Serb territory. The bombing was briefly interrupted due to a ceasefire negotiated by the UNPROFOR commander on 1 September, but it resumed in the early hours of 5 September. Almost all the then sixteen NATO allies contributed in some way to the campaign, which involved a total of 3,515 sorties and the dropping of 1,026 bombs on 338 individual targets.[21]

The opening round of DELIBERATE FORCE included the plan to neutralize the Serbian air defences – Operation DEADEYE – to systematically attack EW, SAM, and Command & Control sites that posed a threat within Bosnia-Herzegovina, focused on force protection through the elimination, or at least degradation, of the Bosnian Serb army's IADS. This operation was later split into two halves, DEADEYE SOUTHEAST and DEADEYE NORTHWEST, targeting first the south-east and then taking on the sites in the north-west as necessary.

The Serbians had reasonably well-equipped, professional air defence forces and were considered a greater threat than had been experienced in Iraq, primarily because the Serbs had imbibed the lessons of the Gulf War and were far better trained although their weapon systems were not as many or as advanced as the Iraqis. The main SAM systems were the SA-32, SA-3 and SA-6 although the numbers were not very large. Of the strategic systems, the Serbs did not have more than thirty SA-2s and forty-eight SA-3s, with about 120 SA-6 missile systems. The tactical SAMs, i.e. the SA-9s and SA-13s, were controlled by the ground forces, as well as SA-7s, SA-14s, and probably SA-16 man-portable SAMs. The Serbs reportedly had only eighty-four SA-9s and four SA-13 units while the holding of SA-7s was reportedly in the hundreds. As the former Yugoslavia produced the SA-7, and several types of anti-aircraft guns, the Serbs were not only well equipped but had sufficient stockpiles of spares and supplies for these systems. Even in the case of the Soviet missile systems, a stockpile of SAM equipment sufficient to maintain the current inventory for the foreseeable future was available to the Serbs.[22] One of the commonly used anti-aircraft guns was the indigenously produced triple-barrel 20mm anti-aircraft gun, mounted on a BVO chassis giving it cross-country mobility. The other anti-aircraft guns were the 20mm M55 triple-barrel AA gun mounted on a truck, the self-propelled two-barrel 20mm FOKA gun system and the 30mm M53/59 Praga.[23]

In August NATO estimated the Serbian air defences to have seven SA-2, six SA-6, and 12 SA-9 SAM batteries, an unspecified number of man-portable missiles, and nearly 1,100 pieces of AAA ranging in calibre from 20mm to 76 mm.[24]

Operation DEADEYE, when it commenced on 30 August, was executed principally by United States Navy and Marine Corps aircraft, operating off carriers in the Adriatic Sea and from Aviano air base in Italy. They performed almost 60 per cent of the SEAD missions in the operation. The first phase was to target the air defence sites in the east only.

On the first night the air strikes by fourteen SEADs with three strike aircraft were led by F-14 Tomcats, launching a volley of tactical air-launched decoys in the vicinity of known air defence sites, luring the air defences to switch on their radars. This was to be followed by the F/A-18 Hornets launching the AGM-88 high-speed anti-radiation missiles at the missile batteries. The Serbs had learnt from the Iraqi experience during the Gulf War and kept most of the SAM radars switched off. The effectiveness of the HARM strikes thus could not be verified but, as the SAM batteries were 'off the air' most of the time, they were effectively self-suppressed although they continued to be a threat until specifically tracked down. The first SAM site attacked was an SA-6 battery north of Sarajevo but the damage done to all the fifteen sites targeted was never known.[25]

To suppress any SAM battery that may have survived the direct attacks, United States Marine EA-6B and Air Force EC-130 aircraft jammed the Serb radar frequencies to prevent them from operating. However, the impact of all these efforts was only on the radar-guided SAMs with the IR-SAM and the anti-aircraft gun threat remaining as viable as before.

The Serbian capability to attrite the NATO air forces was demonstrated when one French Mirage 2000K was shot down near Pale, the Bosnian capital, by a shoulder-fired SAM, most likely the SA-16 Igla.[26] Serb AA gunners and SAMs engaged other aircraft, including US A-10s, Dutch NF-16s, and British Tornados, but did not inflict any damage.[27]

On 30 August the F-18s and F-16s in the second wave targeted Serb ammunition depots and command posts near Sarajevo. On 31 August NATO warplanes continued to strike targets around Sarajevo, hitting at least two ammunition dumps, but bad weather and low cloud prevented wider attacks as a result of which no air defence sites were targeted. The third day only the SEAD and reconnaissance missions were conducted as the Serbs had conveyed their willingness to talk. Over three successive days from 30 August to 1 September NATO had conducted the largest combat operation in its history with over 500 missions flown from bases in Italy and aircraft carriers in the Adriatic.

The assessment of the air strikes carried out showed mixed results. The Serbs' communications capability was degraded but still functioning.

Similarly, the integrated air defence system (IADS) was 'degraded but effective'.[28] Some of the SAM sites, like Sokolac SA-6 site, had sustained considerable damage but DEADEYE had not rendered the IADS impotent. It was still effective as most of the Serbs' SAM radars had not been switched on, and thus were not targeted by the HARM strikes. The Serbs had also relocated and dispersed much of their stock of ammunition to temporary sites, thus retaining the capability of being effective against the NATO air strikes.

During the talks held with the Serbs, they were given until 4 September to comply with the terms of the ceasefire but, as the reconnaissance imagery from Predator and Gnat UAVs on the morning of 5 September showed, the Serbs were only making a half-hearted show of moving weapons around, and the heavy weapons defiantly stayed put. The air strikes resumed the same day against more ammunition dumps, vehicle staging and repair areas and other targets.

The efforts to search for and rescue the French Mirage 2000 pilots had so far not succeeded. The first attempt, made on 6 September by two United States Navy HH-60H helicopters, failed to locate the pilots and came under hostile ground fire during the mission. The third attempt on 8 September, seventy-five miles inside hostile territory, came under intense AA fire and the two of the rescue team helicopters were damaged seriously. The helicopters could be retrieved only after an AC-130 gunship with pairs of A-10s and F-18s engaged the Serb anti-aircraft guns and an EA-6B Prowler jammed the Serb radars.[29] No more search-and-rescue missions were launched thereafter.

During the pause in the air campaign NATO planned to expand the scope of SEAD missions to include the IADS targets in north-west Bosnia as these had hardly been touched and continued to pose a threat to the air operations. As the SAMs and other anti-aircraft weapons had been relocated by the Serbs during the pause in air operations, it was believed that the Serbs may have redeployed their entire IADS in the north-west zone.[30] In view of the threat perception, the use of F-117 Nighthawk Stealth aircraft and Tomahawk land-attack missiles (TLAM) against the IADS was proposed but, as Italy refused to allow the basing of F-117s on its air bases, the plans had to be changed. The new plan was put into effect on 9 September with a package of thirty SEAD aircraft firing thirty-three HARMs at seven SAM sites in the Banja Luka area, including those at Majikici, Donji Vakuf, Sipovo, and Kolonija, without a confirmed kill.[31] The DEADEYE missions continued with forty-two aircraft attacking targets on Lisina Mountain that included the first combat use of GBU–15 and stand-off land attack missiles (SLAM) but the strikes achieved only moderate success, the overall results being disappointing.

Demonstrating their capabilities, the Serb air defences nearly shot down an AC–130 gunship that was on a purely reconnaissance sortie.[32] The gunship had been tasked on reconnaissance missions and had been carrying out these missions following the same general flight profile. Having established the pattern followed by the Spectre gunship, the Serbs opened up with anti-aircraft artillery and SAM fire. The IR-SAMs were deflected by the flares deployed by the AC–130 and the aircraft was luckily not hit by the flak.[33]

The SLAM fired at the Serb air defences the next day missed with not one of the seven missiles hitting the target although the TLAM fired at the Lisina early-warning radar managed to score a hit, rendering the radar non-operational. The radar was attacked again the next night with the SLAM hitting the target this time round. This was the last DEADEYE mission and NATO claimed to have degraded and neutralized the Serbian IADS as 'not one aircraft was shot down by the radar-guided surface-to-air missiles or anti-aircraft artillery during the entire operation.'[34]

DELIBERATE FORCE continued until 20 September when the NATO and UN force commanders concluded that the Bosnian Serbs had complied with the conditions set down by the UN and air strikes were discontinued. The state of the Serbian air defences can be assessed by the fact that Serbian air defence radars locked-on to NATO aircraft at three different locations on 4 October.

On 21 November the Bosnian Peace Agreement between the Republic of Bosnia and Herzegovina, the Republic of Croatia and the Federal Republic of Yugoslavia, was initialled in Dayton, Ohio, USA, bringing to an end one phase of the Balkan crisis. Following the Bosnian Peace Agreement, signed in Paris on 14 December, Operation DENY FLIGHT was terminated with NATO given the mandate to implement the military aspects of the Peace Agreement. The airspace over Bosnia and Herzegovina was subsequently controlled by the Implementation Force (IFOR) as part of its task but the war in Balkans was far from over.

Kosovo 1999

In early 1998 violence erupted within Kosovo between Yugoslavian (Serb) forces and the Kosovo Liberation Army (KLA). The efforts to defuse the crisis did not succeed and by March 1999 the situation had worsened with the Serbs launching a new offensive in Kosovo called Operation HORSESHOE, forcing thousands of ethnic Albanians from their homes north-west of Pristina. The last-ditch effort to stop the Serb atrocities failed and on 24 March NATO launched Operation ALLIED FORCE.

The Yugoslavian Air Force was not much of an opposition with sixteen MiG–29s and eighteen MiG–21 fighters as well as twenty-eight J–22 and seventy G–4M attack aircraft.[35] Of greater concern were the Serbian air defences which posed a bigger threat. Serbian air defences included more than 800 man-portable SA–7, SA–14, and SA–16 surface-to-air missiles and 130 other low-altitude anti-aircraft missiles. Other larger and longer-range missiles included four SA–2s, sixteen SA–3s, and more than eighty SA–6s.[36] The strategic air defence included the vintage S-75s (SA-2) and a small number of partly-modernized S-125 Pechoras (SA-3). The Serbs had only three SA-2 batteries operational with about twenty launchers while there were fourteen batteries of the SA-3 (S-125) with fifty four-rail launchers. The field army had four regiments of 2K12 Kvadrat (SA-6) mobile radar-directed SAMs of which only two regiments were stationed in or near the Kosovo area. Yugoslavia originally had about seventy of these, but high attrition during the civil war left only about twenty-five in the field in 1999. With one 1S91 (Straight Flush) radar vehicle controlling four launchers, the Serbs had only six batteries between the two regiments, seriously undermining the overall air defence cover provided by the Kvadrat system.[37]

Although these missile systems were of 1960s' vintage they had been selectively upgraded. Before the Kosovo air war the S-125 Pechora (SA-3) missile system had been upgraded by including a thermal-imaging camera and laser rangefinder to its fire-control system, allowing the missile to be launched without first acquiring the target using the radar; data could be fed to the system from other radars. As a result, the S-125 held by the Serbs was much more immune to the traditional SEAD measures. The strategic SAMs were served by more than 100 acquisition and tracking radars, networked into an integrated system using secure communication links. A visual observer network acted as the back up to this surveillance network.

Air defence at divisional level was provided by 113 SA-9 and seventeen SA-13 SAMs. As the associated SA-9 missile was being manufactured in Yugoslavia before the war, adequate reserves of the SA-9 were available. Besides these, Serbia had developed improvised air-defence missiles for the air bases using IR-guided air-to-air missiles. Pracka, the simpler of the systems, mounted an R-60 (AA-8 Aphid) missile on an improvised launcher based on the mounting of the towed M55 20mm anti-aircraft gun. The other systems were mounted on the chassis of the Czechoslovak M53/59 30mm self-propelled twin-barrelled anti-aircraft gun. The twin-rail RL-2 used the R-60MK missile while the single-rail RL-4 was based on the R-73 air-to-air missile (AAM). more than 100 of which were in local service.[38] An unspecified number of Bofors 40mm L/70 guns with Giraffe radar were also held for low-level air defence.[39]

In addition, the Serbs had a large number of anti-aircraft guns and a significant number of SA-7 and SA-16/-18 man-portable SAMs. The Strela-2M was being produced in Yugoslavia under the name Strela-2M2J Sava (it had a larger warhead than that of the Soviet SA-7) and was available in large numbers. Serbia had purchased seventy-five of the new SA-16 SAM in the mid-1990s and had, in all, about 850 man-portable IR-guided SAMs in 1999. Aware of the SEAD capabilities of NATO and having learnt from the Iraqi experience during the Gulf War and their own during DELIBERATE FORCE, the Serbs intended to create a killing zone below 10,000 feet by means of AAA, SA-7 infrared SAMs, and Swedish Bofors man-portable air defences.[40]

The overall assessment of the Serbian air defences was of a robust and redundant air defence network, likely to cause attrition. Things turned out differently when the air campaign unfolded with the first strikes on 24 March. The initial strikes were against the integrated air defence system, to enable the conduct of air operations against other targets. NATO committed 400 aircraft on the first night, of which 120 were strike aircraft. The Yugoslavian Air Force launched MiG-29s to intercept the NATO fighters but suffered a loss of three of them, two to United States Air Force F-15s and one to a Dutch F-16.[41] One of the MiG-29s claimed by NATO was reportedly shot down by an SA-6 missile battery instead as it returned to the airport in Niš.[42]

The Yugoslav air defences fired a number of SAMs on the first night but none of the NATO aircraft was hit. It was also due to the fact that the NATO aircraft had been told to maintain a hard deck of 15,000 feet that kept them outside the lethal envelope of the IR-SAM and AA guns. Only the SA-6 was effective at this altitude but, as the incident of friendly fire reveals, there may have been a problem in identification of friendlies from the enemy – due to disruption in the IADS. The threat of being targeted by the anti-radiation missiles (ARMs) also resulted in the launch of most of the SAMs in optical mode without radar guidance, thereby reducing the efficacy of such missiles.

The second night saw more intense air operations, and a lowering of opposition by the air defences who launched less than ten SAMs.[43] Two more MiG-29s were shot down on 27 March, the third day of the operations, by United States Air Force F-15s.[44] The air operations were going on at an uneven pace with the targets being attacked in a gradually escalating manner and the rather slow, uneven pace allowed the Serbs to disperse their air defences and redeploy them. The air situation took a turn on the fourth night when an F-117 Nighthawk stealth aircraft was shot down by an SA-3 missile.[45]

This was a major breakthrough for the Yugoslav air defences as this had been achieved using a missile system of 1960s' vintage against the most advanced aircraft in service – an aircraft that was supposed to be invisible to the radars. The missile was launched by 3rd Battalion of 250th Air Defence Missile Brigade. Colonel Zoltan Dani, the commander of the battalion, had reportedly carried out some modifications on the S-125 'Neva' missile system, enabling it to detect and engage the stealth aircraft.[46]

The loss of the Nighthawk was a serious blow to the United States and equally worrying was the realization that Operation ALLIED FORCE was yet to meet its planned objectives,[47] the main reason being the Serbs forestalling all the NATO efforts and strategies. The air defences and the bad weather were not helping either. NATO was being forced to devote a large part of its air effort on support mission, leaving just about 15 to 20 per cent of the total as strike missions. To have a more concerted air effort, B-1B Lancer bombers were added to the NATO fleet at the end of the second week, two of them carrying out their first mission on 5 April.

The B-1s were to carry out two bomb runs but, on the first run itself, the second B-1 had a malfunction preventing the bomb-bay doors from closing. As they were on the second target, a SAM was fired at them but the B-1 managed to evade it using chaff, ECM and manoeuvring, but as the B-1 was evading the first SAM, a second missile was fired at it. Luckily for the B-1, it was also evaded.[48] B-1s were targeted by SAMs during nearly every sortie they flew although only about ten SAMs were guided on to the B-1s; all were diverted to the Raytheon ALE-50 towed decoy.[49]

As in the case of F-117, the stealth technology did not stop the Serbian air defences picking up the B-1 bombers and firing missiles at them. To detect the aircraft, the Serbians used the radars at Montenegro to acquire and track the B-1s and then hand over the targets to SA-6s. The Kub missile radars locked on to the B-1s in full target-track mode and fired the missiles. The only reason that the missiles did not achieve any hit was that the missiles were diverted on to the ALE-50 decoys.[50]

The Serbian air defences did not shoot down any other manned aircraft for more than a month with the next kill coming only on 2 May when an F-16CG was shot down by an SA-3. Just two days later, two MiG-29s were shot down by a United States F-16CG. Like the previous kills, these were also by beyond-visual-range (BVR) air-to-air missiles. As against the success in the air, NATO was not so successful against the Serbian air defences; for instance, on Day 20 a total of thirty sites were attacked of which only five were destroyed and four damaged severely.[51] The same results, of very few SAM sites being destroyed, continued in the days after.

The altitude limits succeeded in minimizing casualties to IR-guided SAMs. A single aircraft was hit by a shoulder-fired SAM, but the fuse failed to activate and the missile bounced off the aircraft. Several other aircraft were damaged, possibly by this type of weapon. The mere presence of these weapons, however, inhibited air operations to a significant extent.

Due to weather conditions, NATO was forced to abandon air missions when cloud cover precluded operations below the altitude limit, and none of the air forces, other than the US, had munitions such as the Joint Direct Attack Munition (JDAM) that could be used in all-weather conditions. Secondly, it contributed to collateral damage against civilian targets.

The IR-SAMs were the most prolific air defence weapons used during the conflict and brought to the fore an important lesson that, for low-technology armies, the new-generation IR-guided SAM is the most cost-effective solution for tactical air defence and gives them a tremendous capability to harass and deter even the most advanced air forces. The decision not to field the AH-64 Apaches, arguably the most advanced armed helicopters, was partly due to the threat posed by the IR-SAMs. Also, they were very effective in countering the UAV threat, which were used extensively in Kosovo for reconnaissance. Of the twenty-five to twenty-seven UAVs lost in operations, most were downed by IR-guided SAMs, the vehicle-mounted SAMs (Strela-1 (SA-9) and Strela-10 (SA-13)) being more successful due to their higher-altitude capability.[52]

The radar SAMs were kept 'off-the-air' for most of the campaign and used only selectively, giving rise to the impression that they were ineffective. The air strikes aimed at neutralizing them were often assessed as a success with NATO making claims that 'every time the air defence system is turned on, it is destroyed'. NATO claimed that two of the three SA-2 battalions, 40 per cent of Serb SA-3 battalions and a quarter of the SA 6 batteries had been destroyed in air strikes.[53] NATO claims of having destroyed surface-based air defence were misplaced as they were only suppressed. One indicator of the failure of SEAD effort was the repeated and enlarged efforts put in by NATO for the same. As the air campaign progressed, NATO nearly doubled the number of integrated air defence target groups during the fourth week of the war, increasing from thirty to fifty-eight. The air defence targets subsequently went up to 120 by D+50.

One reason for the failure of the SEAD efforts was that it could focus only on the radar-guided SAMs and the radars, whereas the Serbs continued to fire anti-aircraft guns, man-portable surface-to-air missiles, and optically-guided SA-6s against NATO aircraft, without using the radars. As a result, NATO scarcely achieved secure freedom of action, particularly for the more vulnerable systems like the A-10 and AH-64, throughout the conflict.

The assessment of efficacy of Serb air defences based therefore only on the number of aircraft shot down would be erroneous. Even if numbers are considered, it was not a poor performance considering that the Serbs shot down two manned aircraft over the seventy-eight days of the campaign, including the most advanced F-117 Nighthawk aircraft using a SA-3 missile of 1960s' vintage. Moreover, they also shot down twenty-five to twenty-seven unmanned aircraft and twenty cruise missiles.[54] These were achieved by innovative use of the air defence weapons with the AA guns and IR-SAMs sited along the routes frequented by NATO aircraft and UAVs. The air defences forced the NATO aircraft to maintain a 15,000-foot 'floor' to reduce the risks from shoulder-fired SAMs and anti-aircraft guns.[55]

While the restrictions were later removed, the threat remained with the aircraft preferring to engage targets from safer altitudes. The occasional forays to lower latitude, forced by weather or technical reasons, often proved to be a costly lapse as one A-10 pilot found out when he was forced to strafe a target as the AGM Maverick missile was not 'locking-on' to the Serb tanks.[56]

I didn't have any available fighters with LGBs, and the only other option was to strafe the tanks. This was a riskier choice since I would have to dive to a much lower altitude to get in range. I decided to let Andy drop two of his bombs to get their heads down, and I would follow up with a strafe pass … .

Andy had just lost sight of me, a very common occurrence. A good wingman covers his flight lead as he comes off target by focusing on the ground where the threats (AAA and MANPADS) are likely to be fired. A wingman that never goes 'blind' is simply staring at his flight lead and is of no use. 'Lynx 11, copy. One is just west of G-Town climbing … OK! I just got hit! I'm turning to the south.' I never saw what hit me. As I looked up to find Andy, I felt an incredible jolt to the aircraft on the right side. The nose tried to roll off to the right, and I had to put in full left rudder to keep her from flipping over. I was struggling at this point just to keep the jet flying. Dropping the nose, I started a gradual descent to maintain air speed … .

I entered the squadron at Gioia del Colle 24 hours after I had stepped to fly and wanted to get back into the air as soon as possible. The next day, some 48 hours after being hit, I was back in the cockpit. *This time I didn't strafe but dropped CBUs.*

The threat from ground-based air defences remained all through and the assessment by the United States Joint Chiefs of Staff aptly summed up the state of the Serbian air defences at the end of the conflict. It was 'degraded but functional' and it retained 'significant capability to engage with SAMs'.[57]

After seventy-eight days of intense efforts, all that NATO achieved was 'degraded but functional' air defences.

Chapter 11

Syria 2011–2018

The Syrian uprising, known as 'the Day of Rage', began on 15 March 2011 and by April the al-Assad regime had adopted an aggressive approach, but refrained from using its air force against the rebels.

In early June 2011 the rebels ambushed 120 Syrian troops in a move seen as the establishment of formal military resistance to the al-Assad regime. Syria first used its helicopters to obviate reduced mobility due to rebel actions and started using jet aircraft against rebels in August 2011. Although the rebels lacked any dedicated anti-aircraft weapons, they built up an air defence capability over a period of time and had fifteen to twenty-five ZU-23s, two to five 57mm towed air defence guns, or others, and fifteen to thirty SA-7 man-portable air defence systems (MANPADS) by August 2012.[1]

The rebels relied primarily on the ZU-23, which were generally mounted on the back of pick-ups for better mobility, ease of use and getaway and, on at least one occasion, a MANPADS.[2]

The first success came in August 2012 when the Syrian rebels claimed to have shot down a Russian-made MiG-23 on the 12th. This incident came after Syria stepped up its air strikes against rebel strongholds in and around Aleppo and the town of Tal Rifaat, a long-established rebel base.[3] By October, the rebels claimed to have shot down an estimated five rotary-wing and six fixed-wing aircraft. In a pattern similar to the one adopted by the Mujahideen in their fight against the Soviets in Afghanistan, the Syrian rebels sought to attack the air bases to try to destroy the Syrian aircraft, and also to lay ambush as the aircraft came in or took off. Four of the successful aircraft engagements by the rebels took place near the air bases.[4]

In late November and early December 2012, with the Syrian opposition gaining momentum, the rebels overran multiple air bases, using the military stocks of anti-aircraft weapons available in the bases to shore up their air defence capabilities. It is believed that they seized as many as forty MANPADS during this period.[5] This was partly responsible for their enhanced capabilities as they shot down two helicopters and a fighter jet in Aleppo province in the first week of December. With more MANPADS available, the rebels changed tactics and developed the concept of a mixed team of AA guns and MANPADS operating together. They even mounted the heavy AA machine guns and MANPADS on the same vehicle to improvise a composite air defence system. The increased threat was taking a toll of the Syrian Arab Air Force as the rebels claimed to have shot down at least fifty-five Syrian aircraft with their anti-aircraft weapons by December and destroyed the same number in raids and attacks on air bases.

With the situation deteriorating, the Syrian regime used the Scuds for the first time against rebel positions on 12 December although the renewed offensive against the rebels did not deter them from capturing the strategic Taftanaz Air Base in northern Syria. At least twenty Syrian helicopters were destroyed by the rebels at the base.[6] If the outside powers did not intervene at this stage, it was because of the robust Syrian air defences which acted as a strong deterrent. At the start of the civil war, Syria had one of the most formidable air defence systems in the region, perhaps as well-knit and effective as the Israeli air defences. It was sited primarily along the Damascus-Homs-Aleppo corridor and the Mediterranean coast, with 650 air defence sites, of which the SA-5 'Gammon' provided air defence to a range of 200 kilometres. Syria also had over 300 mobile air-defence systems including the SA-11s, SA-17s and SA-22s. Some of these had been captured by the rebels who claimed to be in possession of SA-2 and SA-8 launchers.[7] Some of the SA-5 sites had also been overrun by the rebels, forcing Syria to destroy some SAM sites lest they be captured by the rebels.

By 2013 the Syrian rebels were being supplied with MANPADS that changed the dynamics of the air war in Syria, the first use of which was observed in February when a Chinese FN-6 shoulder-fired missile was used to shoot down a Syrian Mi-8 helicopter.[8] In September 2014 the United States and partner nations intervened militarily, launching air strikes on the 22nd. The United States and other partners carried out the first round of air strikes against targets in Syria using fighters, bombers, and Tomahawk missiles. This also saw the combat debut of the F-22 Raptor stealth fighters. No action was taken by the Syrian air defences which remained 'passive' during the first air strikes, with no attempt to counter US aircraft.

The Russian intervention came a year later, after an official request by the Syrian government for military aid against rebel and jihadist groups. Initially, only air strikes were carried out by Russian aircraft based at the Khmeimim base against militant groups opposed to the Syrian government. Before this the Russian involvement in the Syrian Civil War had been restricted to the supply of arms and equipment. Russian intervention, apart from fighting terrorist organizations such as ISIL, aimed to help the al-Assad regime reclaim its territory and to roll back US influence in the region.

The first Russian Air Force complement was of four Su-30SM fighter aircraft which reached Syria on 18 September, followed by a squadron of twelve modernized Su-25SMs.[9] The Russian Air Force presence was later augmented by twelve Su-24Ms and four advanced Su-34 bombers. In addition, several military transport and reconnaissance aircraft were located at the Khmeimim base. The Russian presence underscored the importance given by Russia to its ties with Syria and the attempts to expand its influence in the region. The Russian air base became operational on 30 September 2015 with squadrons of Su-27SM and Su-30 fighter jets, Su-34 and Su-24 tactical bombers located there. The other deployed aircraft included Il-20M reconnaissance aircraft as well as Mil Mi-24, Mi-28, Ka-52 gunships and Mil Mi-8 support helicopters.[10]

Shortly after the deployment of Russian aircraft, a Su-24M bomber was shot down near the Turkish-Syrian border by a Turkish F-16 on 24 November.[11] Following the incident, Russia deployed the S-400 defensive missile system, allowing it to effectively cover the air space from southern Turkey to northern Israel.[12] The S-400, an upgrade of the S-300 Growler family, is Russia's most advanced anti-aircraft defence system and can hit aerial targets at ranges up to 400 kilometres. The S-400 is capable of hitting tactical and strategic aircraft as well as ballistic and cruise missiles.

On 3 February 2016 a Russian Su-25 attack aircraft crashed over the de-escalation zone of Idlib. The pilot managed to eject but was killed by the rebels. According to the Russian Defence Ministry, the Su-25 attack aircraft was shot down by a man-portable air defence system. The terrorist group Hayat Tahrir al-Sham (HTS), a rebrand of Jabhat al-Nusra, which is the Syrian al-Qaeda affiliate, claimed responsibility for the kill.[13] The incident once again raised the question about the supply of MANPADS to the various rebel and factional groups operating in Syria. Saudi Arabia had long expressed its desire to equip the rebels with advanced man-portable air defence systems[14] but there had been no confirmation that the rebels were ever supplied with the MANPADS. The portable air defence missile systems are, however, believed to have entered Syria in multiple waves via different routes and external sponsors and include the old Soviet models shipped out of Libya, Chinese FN-6s provided by Qatar, and through NATO member Turkey's porous border with Syria. The more likely route remained the missile systems seized from Syrian bases and also the ISIS seizures of Iraqi bases and equipment.

A Syrian fighter jet was shot down on 5 April in southern Aleppo by a surface-to-air missile, making it the second loss for the Syrian Air Force in less than a month. Earlier, on 12 March, the rebel group Jaysh al-Islam claimed responsibility for downing another fighter jet north-west of Hama. The loss of both aircraft was reportedly due to MANPADS although rebel groups stated that the two jets were shot down by anti-aircraft guns, and not anti-aircraft missiles.[15]

After prolonged deliberations and considering the implications of a direct action, the United States launched missile strikes on Syrian airfields on 7 April, making it the first direct attack by the US on the Assad government. The month was a difficult one for the Russians and Syria as they lost a total of three aircraft to rebel air defences – two Syrian jets and one Russian helicopter. While it once again speculated that the rebels may have used MANPADS, their favoured tactic remained the 'flak traps', a Second-World-War-era tactic utilizing multiple machine-gun platforms placed along the paths of jets or helicopters on bombing runs. In March rebels affiliated with the Western-backed Jaish al-Nasr faction had shot down a Syrian MIG-21 near the village of Kafr Nabudah, twenty-five miles north-west of the city of Hama, with the combined firepower of ten machine guns.[16]

Meanwhile, the Russians had supplied Syria with the newer Pantsir S-1 air defence system which was used to good effect. Syrian air defences shot down a number of aerial targets in 2017, the first of which were four artillery rockets shot down over Kmeimim and Masyaf in Hama Province in March with its twelve 57E6 radio-command-guided twenty-kilometre-range missiles and two 30mm 2A38 cannon with 700 rounds per gun and a rate of fire of 2,500 shots per minute. Soon thereafter, an Israeli Heron drone was shot down in April, followed by two more in May and June. The Pantsirs even shot down a Turkish Bayraktar drone near Tartus on 11 May and a US RQ-21A Blackjack drone on the 27th. The Blackjack drone was one of the newer drones in US service and is operated by the United States Navy and the Marine Corps. All these were downed by the Pantsir S1 system.[17]

In January 2018 the Syrian rebels attacked the Russian base at Kmeimim using a drone swarm. The air defences, especially the Pantsirs S-1, engaged and shot down seven of the thirteen drones while the electronic-warfare units took control of the remaining six drones and brought them down. The Pantsir-S anti-aircraft system used a combination of its 30mm auto-cannon with twelve surface-to-air missiles (SAMs) to engage and destroy the drones.[18] Russia has repeatedly accused United States of having orchestrated the drone attack, a charge denied by the United States.[19]

On 3 February the Russian Air Force suffered a setback when an Su-25 attack aircraft was shot down over Idlib province by rebel forces, presumably by a MANPADS[20] while Syrian air defences achieved a rare success against the Israeli Air Force when they shot down an F-16 on 10 February. This incident came after an Iranian Saegheh stealth drone intruded into Israeli airspace and was shot down by an Israeli AH-64. Retaliating against the drone flight, the Israeli Air Force struck T-4 air base. The Syrians launched SAMs at the Israeli aircraft, one of which shot down the F-16, making it the first loss of a combat aircraft for Israel in thirty-five years.[21] After the shooting down of the Israeli aircraft, Syrian anti-aircraft fire reportedly forced an Israeli drone to turn back after it had infiltrated Syrian airspace over the southern province of Qunaitera near the Israeli-occupied Golan Heights[22] although, within two hours of the downing of the F-16, Israel began attacking additional targets inside Syria, including Syrian air-defence batteries and four Iranian targets.

As Israel stepped up the missile strikes, Syria claimed that its air defence systems shot down seventy-one of 103 missiles fired by the US and its allies, the UK and France, in April 2018, a claim denied by the Pentagon. The cruise missiles fired included the first combat use of the JASSM advanced missile, reportedly fired from US B1-B Lancer heavy bombers. The stealthy cruise missiles with a range of 370 kilometres can carry a 450kg warhead and use infra-red sensors to guide themselves towards their targets; each B1B can carry four of these missiles. Russian air defences in Syria, including state of the art S-400 coastal missile batteries located at the Russian naval base at Tartus and elsewhere, monitored the strike but did not engage any of the missiles. That was done only by the Syrians, using the S-200, Pantsir S-1 and Buk-M1 missile systems. The claims could not be verified but if indeed the Syrian air defences shot down the cruise missiles it would confirm that the Syrian air defences had been overhauled and upgraded by the Russians.[23]

Syrian air defences, however, failed to safeguard and protect Syrian air space in May when Israel carried out a massive air strike on the 9th, using twenty-eight F-15s and F-16s to launch sixty guided weapons against Iranian logistical bases and staging areas. During the same raid, Israel claimed to have destroyed five air defence missile batteries that tried to engage the Israeli aircraft. Buk-M2E and Pantsir-S1 systems were claimed to have been included in the missile systems that were destroyed. The destroyed Pantsir system was at the Mezzeh military air base (Damascus). No Israeli jets were shot down during the strikes.[24] One report stated that the Pantsir-S1 missile system was unarmed and was waiting to be reloaded when an Israeli Harpy drone was used to target and destroy it.[25] The failure of Syrian air defences to shoot down the Israeli aircraft was partly due to the degradation suffered over the years and also to the caution that may have been exercised by the air defenders in view of the numerous US, Russian and Turkish aircraft operating in the region.

The next day, 10 May, some twenty rockets were fired at northern Israeli military bases by the Iranian Revolutionary Guard Corps' al-Quds Force from southern Syria, of which four were shot down by the Iron

Dome missile defence system and the rest failed to hit any target. In retaliation, Israel attacked Iranian intelligence centres, weapons depots, storage facilities, observation posts, and logistics centres in Syria. In addition to the strikes on the Iranian targets, the Israelis targeted Syrian air defence systems, with the army targeting 'every battery that fired' at Israeli jets.[26] Syria on its part claimed that its air defences shot down 'most of the seventy rockets' fired by the Israelis.[27] Reports mention that the Israelis were successful in neutralizing the S-200 by jamming its radars, which accounts for its failure to intercept the Israeli aircraft.[28]

After a lull following the first drone swarm attack in January, the rebels stepped up the drone attacks with thirteen in July alone; most of them emanating from the area around Jisr al-Shughur in Idlib province. All the drones were shot down by the Russian air defences, as were those launched later in the year.[29]

On 17 September a Russian Air Force Ilyushin IL-20 'Coot-A' electronic intelligence and radar reconnaissance aircraft monitoring the Idlib province of Syria was mistakenly shot down by Syrian air defence forces after an Israeli air strike on facilities in Latakia, Syria. The Il-20 was shot down by an S-200 system missile, one of the forty-four S-200VE launchers believed to be operated by Syria.[30]

After the accidental shooting down of the Il-20, Russia supplied Syria with its S-300 in early October 2018 as a measure to upgrade its air defences and deter further Israeli induced accidents. The equipment supplied comprised forty-nine units, including radars, control vehicles and four launchers. New electronic warfare systems were also sent to Syria, including systems designed to control a 'near zone' fifty kilometres from the system and a 'far zone' 200 kilometres away that would guard against Israeli attacks.[31]

There was a break in air strikes after the deployment of the S-300, between October and late December. However, Syrian air defence claimed that its radars were jammed on 30 November. This has led to speculation that Syrian air defence was tested several times between October and December. It was also reported that Russia planned to impose electronic countermeasures over Syria's coast line to suppress satellite navigation, onboard radar systems and the communications of warplanes attacking targets on Syrian territory.[32]

On 21 January 2019 Israel struck several targets in Syria that included SAM sites. These strikes were opposed by Syrian air defences which launched several SAMs but they failed to hit any aircraft. Israel claimed that it had targeted and destroyed a Syrian Pantsir S-1 system. The S-300 was reportedly not used during these engagements.[33]

Failure of the Pantsir S-1 was speculated to be because of a saturation attack by the Israelis using Harop (Harpy 2) drones and Delilah cruise missiles. Syrian SAMs shot down a large number of these drones and cruise missiles but as they were followed by waves of missiles and smart bombs, the SAMs were overwhelmed and were not able to counter all of them.

The S-300 was reported to have been made operational by February, based on satellite imagery, with three of the four launchers seen in ready to use position.[34] This would seriously affect the conduct of air operations in the region although Israel had threatened that it would destroy these SAMs if they were used against them. Whether the S-300 is used against Israel and what action is taken by Israel in such a situation is, to date, in the realm of speculation, but their mere presence has raised the cost of air strikes, with Israel forced to use larger quantities of more expensive munitions to saturate and degrade the air defences. In this, the presence of S-300 achieves a goal, even if, a modest one, of shaping the behaviour of the adversaries, increasing the opportunity cost of air raids and making certain types of operations risky or impossible. How far these goals are achieved can only be determined by analyzing the future course of action.

Chapter 12

The Other Wars

T he last four decades have seen a number of conflicts and wars where air power, and air defences, have played a pivotal role. With increasingly lethal air defences, it is becoming all the more important for the air forces to suppress them so as not to be denied control of the air. However, the air defences have proved that they may not have the ability to control the airspace, but they are capable of causing attrition and denying the air forces the freedom so essential for their optimum utilization. Also, with the threat of air defences themselves, air power is restrained and sub-optimally utilized. Of the numerous examples, only a few, viz. Grenada and Kargil in the twentieth century and Georgia in the twenty-first century, are being discussed.

Grenada 1983

The United States invaded Grenada on 25 October 1983. Codenamed Operation URGENT FURY, it was ostensibly triggered by the internal strife within the People's Revolutionary Government and the establishment of a preliminary government, the Revolutionary Military Council, with Hudson Austin as chairman. The invasion resulted in the appointment of an interim government, followed by democratic elections in 1984.

The operation was carried out against a rag-tag army of 1,500 Grenadian soldiers and about 700 armed Cuban nationals manning defensive positions. Grenada had no tanks, only eight BTR-60PB armoured personnel carriers and two BRDM-2 scout cars, and a limited number of M37 82mm mortars and RPG-7 launchers. To take on the United States Air Force, all that Grenada could muster was a dozen ZU-23 anti-aircraft guns and some 12.7mm DShK heavy machine guns.[1]

The air operation started with the 1st Battalion of the 75th Ranger Regiment carrying out an air drop on Point Salines International Airport in face of a moderate resistance from ZU-23 anti-aircraft guns and some BTR-60 APCs. AC-130 gunships were providing support to the mission. When the special operations helicopters tried to approach targets near St George's, Grenadian troops opened fire with anti-aircraft and automatic weapons. As the Rangers' C-130s approached the Point Salines airfield, the Cubans put up stiff resistance, using anti-aircraft guns and automatic weapons. The anti-aircraft fire was soon silenced by a Huey Cobra gunship.

The next day's operation to silence Radio Free Grenada was unsuccessful as the Grenadians had alternative transmitters for the station. Counter-attacks drove the Americans into the jungle in a hasty retreat.

Daylight attacks against objectives at the Richmond Hill prison and Fort Rupert by Delta Force and C Company of the 75th Ranger Regiment embarked in MH-60 and MH-6 Little Bird helicopters also failed after intense anti-aircraft fire severely damaged the helicopters involved in the assault.[2] Two of the helicopters crashed, killing one of the pilots. Worse was to follow when two Marine AH-1T Cobras and a UH-60 Black Hawk were shot down during the air strikes by US Navy A-7 Corsairs and US Marine AH-1 Cobra attack helicopters against Fort Rupert and Fort Frederick.[3]

The heavy anti-aircraft fire even deterred the attacking force from approaching the Governor General's residence in a mission to rescue the Governor General, Sir Paul Scoon, and his wife. The insertion by the SEALs went as planned and they seized the mansion with no opposition. But an enemy counter-attack pinned down the SEALs inside the building, trapping them in the mansion for nearly twenty-four hours until they were relieved by a small marine company-sized unit the following day. In the attempts to rescue the pinned down SEALs, two marine AH-1T Cobra helicopters were shot down, killing three marines; reportedly a UH-60 Black Hawk was also downed.[4] Governor General Scoon, his wife, and nine aides were all safely evacuated without injury.

While firing back at the anti-aircraft guns, one of the A-7s hit a nearby mental hospital, killing eighteen civilians.[5] During the rescue operation to extract American medical students at Grand Anse on Day Two, one CH–46 crashed when its blades hit a palm tree.

On Day Three, during the operation to secure the Calivigny Barracks, as the Rangers approached the objective in four waves of four UH-60 Black Hawk helicopters, the only resistance was by a token force of a few Grenadian soldiers armed with small arms only. There were no anti-aircraft guns to oppose the assault force. Even so, a few rounds from small arms from the ground hit the lead helicopters, severing hydraulic lines and causing one helicopter to crash into another, sending down both helicopters.[6] Nearby, a third helicopter unexpectedly landed in a ditch, striking the tail boom and damaging it. As the helicopter tried to take off, it went out of control and crashed into the wreckage of the other two helicopters. The Rangers had lost three helicopters in a short swift operation opposed by nominal anti-aircraft fire without any radar guidance and without any surface-to-air missiles (SAM).[7]

During the small and swift operation, the United States did not have to face any adversary air force nor was it opposed by organized air defences and yet it suffered the loss of five helicopters with four more severely damaged. This operation brought to the fore the vulnerability of air forces, especially helicopters, to even unorganized air defence with light anti-aircraft guns and small arms.

Kargil 1999

In April 1999 Pakistani troops infiltrated across the Line of Control (LC) in Jammu and Kashmir and occupied positions on the Indian side of the LC on the heights in the Kargil sector, spread over a 160-kilometre-long stretch of ridges overlooking the only road linking Srinagar and Leh.[8] The military outposts on the ridges above the highway were generally around 5,000 metres high, with a few as high as 5,485 metres. Apart from the district capital, Kargil, the only populated areas in the affected areas were the Mushko Valley and the town of Drass, south-west of Kargil, and the Batalik sector, north-east of Kargil. The infiltrating Pakistani troops were from the North Light Infantry and had carried with them heavy, medium and light machine guns, rocket launchers, automatic grenade launchers, mortars, anti-aircraft guns, including shoulder-fired Stingers, and Anza surface-to-air missiles (SAMs).[9] Due to infrequent patrolling and lack of surveillance of these areas, the intrusions remained undetected until May 1999 with the full scale of the incursion being validated on 8 May by the Indian Air Force after surveillance sorties along the Tololing ridge in the Dras sub-sector of the Kargil region.[10]

On 11 May the Indian Army's Northern Command first approached the Indian Air Force with a request to use its armed helicopters against the infiltrators.[11] The Indian Air Force was already carrying out extensive reconnaissance sorties over the Kargil heights, during one of which, on the 12th, a helicopter was fired upon from a forward Pakistani position overlooking Kargil although the helicopter landed back safely, albeit with a damaged rotor.[12]

Following the incident, the Indian Air Force's Western Air Command was put on heightened alert and the bases at Srinagar and Avantipur tasked for quick-reaction launch, if required.[13] On the 13th a forward direction centre for the tactical control of combat aircraft was established at Leh and, in the absence of ground-based radars in the area, an ad hoc air defence control set-up was established.

The reasons for not committing the armed helicopters by the Indian Air Force were twofold. Firstly, Air Chief Marshal A.Y. Tipnis, the Indian Air Force chief, was of the view that the air force could be used only after the necessary 'go-ahead' was given by the government as there was a fear that it could lead to an escalation of the conflict and it was essential that the government was kept in the loop rather than taking a unilateral decision.[14]

The second reason was the need to have a well thought-out and co-ordinated plan for operations that would give the helicopters a fair chance, rather than putting them at avoidable risk in a high risk environment due to the likely presence of infra-red surface-to-air-missiles (IR-SAMs) with the infiltrators. The risks were well underscored when a Canberra PR.57 was hit by a Stinger missile on the 21st while carrying out photo reconnaissance of the Drass, Kargil and Batalik sectors. The Canberra was escorted by two MiG-29s during the mission when, at about 9:00am, after photographing Batalik sector, an infra-red surface-to-air missile[15] hit the aircraft's starboard engine with debris flying off. Wing Commander Alagaraja Perumal, the pilot of the Canberra PR.57 recollects:[16]

On 21 May 1999, prior to the commencement of the Kargil conflict, the Air HQ assigned the Canberra PR aircraft a photo mission task near the LoC (Line of Control). The area of operation covered Drass, Kargil and Batalik sectors. I was detailed to fly the mission along with my navigator, Squadron Leader U.K. Jha. After a thorough study of the area and the restrictions on our manoeuvring posed by the proximity of the LoC, we proceeded for the mission as planned. Over Batalik sector I experienced a violent jolt and explosive thud. I realized that we had been hit by ground fire. Immediately easing up, I checked the aircraft handling and the health of the engines, simultaneously asking the navigator to get back to his seat, strap up and be ready to abandon the aircraft. The aircraft was yawing to the right and was not building up speed.

On the other hand, the bird was still up in the air and flying, posing no problems in handling. After a short discussion with the navigator, I decided against ejection and instead planned to divert for a landing at the nearest airfield at Srinagar. I turned towards Srinagar and initiated a slow descent so as to increase the speed to maintain control of the aircraft. We were now flying over snow-bound mountains on an average height of 2,000 feet.

As the extent of the infiltrations and the gravity of the situation was realized, India took immediate steps to evict the Pakistanis. With the Cabinet Committee on Security giving the 'go-ahead' on 25 May for the use of air force, the stage was set for the Air Force to carry out the strike missions. A restriction was, however, imposed that the Air Force was not to cross the LoC[17].

The first strikes were carried out on the morning of the 26th, with more attacks launched in the afternoon. These were followed by reconnaissance missions by Canberra PR57s and bomb damage assessment (BDA) by MiG-21s.[18]

The first loss for the Indian Air Force occurred on Day Two, 27 May. A MiG-27 experienced an engine failure while coming off a target after a successful two-pass attack with 80mm rockets and 30mm cannon-fire. The MiG-27 was flying well above the operational ceiling at which the 80mm rockets were cleared for firing and it was the likely cause of the engine flame-out.[19] The pilot ejected safely after several unsuccessful air-start attempts and was captured by the Pakistani intruders. Nachiketa, the downed pilot, recollects:[20]

> The hills were fairly close and I turned right by 300–400 to avoid the hill features coming straight ahead. The valley was in an east-west direction, about 5 km away. With no signs of engine restarting, I realized that my height was critical and that I might not clear the northern edge of the bowl. Ejection was inevitable, so I gave an R/T call to my leader, 'Mando! Nachi ejecting!' and pulled the ejection handle.
>
> The parachute opening shock brought me out of the grey-out. The aircraft crashed into the edge of the hill and my seat had cleared the ridge. After about 10–15 seconds of para-descent, I landed on knee-deep snow and soft ice which cushioned the landing. On my landing, I saw some people running towards me from a distance of about 1–1.5 km. Bullets were fired from different directions. I could somehow escape the bullets but got into the enemy hands.

The Indian Air Force suffered another loss, this time of a MiG-21, when it was hit by an infra-red surface-to-air missile hit while assisting in the search for the downed MiG-27 pilot.[21] He also succeeded in ejecting safely, but was executed shortly after he was captured following his landing.[22]

The third day of the air operations saw the IR-SAMs claim another victim when an IAF Mi-17 helicopter was downed while conducting a low-level attack. It was the last in a four-ship flight of armed Mi-17s and the only one without a self-protection flare-dispenser.[23] The Pakistanis fired several SAMs at the formation but they (the SAMs) were distracted by the flares except for one which hit Nubra-3, the last helicopter.[24] Wing Commander A.K. Sinha who led the mission recollects:

> On 28 May 1999, Nubra formation, 4 x Mi-17, were tasked to strike 'Point 5140' feature, located 2 kms north of Tololing. Maj Rakesh Adhikary came on-board Nubra-1 to guide us to locate our armed Mi-17s strike at Tololing, as he came on the 1st day (26 May 99).

Nubra formation took off in time and all went on perfectly well, like clockwork. Notwithstanding the threat of enemy firing, Nubra-1 (my helicopter) struck at point 5140 with two salvoes of 64 rockets each. Simultaneously, enemy started firing shoulder-fired Stinger missiles. Two Stingers skimmed past the windscreen of Nubra-1. Both these were fired from two different locations.

Similarly, Nubra-2, 3 and 4 of Sqn Ldr Verma, Flt Lt Muhilan and Sqn Ldr Nitish respectively struck the enemy positions with 128 rockets each. After Nubra-3 had fired its armament it got hit by the enemy Stinger missile.[25]

After this loss the Indian Air Force pulled back its Mi-17 helicopters from the armed fire-support role. However, they continued to be used for airlift, casualty evacuation, and reconnaissance missions.[26]

All its fighters were equipped with flare dispensers to provide an active countermeasure against any enemy infra-red-guided missiles and henceforth all targets were engaged from outside the threat envelopes of the IR-SAMs.[27]

No Indian Air Force aircraft was lost, or sustained damage, after 28 May even as Pakistanis fired more than 100 IR-SAMs during the conflict.[28] The air strike operations ended on July 12.

The operation was short but very challenging, with restrictions imposed not only by the terrain but also by the political establishment (no crossing of the LoC). The presence of IR-SAMs added to the challenges faced by the Indian Air Force. Remaining outside their lethal envelope meant that the fighters had to remain 6,000 to 8,000 feet above the high ridge lines at all times. The higher weapon release altitude degraded the weapons' performance (already degraded by operating in high altitude with rarefied atmosphere).

The Pakistani infiltrators had other air defence weapons to support them, but it was the IR-SAMs that proved to be the most effective of all. The low attrition rate notwithstanding (three losses from over 6,500 sorties including 1,700 strike missions), the presence and threat of the IR-SAMs forced the Indian Air Force to take defensive measures. The armed Mi-17s were not used for strike missions after the loss of a helicopter on 28 May. The weapon delivery was from outside the threat envelope of the IR-SAMs and that itself was, in a way, the impact of the air defence weapons.

In this, the following two lessons on operations in a SAM environment brought out by the Indian Air Force are self-explanatory:[30]

> Gone are the days of fighters screaming in at deck level, acting as a piece of extended artillery. The air defence environment of today's battlefield just does not permit such employment of airpower anymore, a significant fact that needs to be understood by soldier and civilian alike

And

> during Op Safed Sagar, the abundance of man-portable SAMs in all enemy-held areas precluded the effective employment of attack choppers. As a result, whether Army or IAF, choppers were constrained to operate in SAM-free areas.

Georgia

In August 2008 a short, intense war broke out between Georgia and Russia over South Ossetia and Abkhazia – what is often referred to as the first European war of the twenty-first century. The roots of the Russia-Georgia conflict go back to the early 1990s when both Russia and Georgia were newly independent nations after the dissolution of the USSR. The demand for independence by two Georgian provinces – South Ossetia in eastern Georgia, and Abkhazia on the north-western coast – resulted in a civil war which ended in 1994, but tensions continued to simmer in the two breakaway provinces. In order to retain its sphere of influence in the region, Russia continued to support the Ossetians and the Abkhazians; they had been autonomous earlier in the twentieth century, after the Russian Revolution, and wanted their autonomy back.

Matters came to a head when Georgia accused Russia of supporting the separatist cause, leading to the arrest of four Russian military officers for suspected espionage. This was followed by a series of clashes between South Ossetian militia and Georgian military troops.

August 2008 saw South Ossetian separatists shelling Georgian villages. That met with a sporadic response from Georgia initially but, on 7 August, the Georgian Army moved Georgians to put an end to the shelling; and took control of most of Tskhinvali, a separatist stronghold. Russia responded swiftly by moving troops to the border and conducting air strikes on Georgian positions in South Ossetia as well as Abkhazia.

Russian and South Ossetian forces battled Georgian forces in and around South Ossetia for several days until Georgian forces retreated. Russian and Abkhaz forces opened a second front by attacking the Kodori Gorge held by Georgia. Russian naval forces blockaded part of the Georgian coast. The Russian Air Force attacked targets beyond the conflict zone, in undisputed parts of Georgia.

The conflict lasted for all of five days, during which Russia quickly took control of Tskhinvali and advanced into Georgia, stopping only about thirty miles from Tbilisi, the Georgian capital. A ceasefire on 12 August ended the Russia-Georgia War after Russia had ended its advance into Georgia.

Russian forces temporarily occupied the Georgian cities of Zugdidi, Senaki, Poti, and Gori, holding on to these areas beyond the ceasefire. Russia withdrew its troops from undisputed parts of Georgia on 8 October but continues to occupy Abkhazia and South Ossetia.

The conflict saw an extensive use of air power by Russia during which it lost six aircraft[30] although Georgia claimed to have downed as many as fourteen during the five-day war.[31]

The Russian involvement had begun much before the actual outbreak of hostilities with the Russian Air Force regularly violating Georgian air space. In March 2007 Russian Mi-24 helicopters attacked Georgian government buildings in the Kodori Gorge in the Georgian-controlled area of Abkhazia, followed by the shooting down of a Georgian unmanned aerial vehicle (UAV) by a MiG-29 over Abkhazia.[32] A more serious incident took place in July when four Russian Su-24s flew over the international border and loitered over South Ossetia for about forty minutes, an incident acknowledged by Russia. In August 2007 Russia scaled up its intrusions as a Russian Air Force Su-24 directly attacked a Georgian air defence facility, launching a Kh-58 missile at a radar site.

The missile, however, missed its target and failed to explode. Russia denied any involvement in the incident.[33]

The Georgian air defences were a mix of what had been left behind after the collapse of the Soviet Union and new acquisitions. The Soviet leftovers which Georgia managed to retain were one S-75 and two S-125 SAM battalions, as well as a few P-18 Spoon Rest radars. Of these, only the S-125 were in service in 2008.[34] The later additions by Georgia were two batteries of the Buk-M1 (SA-11) missile system[35] and six Osa-AK (SA-8B) SAM systems, both purchased from Ukraine. The most advanced SAM system was the SPYDER missile system purchased from Israel of which Georgia had one battery worth of equipment[36] while the Igla-1 (SA-16) was the main man-portable missile system, of which it had fifty launchers (grip-stocks) with 400 missiles. In addition, a few Grom MANPADS, purchased from Poland, were also available to the Georgian Army.[37] The anti-aircraft guns included a few C-60 57mm anti-aircraft guns, ZU-23-2 twin 23mm anti-aircraft guns, and ZSU-23-4 Schilka gun systems.

Four P-180U and two 36D6-M radars with one Kolchuga-M passive electronic monitoring system formed the surveillance network that included the civilian air-traffic-control radars called the Air Sovereignty Operations Centre (ASOC) early warning and command control tactical system. The central command centre was located in Tbilisi and was connected to a NATO air situation data exchange (ASDE) through Turkey, which allowed Georgia to receive data directly from the unified NATO air-defence system. All this made the Georgian air defence network a small, compact system capable of providing a reasonable level of opposition to the Russian Air Force. With only eight Su-25 attack aircraft and around twenty-five helicopters, the Georgian Air Force was in any case not expected to offer any resistance to the Russians.

The Russian invasion was spearheaded by its Fifty-eighth Army, consisting of the 19th and 42nd Motorized Rifle Divisions. The additional forces committed included the 76th Air Assault and the 98th Airborne Divisions. A battalion of the 33rd Special Mountain Brigade was also reportedly deployed to South Ossetia. In Abkhazia elements of the 7th Airborne Division, 76th Air Assault Division and 20th Motorized Division were committed. The Russian Air Force component was made up of a force of some 300 combat aircraft, including the Su–24, Su–25, Su–27, and Tu–22[38] of which 120 combat aircraft and seventy helicopters were integral to the Fifty-eighth Army.[39]

The Russian air campaign was not as intense as experienced during the Gulf War, or even the Balkans conflict although the Russian Air Force did carry out 300 to 400 sorties over the five days, with over 120 on the second day alone.[40]

The Russian air campaign started well before the official involvement in the conflict, with three Su–24 attack aircraft attacking civilian and military targets including the military base in Gori, airfields in Vaziani and Marneuli and a radar station 40 kilometres near Tbilisi.

The first loss suffered by Russian Air Force was of an Su–25 shot down by ground fire from South Ossetian forces.[41] Georgian air defences claimed the first Russian aircraft on 9 August when a Tu–22 Backfire was shot down by a surface-to-air missile, believed to be a Buk-M1, while on a reconnaissance mission near Gori. The other losses during the day were of an Su–24 and an Su–25. Of these, one Su–25 was lost to South Ossetian forces. Another Su–25 was shot down by Russian forces using a ZSU-23-4B Schilkas on the 9th in a case of failure of the fighter's 'identification friend or foe' (IFF) system.[42]

Stung by these losses, the Russians targeted both the missile batteries of S-125 Neva and the Buk-M1, and the majority of military and civilian radars. After this Georgian air defences were relegated to the use of portable air-defence systems.

The final aircraft lost in combat was an Su–24, which was shot down by friendly forces while it was escorting a Russian column on the Tskhinvali-Gori highway; it was hit by a Russian SAM.[43] Besides the losses, several Russian Su–25s were hit and severely damaged by Georgian MANPADs but were able to return safely to base.[44]

The Russian air campaign was a mixed bag. While it established air dominance over the Georgian Air Force, it came with unexpectedly heavy losses, especially to friendly fire. No SEAD (Suppression of Enemy Air Defences) missions were launched before targeting the ground troops and it was only after having lost a number of aircraft that the Russians targeted Georgian air defences. The effectiveness of the SEAD was marred by the lack of intelligence about Georgian air defences and lack of suitable weapons. The Russian Air Force did not use any anti-radiation missiles during the war.[45] Moreover, continued use of MANPADS by the Georgians meant that the Russian Air Force was never in total control.

The loss of Su-25s to MANPADS was partly due to the Russian lack of stand-off weapons which could be launched from outside the air defence envelope.

The lack of co-ordination between the air force and ground troops resulted in a large number of fratricide incidents as Russian aircraft were frequently misidentified as Georgian and fired upon without identification by Russian and South Ossetian troops. It also raises questions about the efficacy of the Buk-M1 and SPYDER missile system which claimed just one aircraft (the Tu-22 shot down by Buk-M1 on 9 August) between the two of them. The only air defence system that performed well was MANPADS.

Yemen

The Yemeni Civil War that began in 2015 is a continuing conflict between two factions: the internationally recognized Yemeni government, led by Abdrabbuh Mansur Hadi, and the Houthi armed movement, along with their supporters and allies.

The roots of the conflict lie in the failure of Abdrabbuh Mansur Hadi's regime to ensure a smooth transition when it took over from Ali Abdullah Saleh. The crisis deepened with attacks by jihadists and a separatist movement in the south. Taking advantage of the instability, the Houthi movement took control of the northern heartland of Saada province and neighbouring areas, taking over the capital, Sana'a, in 2015. Unable to control the situation, Abd-Rabbu Mansur Hadi fled the country in March 2015. The Houthis are opposed by Saudi Arabia and eight other, mostly Sunni, Arab states that have been conducting a military campaign aimed at restoring the Hadi government. The intervention started as a bombing campaign by the Saudi-led coalition but later the scope of intervention expanded to include a naval blockade and the deployment of ground forces into Yemen.

Air operations by the Saudi-led coalition form a critical part of these operations with the United States, Britain and France providing intelligence and logistical support for the campaign. The coalition forces managed to take back Aden, pushing the Houthis out of South Yemen. Other militant groups active in the region are al-Qaeda in the Arabian Peninsula (AQAP) and the local affiliate of the rival Islamic State (IS) group.

Backed by Washington, the Saudi-led coalition launched an air campaign, Operation DECISIVE STORM, on 26 March with the aim of restoring exiled President Abd-Rabbu Mansur Hadi to power.[46]

The coalition included the air arms from the Gulf Co-operation Council nations, except Oman, joined by aircraft from Morocco, Egypt, Sudan and Jordan. Saudi Arabia was, and remains, the largest contributor with 100 aircraft that include fighters and support aircraft. The air campaign suffered a setback when Saudi Arabia lost an F-15S Strike Eagle on 28 March when the aircraft crashed into the Gulf of Aden due to technical problems.[47]

With the air operations playing a central role in the military offensive by the Saudi-led coalition, air defence forces of the Houthi rebels were a critical factor that would affect the outcome of the conflict, but the Houthis did not have any significant air defence capability, even though the Yemeni air defence forces had been seized by the Houthi rebels when they assumed control over a large part of the country. These included most of the ex-Soviet SA-2, SA-3, SA-6 and SA-9 SAMs, as also the large inventory of the man-portable air-defence systems.[48]

Most of them were, however, unserviceable and non-operable due to years of poor maintenance and shortage of spares. Moreover, a large number of the fixed-sites missile systems were targeted and destroyed by the coalition in the initial air strikes during the early days of the war in April 2015.

The coalition air forces did not face any serious opposition from the Houthis' air defence systems and the same was reflected in the low level of attrition faced by them during the year.

The Houthis managed to shoot down only four manned aircraft in 2015, the first of which was a Moroccan F-16 brought down by anti-aircraft guns over in the remote Wadi Nashour area in the north-western province of Saada, a Houthi stronghold bordering Saudi Arabia.[49] However, two Saudi AH-64 Apache helicopters and up to a dozen reconnaissance drones were also shot down during the year.[50] The next year Houthi air defences did not achieve much success against the coalition air forces and managed to bring down only one helicopter and one drone although the Houthi claimed that they had destroyed an F-16, four helicopters, and sixteen drones.

This failure to cause any viable attrition on the Saudi-led coalition spurred the Houthis to innovate and develop air defence weapons, using the Russian-made heat-seeking air-to-air missiles. Using the AA-10 Alamo-B, AA-11, AA-8 and probably the AA-7, the Houthis developed truck-mounted anti-aircraft surface-to-air-missiles, the first of which was photographed in February 2017 by a coalition drone in the al-Salif region.[51] Although these missiles did not have radar guidance or cuing facility, the Houthis used them for carrying out SAM-ambushes and claimed to have downed two F-16s in Saudi Arabia's Najran province on 24 February 2017.[52] That same month a United States MQ-9 Reaper UAV was also shot down by the Houthis with their innovative SAM. Another successful kill, of a Saudi AH-64 Apache, was claimed over the Red Sea port of Hudaydah by the rebels in March.

In one of the single biggest losses during the conflict, a Saudi Black Hawk helicopter was lost in April when it was brought down by friendly fire in the Marib province, east of the Houthi-controlled capital Sana'a although the fratricide claims were denied by the Saudis.[53] The other major success was the shooting down of a United States MQ-9 Reaper UAV in western Yemen on 1 October.[54]

Having achieved some success with their innovations, the Houthis warned of a 'new, highly accurate air-defence system' and claimed that the F-15 had been shot down by the 'new' weapons system although no details could be ascertained and only the firing of the R-27T could be confirmed.[55] The Houthis had reportedly used the US-made FLIR (forward-looking infra-red) Systems ULTRA 8500 turrets with makeshift controls for their 'new' SAMs. One such SAM enabled them to fire the R-27T that narrowly missed a Saudi F-15 over Sana'a on 7 January 2018. It was this incident during which the Houthis had claimed to have shot down the F-15.[56]

The failure to bring down an aircraft by the converted SAMs was repeated in another incident on 21 March when a second Saudi F-15 only suffered minimal damages from the R–27T AA–10 0 SAM fired at it. Later that month, on the 26th, two Emirati F-16s were unsuccessfully targeted in an apparent heat-seeking missile attack from the ground. The Houthi air defences were increasingly looking impotent against the coalition air forces, not capable of causing any serious damage. The failure also raises doubts about the capabilities of passive target-tracking systems reportedly acquired by the Houthis from Iran. The Houthis were reportedly supplied with the Sayyad–2C SAMs and transponder interrogators (a virtual radar receiver, or VRR) by Iran which would pose a serious threat to Saudi-led coalition forces although there has been no confirmation of their use by the Houthis.[57]

The one weapon used successfully by the Houthis was the Scud which they had employed from 2015 onwards. These were Scuds left over from the previous regime, of which the rebels reportedly had forty-five. A Scud aimed at the King Khalid Air Base, one of the largest air bases in Saudi Arabia, on 6 June 2015 marked the first time the Scuds had been used by the Houthis to target Saudi Arabia. The Scud was successfully intercepted by a Patriot missile before it could hit the air base.[58]

Saudi Arabia claimed to have intercepted and shot down 40 per cent of the Scuds using Patriots although later analysis points out repeated failure of the anti-missile system. The missiles used during the early stages of the conflict were the Scud-Cs that resembled the Hwasong-6 missiles of North Korea.[59] Scaling up the ballistic missile attacks, the Houthis used the Tochka (SS-21 Scarab) missile at targets in Saudi Arabia in September 2015. This was followed by the use of a Burqan 2H long-range missile targeting Riyadh, in November 2017. The Saudis claim that the Iranian-made missile was intercepted before it could reach its target. The Houthis repeated the tactic in January, firing a ballistic missile, a Qaher2-M, towards Saudi Arabia's southern province of Narjan.[60]

Adding a new dimension to the air defence war, the Houthis revised their strategy in 2017 by attacking the air defence systems of Saudi Arabia using UAVs. Starting in April 2017 the Houthis launched an average of six Qasef-1 UAVs with explosive warheads, aimed at Gulf coalition Patriot missile batteries.[61] These attacks were carried out to disrupt the air defences before the launch of surface-to-surface missiles by the Houthis. The UAVs were programmed using open-source GPS co-ordinates of the Patriots' positions, to crash into the Patriots' radar sets (specifically the circular main phased arrays).[62] The efficacy of these attacks could not be ascertained, but all such attacks coincided with the launch of ballistic missiles, indicating that they did achieve some degree of success. The Scud attacks continued with the first four months of 2018 seeing thirty such launches. Saudi Arabia claimed to have intercepted seven ballistic missiles fired by Houthi forces from Yemen using the MIM-104 Patriot missile defence system, but reports suggest that the Patriot missiles failed on a number of occasions.[63]

With no end to the conflict, the region will continue to see the Scuds and Patriots battle it out in the times to come with the drone attacks being a regular feature.

Conclusion

On 6 October 1973, as the Israeli Air Force (IAF) retaliated against the Egyptian and Syrian offensives, it was opposed by an unexpectedly effective air defence network, losing at least ten aircraft in its initial strikes across the two fronts, with the number going up to thirty in the first twenty-four hours.[1] This was less than the loss it had suffered during the pre-emptive strikes of 1967, but the sheer scale and lethality of the air defences came as a shock to the Israelis. Their efforts to supress the SAMs failed as the Israelis had no answer to the SA-6, the newer SAM, and the IAF gave up trying even to target the missile sites. It was not without reason that Eric Weizmann said 'missile [had] bent the aircraft's wing'.

It was the air defence that was dictating terms to the air, rather than just reacting to it.

It was not the first time that the SAMs had taken a toll of Israeli aircraft. Between July 1967 and May 1973 Israel lost a total of twenty-five aircraft in clashes with Egypt, of which the majority were to SAMs.[2] The main challenge for the Israelis was the SA-6. It was not a new system as it had already been encountered in August 1970. Yet it was technologically a surprise with the existing electronic countermeasures (ECM) impotent against the SA-6 radar.[3] The mobility and small size of the SA-6 launchers meant that they were difficult to target and at times it seemed futile trying to attack them. As one Israeli pilot described the experience:

> We had no response to the overlapping missile systems, which complemented each other... . This was no longer a missile fired from a bunker but one fired from a vehicle, something tiny, seeing but unseen, with almost unlimited range of operation.... The pilot's response time is reduced to almost nothing. A lot of time passes

before the aircraft's radar detects the location of the firing and until the opposition missile homes in on the target. In this time, the mobile missile carrier can turn and run, and it is not worth wasting ammunition chasing it.[4]

In 1973 the Arabs had tried, for the first time, to compensate for their inferior air forces with an integrated air defence system and had succeeded to a large extent. They were helped by the Israelis who mistakenly believed that they could eliminate the Arab integrated air defences in a large first strike. The belief was, however, not backed up by practical measures like self-protection suites for the aircraft and the munitions to counter the Arab air base defences.[5]

In the end, Israel managed to destroy only one hangarette and twenty-two aircraft during the war.[6]

More than the failure in their attacks on air bases, it was their ineffectiveness in providing close support and the greater losses over the battlefield that were a big setback to the Israeli Air Force. All the efforts to neutralize the SAMs using air strikes failed although, as the war progressed, the air defences, more specifically the SAMs, were eventually defeated by ground action and that too only in the south. On the Syrian front, the SAMs remained unbeaten right to the end of the war. It was truly the 'coming of age' of the SAMs. Commenting on the impact of the SAMs, the official USAF report concluded:[7]

The enemy's improved capabilities and massive use of surface-to-air missiles has shifted the balance over the battle arena. Improved air delivered munitions and modern electronic countermeasures are needed to insure [sic] support of the ground forces.

It was not that the SAMs were, or are, unbeatable as the subsequent wars have shown, of which the Bekaa Valley stands out as the prime example of air power totally decimating the adversary's air defences. But just as the Yom Kippur War is not the best example of studying the application of air power, the Bekaa Valley episode is the wrong example to assert the supremacy of air power over air defences. The IAF failed in Yom Kippur as they had not adopted the lessons learnt in the previous wars in their tactics and practices, just as the Syrians failed to adopt the basic tactical lessons of the previous wars in the Bekaa valley in 1982.

While SEAD (suppression of enemy air defences) succeeded in the short term, the Syrian air defences were soon operational at their previous capabilities, highlighting a simple fact that air defences are resilient and can be neutralized or suppressed only for short periods. This remains true to date, as experienced by the NATO air forces in the Balkans when the Serb air defences continued to fire back at the NATO aircraft right to the end of the seventy-eight-day air campaign. It is equally relevant in Syria and Yemen where even the poorly-equipped insurgent groups continue to fight back with improvised air defence weapons. This continued capability of air defences and even the threat of air defence systems alone pushes up the cost of using air power with the presence, or the mere possibility of use of air defence systems, shaping and restricting the use of air power.

The Indian Air Force withdrew its armed helicopters from front-line use during the Kargil conflict of 1999 when an armed Mi-17 was shot down by a MANPADS. Similarly, the United States did not use its AH-64 Apaches advanced attack helicopters due to the threat of Serb air defences. The need to 'shape' the battlefield by suppressing the enemy air defences will remain a prerequisite and this means that even the most advanced aircraft will be fielded reluctantly, even if they ever are, thereby limiting the strike power available.

Another unintended effect of the air defence threat is the use of advanced high-technology aircraft for routine operations as the air defence environment may not be conducive for employing the other aircraft. The examples of F-117 Nighthawk and F-22 Raptor are illustrative. During their use in the Gulf War, F-117s were used only at night and were escorted by support aircraft to suppress the Iraqi air defences. Similarly, the F-22 Raptor was intended for the air defence role and was declared operational in 2005. The then head of US Air Combat Command, General Robert Keys, had declared, 'If we go to war tomorrow, the Raptor will go with us,'[8] but its first combat use was nine years later, in 2014, when it was used in the second wave (cruise missiles were the first wave) against Islamic State targets near Tishrin Dam in Syria. This trend is likely to continue in view of future air defence threats.

The need to support the strike missions will again restrict the strike power available to an air force as more and more effort will be demanded for SEAD, resulting in 'virtual attrition'.

Trends in Air Defences

The proliferation of man-portable air defence systems (MANPADS) presents a challenge that needs to be addressed more seriously. Since the 1970s more than thirty countries have manufactured complete MANPADS systems, produced important components, or upgraded existing systems. Not only the state but the non-state actors have access to these weapons that make them more than just a 'clear and present danger'. Unfortunately, the trend of arming various groups and factions with these weapons is likely to continue as in the case of the continuing Yemen crisis where Saudi Arabia has reportedly made MANPADS available to the warring factions. It is difficult to control them and keep them safe, no matter what the means employed. Ultimately, as in the case of Afghanistan, these weapons end up being used against the 'benefactors' with deadly results.

Anti-aircraft guns will continue to be used, in spite of the wider acceptance and use of missiles as the primary air defence weapon. There may be fewer new air defence guns being developed but the existing inventories are likely to be upgraded and used in the days to come.[9]

Innovations and improvised air defence weapons have been used in the past and will continue to be used in the future. The innovations and improvisations will not only be in developing 'improvised aerial explosive devices' but also in the tactical employment of existing weapons, as seen in Afghanistan and Iraq where a large number of heavy anti-aircraft machine guns were used to lay air defence ambushes. The manner in which the air defence weapons are used in the future may well be different and a totally new innovation. As all contingencies cannot be catered for, these innovations will continue to take a toll.

Limitations of Air Defence Systems

Saturation of air defences is a major limitation that restricts the capabilities of air defence systems in countering the air threat. The use of drone swarms in an attempt to overwhelm Russian air defences is a recent example. Although the Russians managed to shoot down/neutralize all the drones, in a later incident, the newer S-400 system did not engage the sixty BGM-109 Tomahawk land attack cruise missiles (TLAMs) launched by the United States against the Syrian Air Force base at Shayrat. Even if the Russians had attempted to engage the TLAMs, it is possible that the S-400 would not have been able to destroy more than about half the incoming missiles, even assuming all of the SAMs loaded and ready were fired and hit their intended individual targets. TLAMS are of 1960s' vintage and otherwise simple to engage but the sheer scale of the attack made it difficult for the world's most advanced air defence system to counter it.[10]

The problem of countering cruise missiles and UAVs is accentuated by the wide proliferation of these systems – even with non-state actors. With technological advancements, the non-state actors are now able to deploy small UAVs capable of delivering payloads of up to 20kg over continental ranges.[11] Detection of these UAVs is difficult because of their small size and use of composite material, but what is of greater concern is the minimal response time, at times as low as tens of seconds to a minute, available to counter them. As the conventional air defence systems are not designed to counter such threats, there is thus a need to develop new technologies and weapons.

On the other end of the threat spectrum, the conventional threat of fixed- and rotary-wing aircraft will become more difficult to counter due to the wider use of stealth and very-low-observable (VLO) characteristics which will be the rule and not the exception in modern combat aircraft. Even if this threat remains limited to a handful of nations, the armament used by almost all aircraft will be smaller and more capable guided munitions. Coupled with advances in computer electronic warfare and cyber operations capabilities, the conventional air threat will be a challenge for traditional air defences.[12]

The Future

As the air defences will become more complex to counter the emerging air threat, it will become more expensive to develop the countermeasures to such defences. And the duel between the air defences and air power will continue.

In real terms, every war is a duel involving dynamic partners. To win, the need is not only to learn from the previous engagements but also innovate and employ new tactics and strategies for which the opponent may have no counter. It is not only that new weapons and technology provide the 'new tactics'; the way that the available weapons and systems are used is more important. All the previous wars and operations have shown that whichever side learns from the past conflicts, and adapts and changes its tactics and practices, will prevail. To ignore the lessons of the past makes it inevitable that the follies of the past will be repeated at a cost that may be too heavy to be paid.

Notes

Yom Kippur War

1. Mohamed Hassanein Heikal was an Egyptian journalist with the Cairo newspaper *Al-Ahram* for 17 years. He was a member of the Central Committee of the Arab Socialist Union and served as minister of information from 1970 to 1974.

2. Muhammad Hassanayn Heikal, 'al-Jaysh al-Israeli wa al-dawa'i al-mulha li-hazima fi ma'arka,' *al-Ahram*, 11 April 1969. An English translation appears as 'The Strategy of Attrition' in *The Israel–Arab Reader*, edited by Walter Laqueur and Barry Rubin, 4th ed., pp. 423–4.

3. Egyptian and Soviet air defences claimed to have shot down nine Israeli Air Force Phantoms and damaged three more during the period from 30 June to 3 August 1970. (*'Operation KAVKAZ: Israeli Phantoms against the Soviet air defense'*, Centre for Strategic Assessment and Forecasts, 27 September 2018, http://csef. ru/en/oborona-i-bezopasnost/423/operacziya-kavkaz-izrailskie-fantomy-protiv-sovetskoj-pvo-8646)

4. Hopkins, *Anatomy of a Failure: Soviet Military Assistance to Egypt*, US Army Institute for Advanced Russian and Far Eastern Studies, 1978.

5. Of the 770 aircraft, 120 were in storage, leaving 550 available for combat. Ballance, *No Victor, No Vanquished: The Yom Kippur War*, p. 280.

6. Ibid., p. 281.

7. Palit, *Return to Sinai*, p. 69.

8. O' Ballance, p 282.

9. Major General Hassan el Badri, Major General Taha el Magdoub, and Major General Mohammed Dia el Din Zohdy, *The Ramadan War, 1973*, p. 146.

10. SA-6 Kub (export name 'Kvadrat') used a continuous wave (CW) transmitter unlike those of SA-2 and SA-3. The Israeli ECM equipment was not designed to operate against the CW. Please refer *'The Development of Soviet Air Defence Doctrine and Practice'* prepared for Sandia National Laboratory by Historical Evaluation and Research Organization, Dunn Loring, Virginia, July 1981.

11. The Soviet practice that was also followed by the Arabs was to engage each target with at least a salvo of two missiles. This meant that the battery (with four launchers) fired two missiles at a target – not that each launcher fired two missiles each. These details were apparently not known to the west and its (SA-6) capabilities were overhyped to an extent that each launcher was generally considered to be capable of taking on a target independently.

12. Clarence E. Olschner, *The Air Superiority Battle in the Middle East, 1967–1973*, p. 34.

13. Riad N. El-Rayyes and Dunia Nahas, eds., *The October War*, p. 5.

14. Insight Team of the London *Sunday Times*, 'The Yom Kippur War', 1 Oct 2002, pp. 94–7; Anthony H. Cordesman, *After The Storm: The Changing Military Balance in the Middle East*, p. 337.

15. Pollock, *Arabs at War: Military Effectiveness, 1948–1991*; 'Syrian Arab Air Force (SyAAF) in combat', *The Aviationist*, https://theaviationist.com/special-reports/syrian-arab-air-force-syaaf-in-combat/

16. O' Ballance, op. cit., p. 285.

17. Ibid., p. 286.

18. *The Military Balance, 1971–1974*, p. 34; O'Ballance, op. cit., p. 287.

19. Brower, '*The Israeli Defense Forces, 1948–2017*', Mideast Security and Policy Studies No. 150.

20. Olschner, op. cit., p. 34.

21. Kreis, *Air Warfare and Air Base Air Defense, 1914–1973*.

22. Brower, op. cit.

23. '*Preparation and Planning: Air Strikes on October 6, 1973*', http://www.skywar.ru/Ramadanwar.html

24. Israel claimed 13 Syrian aircraft for the loss of one of its own while Syria admitted the loss of 8 and claimed to have shot down 5 Israeli aircraft while the generally accepted figure for Syrian losses is of 12 Syrian aircraft shot down. The total Syrian aircraft losses since the 1967 war were reported to be 60, including these 12: these included 48 MIG-21s, nine MIG-17 interceptors and three Sukhoi-7 fighter bombers. Israel lost 3 planes in all its clashes with Syria since 1967. ('13 Syrian MiG-21s Downed, 1 Israeli Plane Downed in Biggest Air Clash Since the Six Day War', *Jewish Telegraphic Agency*, 14 September 1973); David Buckwalter, *1973 Arab-Israeli War* (United States Air Force University, http://www.au.af.mil/au/awc/awcgate/navy/pmi/1973.pdf)

25. Bar-Joseph, *The Watchman Fell Asleep: The Surprise of Yom Kippur and Its Sources*; Bar-Joseph, 'The Wealth of Information and the Poverty of Comprehension: Israel's Intelligence Failure of 1973 Revisited', (*Intelligence and National Security 10, No. 4*, October 1995), p. 232.

26. Egyptian Air Force fighter jets attacked the IDF's airfields, Israeli Air Force, http://www.iaf.org.il/843-13276-he/IAF.aspx

27. Israel used captured 57mm Soviet AA guns also for base defence. No Egyptian aircraft was shot down by Israeli AA guns deployed on the air bases although seven aircraft were shot down by two Israeli F-4 Phantoms at Ras Nasrani air base on 6 October.

28. Levav & Almadon, *The Closest Call, Israeli Air Force*, (http://www.iaf.org.il/4477-50456-en/IAF.aspx)

29. Upon the outbreak of the war, Egyptian Air Force fighter jets attacked the IDF's airfields (http://www.iaf.org.il/843-13276-he/IAF.aspx)

30. Sherman, *When God Judged and Men Died: A Battle Report of the Yom Kippur War*, p. 37.

31. Insight Team of the London *Sunday Times*, The Yom Kippur War, (1 Oct 2002), pp. 93–4.

32. Nordeen, *Air Warfare in the Missile Age*, p. 256.

33. Perman, *Spies, Inc.: Business Innovation from Israel's Masters of Espionage*.

34. During the strike the squad leader's aircraft was hit by an SA-2 missile, killing the pilot (Major Eitan Chanan), making him the IAF's first casualty of the war. (*The Valley Squadron*, http://www.iaf.org.il/4968-33525-en/IAF.aspx)

35. Israel claims to have shot down 42 aircraft during 6 October. (http://www.iaf.org.il/843-13277-he/IAF.aspx) and Nordeen, op. cit., p. 257.

36. Bar-Joseph, op. cit., p. 219; Emanuel Sakal, *Soldier in the Sinai: A General's Account of the Yom Kippur War*.

37. 'The results were harsh: in only five minutes, 6 of the squadron's aircraft were hit – 4 of them were abandoned by their crews and some of the airmen were taken captive; 2 others were hit but managed to safely land in Ramat-David air base. (Extract from *The 'One' Squadron's Yom Kippur War* from Israeli Air Force's official website http://www.iaf.org.il/4452-47077-en/IAF.aspx)

38. Kreis, op. cit., p. 328.

39. During the war, five Chukars were shot down by Syrian and Egyptian air defences though the losses were made up by Israel as more UAVs were received from the US. '*The First UAV Squadron*', http://www.iaf.org.il/4968-33518-en/IAF.aspx; Kreis, op. cit., p. 328.

40. The IAF reportedly lost 30 aircraft in the first two days. The exact breakdown is not known with various sources claiming different figures. With an accepted loss of six aircraft on day one, the figure should be 24 losses on day two. ('*The second day of the war: Tagger and Dogman*', http://www.iaf.org.il/843-13281-he/IAF.aspx.)

41. *The attack on the bridges in the Suez area*, http://www.iaf.org.il/843-13285-he/IAF.aspx

42. Ibid.

43. As claimed by General Mordechi Hod, Commander of the Israeli Air Force in the North as quoted by Nordeen, op. cit., p. 262.

44. Only seven of the eight Phantoms managed to reach Damascus as one aircraft developed a mechanical fault and had to return. The second squadron could not locate the targets in Damascus due to cloud cover and attacked alternative targets instead. The third squadron returned without attacking targets after dumping their bombs and excess fuel over the Mediterranean.

45. *Ramat David attacked with FROG missiles* http://www.iaf.org.il/843-13289-he/IAF.aspx

46. 'Israeli Planes Attack Damascus'. *Beaver Country Times* (United Press International. 9 October 1973) Retrieved 27 October 2010. Israeli account of the raid is available at '*Ramat David attacked with FROG missiles*', op. cit.

47. Nordeen, op. cit., p. 260.

48. '*Ramat David attacked with FROG missiles*', op. cit.

49. Israel admits to a loss of only three aircraft – a Phantom and two A-4 Skyhawks. (*New York Times*, 10 Oct 1973); *The commander of the corps, Benny Peled, presents the plan of action to the chief of staff*, http://www.iaf.org.il/843-13290-he/IAF.aspx

50. Kreis, op. cit., p. 340.

51. Nordeen, op. cit., p. 260.

52. '*The effort to remove Syria from the cycle of fighting*', http://www.iaf.org.il/843-13297-he/IAF.aspx

53. Nordeen, op. cit., p. 260.

54. '*The effort descends south*', http://www.iaf.org.il/843-13301-he/IAF.aspx

55. Nordeen, op. cit., p. 266.

56. '*The First Fighter Squadron*', http://www.iaf.org.il/4968-33529-en/IAF.aspx

57. Schul and Hope, 'Anti-aircraft missile batteries destroyed', *Jerusalem Post*, 17 October 1973.

58. Shlomo Aloni, *Israeli A-4 Skyhawk Units in Combat.*

59. Schul and Hope, 'Israel expands bridgehead, downs 32 enemy aircraft', *Jerusalem Post*, 22 October 1973.

60. As claimed by an Egyptian Air Defence officer (as recounted by Nordeen, op. cit., p. 274). The equipment provided in the later part of the war included Shrike anti-radar missiles (ARMs), Maverick missiles and Walleye glide bombs. The stand-off weapons also contributed to neutralizing the air defences as the aircraft could launch the weapons while staying outside the lethal zone of the missile/gun.

61. Laur, & Llanso, *Encyclopaedia of Modern U.S. Military Weapons*, pp. 273–4.

62. Earlier accounts had credited the IAF with more success against SAMs. Col Eliezer 'Cheetah' Cohen, *Israel's Best Defense: The First Full Story of the Israeli Air Force*, trans. Cordis, pp. 352–4.

63. Brower, op. cit.

64. Kis, 'Techniques of gaining Israeli air superiority in the 1973 war, better known as 'The Yom Kippur War', (*AARMS*, Vol. 7, No. 3, Miklós Zrínyi National Defence University, Budapest, Hungary, 2008), pp. 407–23.

65. Report, Naval Weapons Center, NWC TP 5885, '*The Yom Kippur War, Analysis of Weapon Implications*', July 1976, pp. 33–5 quoted by Kreis, op. cit.

66. al-Sanjak, 'We dropped the Phantoms by ambushes of air defence', *El- Watan News*, https://www.elwatannews.com/news/details/333990

67. By the end of the war the IAF had only managed to destroy 3 of the 31 SAM systems and damage five others. Cohen, op. cit., pp. 352–4. See also, Chaim Herzog, *The Arab-Israeli Wars*, p. 310; Herbert J. Coleman, 'Israeli Air Force Decisive in War', *Aviation Week & Space Technology* 99, No. 23 (3 December 1973), p. 18; Robert Frank Futrell, *Ideas, Concepts, Doctrine, vol. 2, Basic Thinking in the United States Air Force, 1961–1984.*

68. '*The first days of the northern front*', http://www.iaf.org.il/843-13282-he/IAF.aspx

69. Werrell, op. cit., p.154.

70. The Israeli Air Force mentions a figure of 109 combat aircraft with 3 more helicopters and 2 light planes destroyed, making it a total of 114 aircraft destroyed (Yossi Abudi, *The Missile did not bend the Wing*, Israel Air Force, http://www.iaf.org.il/1213-21478-he/IAF.aspx). See also, Gen. Peled briefing Dr Henry Kissinger during a meeting between the Israeli Prime Minister and US Secretary of State held on 22 October 1967 at a Guest House at Herzliyya near Tel Aviv. *White House Military Briefing*. Retrieved 29 November 2015. https://nsarchive2.gwu.edu//NSAEBB/NSAEBB98/octwar-56.pdf

71. US Army Combined Arms Centre, '*Analysis of Combat Data – 1973 Mideast War*' quoted by Kreis, op. cit., p. 336.

72. Ganin, Korovin, Karpenko, & Angelsky, 'Combat Use Of C-125 Anti-Aircraft Missile System', *Equipment and Armament: Yesterday, Today, Tomorrow*, No. 9/2003, http://otvaga2004.ru/boyevoe-primenenie/boyevoye-primeneniye02/s-125/

73. *'Assessment of The Weapons and Tactics Used in the October 1973 Middle East War'*, WSEG Report 249, Weapon Systems Evaluation Group, Institute for Defense Analyses, Systems Evaluation Division, Arlington, Va, Oct. 1974 accessed at https://www.cia.gov/library/readingroom/docs/LOC-HAK-480-3-1-4.pdf

74. The article also claims that during the war of attrition, from 8 March to 30 May 1974, only 8 SA-6 missiles were spent to destroy 6 aircraft. (Igor Nikolaev, 'Hunt for the Cube', *Soldier of Fortune Magazine*, No. 4, 17 Sep. 2008) http://otvaga2004.ru/ kaleydoskop/kaleydoskop-miss/oxota-za-kubom/

75. *'Assessment of The Weapons and Tactics Used in the October 1973 Middle East War'*, op. cit.

76. *'UAV Squadron, Israel Air Force'*, http://www.iaf.org.il/4968-33518-en/IAF.aspx

77. Gen. Peled's briefing of Dr Henry Kissinger during a meeting between the Israeli Prime Minister and US Secretary of State held on 22 October 1967 at a guest house at Herzliyya near Tel Aviv. op. cit.

78. It is believed that 35 Egyptian aircraft were brought down by their own air defences during the war, however no firm figures/data is available to confirm this.

79. Egypt lost 279 aircraft with another 11 probable losses. Of those, 180 aircraft were shot down in air combat, 39 were shot down by anti-aircraft and helicopter gunships, 17 were hit and felled by ground forces, 12 were destroyed on the ground in an attack on air bases, and 32 were shot down in fratricide incidents or lost to technical failures. Syria lost 153 planes with 6 probables; 97 aircraft were shot down in air, seven by anti-aircraft guns and HAWK units, 17 by the ground forces, 9 were destroyed in the airfields during their attack, and another 23 were fratricide incidents or lost to technical failures. (Details accessed at http://www.iaf.org. il/1213-21478-he/IAF.asp)

80. *'Assessment of The Weapons and Tactics Used in the October 1973 Middle East War'*, op. cit.

81. US Army Combined Arms Centre, *'Analysis of Combat Data – 1973 Mideast War'*, op. cit., ACN 22216, pp E-11 to E-21.

82. Cordesman and Wagner, *The Lessons Of Modern War: Volume I: The Arab-Israeli Conflicts, 1973–1989*, p. 18.

83. Herzog, *The War of Atonement: The Inside Story of the Yom Kippur War*, p. 261.

Iran Iraq War

1. Wessel. ed., *The Iran-Iraq War: New Weapons, Old Conflicts*, p. 43.

2. Nordeen, *Air Warfare in the Missile Age*, p. 369. As per Major General 'Alwan Hassoun 'Alwan al-Abousi of Iraqi Air Force, Iraq had only seven operational fighter squadrons at the war's beginning; of MiG-21s and MiG-23s. (Woods & others, *Saddam's Generals: Perspectives of the Iran-Iraq War*, p. 201.

3. The reasons for low serviceability rate were poor maintenance standards and old, vintage aircraft at the start of the war. It was only later that Iraq received the more capable and advanced MiG-25 and the Mirages F-1. As per some reports, Iraq had

already received the MiG-25 but it was not used for the initial strikes and after the Iranian counter-attack, was withdrawn to air bases in the west.

4. Bishop & Cooper, *Iranian F-4 Phantom II Units in Combat* mentions a figure of 252 sorties by Iraq on the first day, 192 in the first wave with 60 in the second wave.

5. Ronald E. Begquist, *The Role of Airpower in Iran-Iraq War.*

6. Nordeen, op.cit., p. 370.

7. Major General 'Alwan Hassoun 'Alwan al-Abousi served as commander of multiple squadrons, groups, and air bases during the Iran-Iraq War. Late in the war, he became the director and deputy commander of air force training. (Woods & others, op. cit.), p. 191.

8. Mottale, *The Arms Buildup in the Persian Gulf.*

9. Nordeen, op. cit.

10. Bishop & Cooper, *Iranian F-4 Phantom II Units in Combat.*

11. Ibid.

12. The number of SAM systems varies as per the source referred to. Werrell mentions a figure of 70 SAM systems while others mention a higher figure of over 120 Soviet missile systems plus 60 Rolands.

13. Bishop & Cooper, op. cit.

14. Ibid.

15. Murray, Woods, *The Iran-Iraq War: A Military and Strategic History*, p. 103; and Begquist, op. cit., p. 46.

16. 'Iraqi Tank Guns Stop Missile Helicopters', *Aerospace Science and Technology* 113 (24 November 1980), p. 66 and Begquist, op. cit.

17. Murray, Woods, op. cit., p. 103.

18. Ibid.

19. Woods & Ors, op. cit., p. 206.

20. Abousi, op. cit.

21. The Iranians were less successful against Iraqi SA-6s as they had no EW equipment to jam it, nor were they able to jinx the faster and more agile SA-6.

22. Middleton, 'Tactics in Gulf War', *New York Times*, 19 October 1980, p. 12.

23. Though the number of losses to friendly fire is not reliably known; by all accounts, they were a large part of the overall attrition caused to both sides.

24. Cooper and Bishop, 'Target : Saddam's Reactor', *Air Enthusiast*, (March/April 2004, Issue 10).

25. Murray, Woods, op. cit., p. 104.

26. Fairhall, 'The Iran-Iraq War at First Hand,' *Defense Week*, No .31 (3 November 1980).

27. Woods and others, *Saddam's War: An Iraqi military Perspective of Iran-Iraq War*, McNair paper 70, Institute for National Strategic Studies, National Defence University, Washington, D.C., 2009, p. 36.

28. Murray, Kevin, op. cit., p. 105.

29. Cordesman and Wagner, *The Lessons of Modern War, vol. 2, The Iran-Iraq War*, 98.

30. Murray, Kevin, op. cit., p. 107.

31. In October alone, the Iranian Air Force had shot down 25 Iraqi fighter aircraft. (Murray, Woods, op. cit., p. 103).

32. *Military Balance*, International Institute of Strategic Studies, 1980–81, p. 42.

33. Nordeen, p. 368. As per Werrell, Iran had an unspecified number of British Tiger Cat Surface-to-Air-Missiles also.

34. Operational readiness of the HAWK missile system suffered due to lack of spares. (Maedh Ayed Al-Lihaibi, *An Analysis of the Iran-Iraq War: Military Strategy and Political Objectives*, Air War College, Air University Maxwell Air Force Base, Alabama, May 1989)

35. Begquist, op. cit.; O'Ballance, *The Gulf War*, p. 42.

36. The Iraqi Air Force used the Tu-22 Bombers from October 3 to 29 for strikes against Iranian cities. Not more than four Tu-22 were used in a single raid. Pierre Razouk, *Iran Iraq War*, p. 128.

37. Razouk, op. cit., p. 128.

38. *Assault on Al-Walid*, Iranian Air Force, ttp://www.iiaf.net/stories/warstories/s1.html

39. Cordesman and Wagner, op. cit., p. 549; Bergquist, op. cit., p. 52.

40. O'Ballance, *The Gulf War*, p. 546.

41. Cordesman and Wagner, *The Lessons of Modern War, Vol. 2, The Iran-Iraq War*, p. 119.

42. Berquist mentions that only two IIAF planes were used in an attack on Baghdad on one occasion while in another IIAF attack on Baghdad, two planes carried out the bombing while two covered for them (Berquist, op. cit., p. 47).

43. O'Ballance, The Iran Iraq War First Round, *Parameters,* (Journal of US Army War College, Vol XI, No 1, March 1981), pp. 54–9.

44. Cordesman and Wagner, *The Lessons of Modern War Volume II: Iran-Iraq War* (Chapter XIII). 'The Air and Missile Wars and Weapons of Mass Destruction'.

45. Karsh, *The Iran-Iraq War: A Military Analysis*, p. 38

46. Cordesman, *The Gulf and the West: Strategic Relations and Military Realities*, p. 671.

47. Karsh, op. cit., p. 40.

48. Ibid. 38.

49. Nordeen, *Air Warfare in the Missile Age*; and David Segal, The Iran-Iraq War: A Military Analysis, *Foreign Affairs*, Summer 1988 accessed at https://www.foreignaffairs.com/articles/iran/1988-06-01/iran-iraq-war-military-analysis.

50. Razouk, op. cit., p. 196.

51. Ibid. pp. 196–200.

52. The first use of armed helicopters was reported as early as October 1980 when Iran used the AH-1 Cobra armed helicopters armed with tube-launched, Optically-tracked, wire-guided (TOW) anti-tank missiles against Iraqi armoured columns. 'Iraqi Tank Guns Stop Missile Helicopters', *Aviation Week & Space Technology*, No. 113, November 1980), p. 66.

53. Politi, 'Iran-Iraq', *Defense Today*, (Issue No 9–10, 1989), p. 328.

54. Farrokh, *Iran at War: 1500–1988*.

55. Ibid.

56. Aboul-Enein, Bertrand, & Corley, *The 'Dawn of Victory' campaigns to the 'Final Push'*, Small Wars Journal.

57. Farrokh, op. cit.

58. MiG–29 was received in 1986. The Su–25s were first used in the al–Faw Offensive. Iraq received the B–6D Bombers from China in 1986 to supplement its fleet of Tu–22 Blinders Bombers it had earlier received from Soviet Union. The Tu–22 had been used by Iraq in the early days of the war.

59. Hiro, *The Longest War: The Iran-Iraq Military Conflict*, p. 144.

60. Despite some acquisition of spare parts during the US arms embargo, Iran was unable to maintain more than a third of the needed radars. Destruction of I–HAWK radars during the early years of the war played a significant part in limiting the number of system available to defend economic targets and the battlefield defence. With limited technical support, Iran was unable to maintain more than a third of the radars at any one time. Further destruction of I–HAWK radars during the early years of the war limited the number of systems available. 'Electronic Warfare Forces Study- Iraq', Defence Intelligence Reference Series, 1 April 1990 (Declassified 21 November 2017) accessed at https://www.archives.gov/files/declassification/iscap/pdf/2014-033-doc01.pdf

61. The war of the cities was halted by Iraq in April though resumed the next month. One of the aims of the air raids was to escalate the war to a point that international intervention would become inevitable, giving Iraq a way out (Farrokh, op. cit.).

62. Schroeder, Smith, Stohl, *The Small Arms Trade: A Beginner's Guide*, and Farrokh, op. cit.

63. Additionally, Iranian Hawk sites shot down three friendly F-14 Tomcats and one F-5 Tiger II.

64. These claims were almost certainly exaggerated, but Iraq did lose at least 5 to 12 fighters during the fall and early winter. Iraq also later claimed that its losses to the HAWKs were forcing it to sharply reduce its attacks on the island, although many of its losses may actually have occurred to guns and light Swedish-made RBS-70 missiles.

65. Farrokh, op. cit.

66. Iraq claimed to have lost a MiG- 25 to a HAWK missile on 9 January, two Tupolev bombers on 14 January and a MiG-23 flying at 13,000 feet at Basra on 28 January, 1987.

67. *Iraq: Major Weapon Deliveries and their Impact on capabilities*, Directorate of Intelligence, Central Intelligence Agency, February 1987, p. 13 (Sanitised copy approved for release 21 March 2012).

68. Cordesman and Wagner, The Lessons of Modern War Volume II: Iran-Iraq War.

69. *Iraq: Major Weapon Deliveries and their Impact on capabilities*, Directorate of Intelligence, Central Intelligence Agency, op. cit.

Soviet Afghan War

1. Nordeen, *Air Warfare in the Missile Age* (Kindle Edition) p. 322; Flintham, Victor, *Air Wars and Aircraft, A Detailed Record of Air Combat, 1945–Present*, pp. 202–10.

2. Forger (Yak-38) was a carrier-borne aircraft which was tried out in Afghanistan but because of problems due to climatic conditions and the limited payload, was used only selectively. The Frogfoot served well and earned the respect of even the Mujahideen. Tucker-Jones, *Soviet Cold War Weaponry: Aircraft, Warships*

and Missiles, p. 25; and Hirschberg, S*oviet V/STOL Aircraft: The Struggle for a Shipborne Combat Capability*, p. 21.

3. Su-25 was introduced in April 1980 and was first used only 11 days after its arrival in Afghanistan during Operation Romb. The first unit formed with the Frogfoot for deployment in Afghanistan was the 200th Independent Attack Squadron. Mladenov, *Sukhoi Su-25 Frogfoot*, p. 43 and Alexey Zakharov, 'Afghan Rambos', *Air Forces Monthly*, June 1996, pp. 37–40.

4. Nordeen, op. cit., p. 324; Martin, *Afghanistan: Inside a Rebel Stronghold*, p. 74; and Amstutz, *Afghanistan: The First Five Years of Soviet Occupation*, pp. 149–51.

5. Nordeen, op. cit., pp. 324–6; Nawroz and Grau, *The Soviet War in Afghanistan: History and Harbinger of Future War*.

6. Nawroz and Grau, op. cit., p.10.

7. Dimitrakis, *The Secret War in Afghanistan: The Soviet Union, China and Anglo-American Intelligence in the Afghan War*, p. 160; and Lansford, *Afghanistan at War: From the 18th-Century Durrani Dynasty to the 21st Century*.

8. According to a report by the Federation of American Scientists, during the 1980s, in an effort to topple the Soviet-backed government of Afghanistan, the U.S. government provided Mujahideen with Soviet-made SA-7s. They were supplied, along with RPG-7 rocket-propelled grenades and AK-47s, by CIA through Egypt and Pakistan. Rubright, *The Role and Limitations of Technology in U.S. Counterinsurgency Warfare*, p. 120; Ali, *US-China Cold War Collaboration: 1971–1989*, p. 175. See also McMichael, *Stumbling Bear: Soviet Military Performance in Afghanistan*, p. 89

9. Stalder, *The Air War in Afghanistan*.

10. Giradet, *Afghanistan: The Soviet War*.

11. Winkler, '*The Soviet Invasion of Afghanistan*', National Defense Review, April 1980.

12. Jalali & Grau, *The Other Side of the Mountain, Mujahideen Tactics in the Soviet–Afghan War*.

13. Ibid.

14. Jalali & Grau, *Afghan Guerrilla Warfare: In the Words of the Mujahideen Fighters*, pp. 286–7.

15. Ibid.

16. Mladenov, *Su-25 'Frogfoot' Units In Combat*, Kindle Edition.

17. Jalali & Grau, *Afghan Guerrilla Warfare: In the Words of the Mujahideen Fighters*, p. 227.

18. The wrong tactics adopted by the Mi-24 pilots were highlighted by Soviet writers also. 'Suddenly, Swiftly' in the Soviet journal *Aviatsiya iKozmonautica* Issue No 9, 1980 and 'Firing Against Abandoned Trenches' in *Krasnaya Zvezda* 16 April 1982 are two such articles.

19. Stalder, *The Air War in Afghanistan*.

20. Dick, *Mujahideen tactics in the Soviet-Afghan War*, (Conflict Studies Research Centre, January 2002, Accessed 8 January 2019 at http://edocs.nps.edu/AR/org/CSRC/csrc_jan_02.pdf

21. This claim is based on account of an Afghan defector and is highly exaggerated on two counts – firstly, it credits SA-7 with a kill rate never seen before (or later) and it is highly improbable that the missiles would have performed so well in an operation

especially in the mountains and secondly, the same source pegs the Soviet aircraft losses in the first three years, from 1979 to 1983, at 543 which is also an exaggeration and not supported by other sources. Amstutz, op. cit., p. 164.

22. The SA-7s were supplied by China or other third-party sources. McMichael, *Stumbling Bear: Soviet Military Performance in Afghanistan*, p. 89.

23. O'Ballance, *Afghan Wars 1839–1992. What Britain Gave Up and the Soviet Union Lost*, p. 145.

24. 'Soviets Use Flares to Counter Missiles', *Aviation Week & Space Technology*, 26 March 1984, pp. 54–5.

25. Goodwin, *Caught in the Crossfire*, pp. 111, 123 & 153.

26. Zakheim, 'New Technologies & Third World Conflicts', *Defense 86* (July/August 1986), p. 16.

27. Arnett, *Live from the Battlefield. From Vietnam to Baghdad 35 Years in the World's War Zones*, p. 426.

28. Yousaf, Adkin, *The Battle for Afghanistan: The Soviets Versus the Mujahideen During the 1980s*, (Kindle Edition).

29. Collins, 'The Soviet Military Experience in Afghanistan', *Military Review*, (May 1985)

30. In all, Su-25s represented a quarter of Soviet Air Force fixed-wing losses in the campaign. Alexander Mladenov, *Sukhoi Su-25 Frogfoot*, and *Su-25 'Frogfoot' Units In Combat* (Kindle Editions).

31. In 1985, 27 per cent of the combat losses of the Mi-8 came from small arms, 40 per cent from DShK, 27 per cent from RPGs and only 6 per cent were due to MANPADS.

32. Yousaf, Adkin, op. cit.

33. Corera, *The Art of Betrayal: Life and Death in the British Secret Service*.

34. Yousaf, Adkin, op. cit.

35. In November 1986 Gorbachev expressed his annoyance with the pace of negotiations at a Politburo meeting. 'At this point, we have been fighting in Afghanistan for six years. If we do not change our approaches, we will fight there for another 20 to 30 years. We must bring this to an end in short order.'

36. Mladenov, *Su-25 'Frogfoot' Units In Combat*, pp. 24–5; and Gordon; Alan Dawes, 'Russian Air Power', p. 31.

37. By the latter half of 1986, about 100 Stingers had been delivered but were still restricted to groups operating around Kabul and Jalalabad. 90 Soviet aircraft were claimed to have been shot down in 1986 alone which translates to a 100 per cent kill rate which is highly unlikely.

38. Yousaf, Adkin, op. cit.

39. *Echo 'Stinger': the danger for Russian aviation American MANPADS in Syria*, RIA, 16 January 2018, https://ria.ru/20180116/1512717432.html

40. Mahmood, *Stinger Saga*, pp. 49–51.

41. *Soviet aircraft lost in Afghanistan 1986*, http://www.skywar.ru/afghan4.html

42. Mahmood, op. cit., pp. 49–51.

43. Ibid., p. 50; Mladenov, *Mil Mi-24 Hind Gunship*.

44. The new flares used by the transport aircraft burned at 6,000 degrees Celsius while the one with the helicopters and fighter aircraft was of a lower intensity (3,000 degrees Celsius).
45. Gordon, *Russian Gunship Helicopters*, pp. 11–12.
46. The number of such night sights was rather limited and only about six were made available to the Mujahideen. (Mahmood, op. cit., pp. 53–5).
47. Ibid.
48. Ibid.
49. The Soviet account is given at '*Why were the Soviets hellbent on finding U.S.-made Stinger missiles in Afghanistan?*' by Alexey Timofeychev in 'Russia Beyond the Headlines', February 17, 2019 accessed at https://www.rbth.com/history/329988-why-soviets-look-for-stingers while Mohammed Yousaf also mentions the incident in '*The Battle for Afghanistan: The Soviets Versus the Mujahideen During the 1980s*'.
50. Giving details of the Stingers fired in 1987, Mohammed Yousaf of the Inter-Services Intelligence (ISI) of Pakistan, mentions that in the first ten months, 187 Stingers were fired and 75 per cent of them hit the target. He was in charge of the arms training for the Mujahideen and was the main person responsible for training and supply of Stingers to the Mujahideen. He only mentions 'hits' but does not give details of aircraft shot down. (Mohammed, Adkin, *The Battle for Afghanistan: The Soviets Versus the Mujahideen During the 1980s*). These figures are also mentioned by Werrell in his book *Archie to SAM: A Short Operational History of Ground-Based Air Defense*, p. 172 and by Case, Henry in the *Air Defense Artillery Yearbook 1993*, US Army Air Defense Artillery Branch. p. 20. Also, Jalali and Grau, *The Other Side Of The Mountain: Mujahideen Tactics in the Soviet-Afghan War*.
51. Werrel, op. cit., p. 171.
52. The losses included both the Soviet and Afghan Air Forces but the details of aircraft shot down by Stingers, Blowpipes, other anti-aircraft missiles or heavy machine guns was, however, not clear. (Ottaway, 'U.S. Missiles Alter War In Afghanistan', *Washington Post*, 19 July 1987) and Cassidy, *Counterinsurgency and the Global War on Terror: Military Culture and Irregular War*, p. 56; and Cordesman and Wagner, T*he Lessons of Modern War, vol. 3, The Afghan and Falklands Conflicts*.
53. Gordon, *Russian Gunship Helicopters*, p. 30.
54. Steele, 'Afghan Ghosts: American Myths', *World Affairs*, March/April 2010 quoting Harrison in 'Out of Afghanistan' http://www.worldaffairsjournal.org/article/afghan-ghosts-american-myths. Many accounts mention 'aircraft/helicopter hit by Stingers' rather than give details of aircraft shot down making it difficult to ascertain the true number of aircraft actually shot down by Stingers. Even though the Stingers may have hit the helicopter (or an aircraft), it did not always result in the helicopters being destroyed as it happened during an incident in Ghazi in 1987 when the Stinger broke off part of the tail rotor of the Mi-24 smashing the blades but the Hind was able to land and was repaired later (Gordon, op. cit., p. 30).
55. As per Urban, kill rates exceeding 50 per cent claimed by some analysts cannot be accepted (Urban, *War in Afghanistan*). A look at the total losses before and after the introduction of Stingers is quite illustrative; of the total 114 aircraft lost in the war, 62 were lost between 1979 and 1985, i.e. before Stingers were given to

the Mujahideen while 52 were lost in the last three years and not all were lost to MANPADS let alone Stingers. Similarly, 107 aircraft were lost in the last three years of the war and 226 before 1986. 1988 in fact saw one of the lowest rate of losses with only 16 aircraft and 14 helicopters being lost in combat.

56. Aigner, *The Bear Flew Over The Mountain: (Re)Assessing the Soviet Air Force's Air Campaign in Afghanistan*, 1979–89 accessed at https://www.academia.edu/4875441/The_Bear_Flew_Over_The_Mountain_Re_Assessing_the_Soviet_Air_Force_s_Air_Campaign_in_Afghanistan_1979-89

57. Galeotti, (1995) *Afghanistan: The Soviet Union's Last War*, pp. 80–6.

58. Hawkins, *Soviet Counterinsurgency Operations In Afghanistan (1979–1988)*, USMC Command and Staff College, Marine Corps University, Quantico, Virginia, 2010, accessed at https://apps.dtic.mil/dtic/tr/fulltext/u2/a603257.pdf.

59. Urban, op. cit., p. 270.

60. Kuperman, 'Stinging Rebukes', *Foreign Affairs*, (January/February 2002), https://www.foreignaffairs.com/articles/afghanistan/2002-01-01/stinging-rebukes

61. Kuperman, 'The Stinger missile and U.S. intervention in Afghanistan', *Political Science Quarterly* (Summer 1999).

Falklands (Malvinas) War

1. Argentina reportedly had 240 aircraft although this figure varies as per different sources. There are minor variations. The ANA was in the process of inducting a dozen Super Étendards but had only five operational aircraft at the time of going to war.

2. Boyce, *The Falklands War: Twentieth Century Wars*, p. 35.

3. Apple, 'British Blockade Around Falklands Goes Into Effect', *The New York Times*, 12 April 1982.

4. Brown, *The Royal Navy and Falklands War*, p. 85.

5. The aircraft carrier *Veinticinco de Mayo* was used to support the invasion but as the British Task Force approached the Falklands, it returned to port. The ANA thereafter operated from shore bases only with the bulk of MB-339s stationed at Port Stanley.

6. The number of Tiger Cat launchers is given as four by van der Bijl in *Victory in the Falklands*, manned by the 1st Marine anti-Aircraft Battalion. The other sources give the number of Marine Tiger Cat launchers as three. See also Brown, *The Royal Navy and Falklands War*, pp. 85–6. Argentina is reported to have some SA-7 also (Nordeen, op. cit., p. 342). 120 SA-7s were allegedly supplied to Argentina by Libya. See also, *Argentine Fight for the Falklands* by Middlebrook.

7. Brown, op. cit., pp. 85–6.

8. The RAF F-4 Phantoms were also reported to have been deployed in Chile, presumably to hold back the Argentine Air Force. *Aerospace Power in the Twenty-First Century: A Basic Primer – Air and Space Power, Doctrine and Strategy, Airpower, Satellites, Billy Mitchell, Claire Chennault, Reconnaissance*, pp. 229–31; and Chant, *Air War in the Falklands 1982*, p. 33.

9. 'South Georgia Seized', *The Guardian*, 26 April 1982.

10. Blackman, *Vulcan Boys: From the Cold War to the Falklands: True Tales of the Iconic Delta V Bomber*.

11. At least one Roland and two Tiger Cat missiles were claimed to have been fired as also the 35mm AA guns. At Port Stanley, the AA guns and Tiger Cat missiles claimed one aircraft each. Only one hit was claimed by the Coast Guard ship *Islas Malvinas*. Middlebrook, *Argentine Fight for the Falklands*, pp. 77–8; and Chant, op cit., p. 32.

12. Corum, *Argentine Airpower in the Falklands War: An Operational View*, USAF School of Advanced Airpower Studies and Middlebrook, op. cit., pp. 77–8.

13. The Official History of the Argentine Air Force put the blame on the lack of coordination between the Joint Anti-aircraft Command and infantry troops on the ground, who started to fire their rifles at the aircraft, unleashing a chain reaction among the Navy and Army's gunners (*Flight*, 15 December 1949, pp. 766–72).

14. The Mirages were held back due the threat of an air attack on the mainland. (Chant, op. cit.; *The Falkland Islands Conflict, 1982: Air Defense of the Fleet*. Globalsecurity. org.

15. Hastings and Jenkins, *The Battle for the Falklands*, 'Official MOD report into the sinking of HMS *Sheffield*' Archived 6 February 2012 at the Wayback Machine at https://web. archive.org/web/20120206212020/http://www.mod.uk/NR/rdonlyres/9D8947AC-D8DC-4BE7-8DCC-C9C623539BCF/0/boi_hms_sheffield.pdf; 'A Rip in Time for *Sheffield*', *Navy News*, April 2007; Woodward & Robinson, '*One hundred days: the memoirs of the Falklands battle group commander*', p. 11. See also Nordeen, *Air Warfare in Missile Age*, p. 346. Air Force Grupo 1 also claimed that its 20mm AA guns hit and destroyed another Sea Harrier but it was neither confirmed nor acknowledged.

16. ARA *Vienticino de Mayo* remained in port for the remainder of the war, missing all action. Her A-4Q Skyhawks, however, flew the rest of the war from the air base in Río Grande, Tierra del Fuego, and had some success against the Royal Navy, sinking HMS *Ardent*. Middlebrook, op. cit.

17. Middlebrook, op. cit.; DeHoust, *Offensive Air Operations Of The Falklands War*, (Marine Corps Command and Staff College, Quantico, Virginia, 1984); Dyke, *Four Weeks In May* p. 150 and Morison, 'Falklands (Malvinas) Campaign: A Chronology', *Proceedings*, (United States Naval Institute, June 1983), p. 122.

18. Fernández Reguera, *La Guerra De Las Malvinas : El Final De Una Batalla; La Ultima Mision De Bombardeo; El Ultimo Round De Una Pelea Desesperada; (No. 22 Version Argentina)*, (1987), p. 572 (in Spanish).

19. Davis, *The Complete Encyclopaedia of the SAS*, p. 133; Middlebrook, op. cit. and Chant, op. cit.

20. Over 100 Blowpipe missiles were fired by the Argentine forces with this being the only successful hit. Even the British had similar experience with one kill of an Aermacchi MB.339. from 95 launches. (Nordeen, op. cit., p. 351).

21. 'Jump jet war hero is selling off his medals', *Peterborough Telegraph*, September 7, 2007. https://www.peterboroughtoday.co.uk/news/environment/jump-jet-war-hero-is-selling-off-his-medals-1-84731

22. Chant, op. cit.

23. Most of the accounts mention 'several' missiles fired and do not specify the actual numbers. van der Bijl, *Victory in the Falklands*, p. 89; Chant, *Air War in the Falklands* and Morison, *Falklands (Malvinas) Campaign: A Chronology and San Carlos Air*

Battles – Falklands War 1982, (Naval-history.net, http://www.naval-history.net/F44airbattles.htm), all mention several missiles without giving exact details.

24. The British engaged Crippa's Pucara by a Blowpipe and GPMG fire from the *Canberra*, Sea Cat from HMS *Intrepid* and main 4.5 in gun fire from HMS *Plymouth*. The Pucara received only minor damage. Crippa was awarded Argentina's highest gallantry award – the only pilot to be so awarded during the war. (Chant, op cit., p. 62).

25. Chant in *Air War in the Falklands* mentions that the Argentines managed to attack the ships unhampered as they were not detected while the other accounts, notably by Argentinians, mention intense anti-aircraft fire engaging the aircraft as they went in for the attack. The details of TV tracking used to guide the Sea Wolf missile are given by Hastings and Jenkins in *The Battle for the Falklands*, p. 258.

26. Middlebrook, op. cit.

27. The figures for Argentinian losses vary between 12 and 15. While the Argentine accounts accept the loss of 12 aircraft, Chant and Nordeen give the figure of 13. Another account, by Corum in *Argentine Airpower in the Falklands War: An Operational View* (USAF School of Advanced Airpower Studies) mentions the Argentine losses as 13 – 5 Daggers and 4 Skyhawks of the FAs and 2 Pucaras and 2 helicopters based at the Falklands. The disparity may also be due to the inclusion of helicopters in the figures for total losses. The Rapier did not score any kills as the 'tests and adjustments' had not been carried out and were not orientated properly. (Nick van der Bijl, op. cit., p. 91).

28. 'Rapier' Falklands Performance Praised', *Flight International*, 25 December 1982, pp. 1799–80.

29. Darling, *RAF Strike Command, 1968–2007*, p. 159.

30. Moreno, *Comandos en Acción*, Emecé Editores (Claridad, 1986).

31. Some sources mention 8 Argentine aircraft destroyed that day, 3 each by Harriers and Rapier surface-to-air missiles and 2 by Bofors anti-aircraft fire. The claims by Rapiers were not corroborated and were later found to be untrue. DeHoust, *Offensive Air Operations Of The Falklands War* (Marine Corps Command and Staff College, Quantico, Virginia, 1984); Nordeen, op. cit., pp. 351–2.

32. DeHoust, op. cit.; Hastings, op. cit.; Nordeen, op. cit., p. 365.

33. Privratsky, *Logistics in the Falklands War*.

34. Pook, *RAF Harrier Ground Attack-Falklands*, p. 109; Ethell, and Price, *Air War South Atlantic*, pp. 248–51; and Nordeen, op. cit., p. 353.

35. Ward, *Sea Harrier Over the Falklands*, p. 227.

36. This was the only confirmed kill by a British Blowpipe missile. In some accounts, the shooting down of the Pucara is wrongly credited to the Blowpipe. The second success for the Blowpipe was by the Argentine Army special forces (Commandos Company). Corum, *Argentine Airpower in the Falklands War: An Operational View*, USAF School of Advanced Airpower Studies and Jeffery Ethell, 'Flying the Pucara', *Air Progress*, May 1983.

37. Chant, op. cit.

38. *London Gazette*, No. 49134 (Supplement). 8 October 1982. p. 12854. Argentine authors on the other hand claim that the aircraft was hit by 35mm AA fire from GADA's 1st Section, B Battery:

During another action, an enemy aircraft fell victim to the 601 Air Defence's 35mm batteries. The plane came down in the water and the pilot, Maj. Jerry Pook, was rescued shortly after. [Moro, *The History of the South Atlantic Conflict: The War for the Malvinas*, p. 272. Also, Rodríguez Mottino, (1984). *La Artillería Argentina en Malvinas*, pp. 158–9.

The British account of the incident is as follows:

'Ingress was from the South crossing the main road which runs into Stanley. As Pook's aircraft crossed the road it was hit by small arms fire from troops and SSvs parked on the road. Pook felt the the the impact of the small arms and was told that he appeared to have a fuel leak.' (*The Falkland Islands, A history of the 1982 conflict, The Harrier Goes to War*, The No 1 (Fighter) Squadron Operation Corporate Diary. Reproduced by kind permission of Air Chief Marshal Sir Peter Squire, Chief of the Air Staff, 30 May Entry, Accessed 2011-12-18 at http://www.radarmalvinas.com.ar/relatos/diariosquiretraba.pdf)

39. No claims were made by the British Special Forces and it was considered that the Puma was brought down in error by Argentine Forces. 'Argentine Puma Shot Down By American "Stinger" Missile', En.mercopress.com. 12 April 2002.

40. The British account mentions the damage from debris as follows: 'As a result of debris damage to one aircraft and relative lack of effective penetration of the runway, Command decides that the future bombing efforts should be high-angle.' *The Falkland Islands, A history of the 1982 conflict, The Harrier Goes to War*, op. cit.

41. Brown, op. cit., p. 259.

42. The post-strike reconnaissance mission failed to find any evidence of the damage and the result of the strike was classified as 'unquantifiable'. Blackman, op. cit., pp. 181–4; and Brown, op. cit., p. 259

43. Brown, op. cit., p. 272, and Smith, *Battle Atlas of the Falklands War 1982*, (Naval-History, 2006).

44. Blackman, op. cit., pp. 186–7; Brown, op. cit., p. 277; and Middlebrook, op. cit.

45. The Harrier managed to reach *Hermes* but caught fire on the flight deck. After attempts to repair it, the aircraft was declared out of service and shipped back to Britain.

46. Werrell, op. cit., p. 162.

47. Hastings, & Jenkins, *The Battle for the Falklands*.

48. Squire, 'Biggest threat: AA and small arms', (*Astronautics & Aeronautics*, May 1983), pp. 99–100.

49. A total of 102 aircraft were lost. 32 Argentine aircraft were destroyed by Sea Harriers using their AIM-9L Sidewinders or the 30mm cannon, 20 were destroyed by surface-to-air missiles and small arms fire: 32 were captured on the East Falklands, and 18 aircraft were destroyed during the SAS attack on Pebble Island, on *General Belgrano* and in operational accidents. Ethell and Price, *Air War South Atlantic*, p. 207. See also, Werrel, op. cit., p. 164.

50. The other three, a A-4B Skyhawk of FAA Grupo 5 on 23 May and 2 A-4C Skyhawks of FAA Grupo 4 on 24 May and 25 May 1982, were subjected to the full force of

the San Carlos Air Defences, with claims going to Sea Wolf, Sea Cat, Blowpipe and small arms, as well as T Battery. Ethell and Price give the kills at five, with one confirmed, two probable, and two possible kills.

51. The MoD had exaggerated the capabilities of Rapier and it was later observed that the reason was that 'if this (the true) assessment became publicly known it could have a serious adverse effects on sales prospects for Rapier, which is the staple revenue-earner for BAe's Dynamic Group'. Freedman, *The Official History of the Falklands Campaign*. Volume II, pp. 732–5 and Navy Command HQ *Board of Inquiry into the Loss of AAC Gazelle XX377* (PDF), Ministry of Defence, p. 4. Retrieved 19 November 2008.

52. In all, 195 Blowpipe missiles were fired during the war, 100 by Argentine troops and 95 by the British. Only 2 kills can be attributed to Blowpipe: a British Harrier GR3 shot down by Argentine Army special forces (Commandos Company), and an Argentine Aermacchi MB-339 by the British during the Battle of Goose Green. Freedman, op. cit., pp. 732–5; and 'Barrage Balloons For Low-Level Air Defense', *Airpower Journal* (Summer 1989). Archived 12 August 2007 at the Wayback Machine.

53. The Argentine forces solved the problem by fitting improvised retarding devices, allowing the pilots to effectively employ low-level bombing attacks on 8 June but it was too late by then.

Lebanon

1. David Ivry, Deputy Chief of Israeli Air Force quoted by Grant in 'The Bekaa Valley War', *Air Force Magazine*, (June 2002), pp. 58–62.
2. Ibid.
3. Schnell, 'Experiences of the Lebanon War', (*Military Technology*, July 1984), p. 32.
4. Dupuy and Martell, *Flawed Victory: The Arab-Israeli Conflict and the 1982 War in Lebanon*, pp. 62–3.
5. The SAM suppression operation was originally called 'Mole 3', the figure 3 referring to the number of SAM batteries detected and to be destroyed. The number of SAM batteries was later revised to '19', and the name of the operation accordingly changed to 'Mole Cricket', after the name of the plan for a general war since 1973. Evron, *War and Intervention in Lebanon: The Israeli-Syrian Deterrence Dialogue*, p. 95.
6. Dupuy and Martell, op. cit., p. 63.
7. Lambeth, *Moscow's Lessons from the 1982 Lebanon Air War*, p. 5.
8. Eshel, *The Lebanon War, 1982*. p. 12.
9. *The Lebanon War: Operation Peace for Galilee* (1982), Israeli Ministry of Foreign Affairs, https://mfa.gov.il/mfa/aboutisrael/history/pages/operationpeaceforgalilee201882. aspx
10. Dupuy and Martell, op. cit., p. 81.
11. Grant, op cit., pp. 58–62.
12. Gabriel, *Operation Peace for Galilee: The Israeli-PLO War in Lebanon*, p. 95.
13. Dupuy and Martell, op. cit., p. 120.
14. CIA Intelligence Memorandum '*Israel: Options in Lebanon*', National Foreign Assessment Centre, NESA 81-10066, December 1981.
15. *The First UAV Squadron – Israel Air Force*, http://www.iaf.org.il/4968-33518-en/ IAF.aspx

16. Samson is also referred to as Sampson. Ofir and Yaakov, 'Delilah's Story', *Air Force Magazine*, Israeli Air Force. Accessed at http://www.iaf.org.il/5642-35312-en/IAF.aspx.

17. General Dynamics denies any knowledge of the programme and it was speculated that the system was actually developed by MBT, a subsidiary of Israel Aircraft Industries (IAI). However, Israeli sources continue to insist that General Dynamics was involved in its development.

18. Israel had developed Kilshon, an M4 Sherman tank fitted to launch AGM-45 Shrike anti-radiation missiles. Later, this system was fitted with AGM-78 Standard ARMs and then the Keres. Some sources had indicated that the Keres was similar to the IAI Harpy ground-launched anti-radiation drone, but this has been dismissed by Israeli military sources who stated that Keres is nothing like the Harpy. It's possible that only 300 Keres were produced.

19. Cohen, *Israel's Best Defense: The First Full Story of the Israeli Air Force*, p. 611.

20. The Syrians are often criticised for presenting an easy target to Israeli air strikes by keeping the radars switched on but it takes a good standard of training to differentiate between a decoy and an actual target (aircraft) which apparently the Syrians lacked.

21. The details of the number of Keres and Wolf missiles launched and their efficacy in destroying the SAMs, however, are not known.

22. Lambeth, *The Transformation of American Air Power*, p. 94.

23. Millis, 'RPVs Over the Bekaa Valley', (*Army*, June 1983), p. 50.

24. Hurley, 'The BEKAA Valley Air Battle, June 1982: Lessons Mislearned?', *Airpower Journal*, Winter 1989.

25. Ibid.; Grant, op. cit., pp. 58–62.

26. Grant, op. cit., pp. 58–62.

27. Dupuy and Martell, op. cit., p. 145 and Eshel, op. cit., p. 47.

28. *UAV Squadron*, Israel Air Force, http://www.iaf.org.il/4968-33518-en/IAF.aspx

29. 'The Rape of Lebanon (Special Issue)', (*Monday Morning*, June 1982), pp. 14–16.

30. Olivier, 'A history of South African UAVs', *African Defence Review*, 5 Aug 2015 and Kamm, 'Israel reports its Air Force has wrecked Syria's Anti-Aircraft Missiles in Lebanon', *The New York Times*, 10 June 1982.

31. Cutter, 'ELTA Plays a Decisive Role in the EOB Scenario', *Military Electronics/Countermeasures*, January 1983, p. 136.

32. Korytko, '*Battalion Air Defense on the Defensive,*' Soviet Awareness Red Eagle Reader (AF Intelligence Service, Bolling, AFB, Washington, D.C., 1982), p. 78.

33. Miller, 'The Soviet Air Force View of the Bekaa Valley Debacle', *Armed Forces Journal International*, June 1987, p. 54.

34. 'IAF vs. SAM: 28-0', (*Defense Update International*, December 1986), p. 54.

Lebanon 1983

1. The British joined the Multi-National Force later. Kelly, *U.S. and Russian Policymaking With Respect to the Use of Force, Chapter VI: Lebanon: 1982–1984*, (RAND Corporation, September 1982), p. 4.

2. US Marines in Lebanon 1982–1984, Beirut V Disaster Strikes, 30 May – 19 November 1983. Accessed at https://www.marines.mil/Portals/59/Publications/USMarinesInLebanon1982-1984PCN19000309800_3.pdf

3. Frankel, 'French Jets Strike Shiite Position in Eastern Lebanon', *Washington Post*, 18 November 1983.

4. Friedman, 'French Jets raid Bases of Militia Linked to Attacks', *The New York Times*, 18 November 1983.

5. There are reports that following the suicide truck bomb attack, the United States President had approved a joint U.S.-French air raid on 14 November, to be carried out two days later but owing to differences between the US State Department and the Department of Defence, the United States did not carry out any retaliatory air strikes. Crist, *The Twilight War: The Secret History of America's Thirty-Year Conflict with Iran*, (Kindle Edition).

6. Zenko, 'Why America Attacked Syria', *Council for Foreign Affairs*, 13 February 2012.

7. Trainor, ''83 Strike; Hard Lessons for United States', *The New York Times*, 8 August 1989.

8. Wilson, 'The Day we fouled up the Bombing of Lebanon', *Washington Post*, 7 September 1985; Trainor, op. cit.

9. Ibid.

10. Ibid.

Libya
1. Boyne, 'El Dorado Canyon', *Air Force Magazine*, March 1999, pp. 56–62 and Davies, *F-111 & EF-111 Units in Combat*, (Kindle Edition).

2. Arnold, 'Conflict with Libya: Operational Art in the War on Terrorism', (Naval War College, November 1993), pp 12–13. Accessed at https://apps.dtic.mil/dtic/tr/fulltext/u2/a265318.pdf

3. SA-5 Gammon is also referred to as the S-200 Vega.

4. Martin and Walcott, *Best Laid Plans: The Inside Story of America's War Against Terrorism*, p. 281.

5. Arnold, op. cit., p. 13.

6. Pochtarev, 'Debut of Vega', *Red Star*, 29 August 2001.

7. 'High-Tech Firepower', (*Time*, 7 April, 1986) and *Libya: Encounters with the United States*, Country Data, Based on the Country Studies Series by Federal Research Division of the Library of Congress, http://www.country-data.com/cgi-bin/query/r-8251.html

8. Arnold, op. cit., p. 13 and Boyne, op. cit., pp. 56–62.

9. Excerpts from the News Sessions on 'The Clash with Libya's forces', *The New York Times*, 25 March 1986.

10. Pochtarev, op. cit.

11. Belash, 'Operation Canyon Eldorado: US shows muscles', *Warspot*, 15 April, 2016. Accessed at https://warspot.ru/5870-operatsiya-kanon-eldorado-ssha-pokazyvayut-muskuly.

12. 'Pentagon Revises Libyan Ship Toll', *New York Times*, 27 March 1986.

13. Parks, 'Crossing the Line', *U.S. Naval Institute Proceedings*, November 1986, p. 45.

14. Bailey, Kennedy, David; Cohen, *The American Pageant* (Eleventh ed.), p. 1000; Boyne, 'El Dorado Canyon', *Air Force Magazine*, March 1999, pp. 56–62.

15. 'Operation El Dorado Canyon', *Global Security*, retrieved 30 January 2019.

16. Endicott, *Raid on Libya, Operation El Dorado Canyon*, pp. 145–55.

17. Ibid.

18. Kopp, 'The Libyan Strike: how the Americans Did It', *Australian Aviation*, July 1986.

19. Boyne, El Dorado Canyon, *Air Force Magazine*, March 1999, pp. 56–62.

20. Endicott, op. cit.

21. Bolger, *Americans at War: 1975–1986 — & Era of Violent Peace*, p. 424.

22. Stanik, *El Dorado Canyon: Reagan's undeclared war with Qaddafi*; Endicott, op. cit.; Boyne, op. cit.

23. Some US sources suggest that the lost F-111F was fatally damaged by one of these weapons while attacking this target.

24. Pochtarev, op. cit.

25. The Soviets claim that the targets destroyed were Unmanned Aerial Vehicles (UAVs) used by the USAF for deception. (Pochtarev, op. cit.)

26. Wilson, 'Libya Upgrades Air Defences With New Missile Site on Gulf', *Washington Post*, 13 June 1986.

27. Belash, op. cit.

28. 'Libyan website reports rebels sink Gaddafi ships', *Reuters*, 15 March 2011.

29. Potter, 'The Star in Libya: Rebels quash Gadhafi raid', *The Star*, 2 March 2011 https://www.thestar.com/news/world/2011/03/02/the_star_in_libya_rebels_quash_gadhafi_raid.html

30. At least six of the total 15 aircraft are claimed to have been shot down by the ZPU-4 guns and one by a MANPADS, likely to be a SA-7.

31. 'Syrian pilots said to be flying Libyan fighter jets', *The World Tribune*, 10 March 2011, http://www.worldtribune.com/worldtribune/WTARC/2011/me_libya0257_03_10.asp

32. The anti-aircraft guns had even been used on the demonstrators by Gaddafi's forces at Ra's Lanauf and Zawiyya in February 2001. Bassiouni (Ed.), *Libya: From Repression to Revolution: A Record of Armed Conflict and International Law Violations, 2011–2013*, International Criminal Law, pp. 164–7 and 576.

33. 'Security Council Authorizes 'All Necessary Measures' To Protect Civilians in Libya' *UN News Centre*, 17 March 2011. The first United Nations intervention was in February when the Security Council passed an initial resolution, freezing the assets of Gaddafi and his inner circle, restricting their travel and referring the matter to the International Criminal Court for investigation. (Wyatt, 'Security Council Calls for War Crimes Inquiry in Libya', *New York Times*, 27 February 2011.

34. Rayment, 'Libya: moment a rebel jet crashed to earth in flames', *The Telegraph*, 19 March 2011; 'Benghazi bombarded by pro-Gaddafi forces', BBC News, 20 March 2011.

35. Operation Odyssey Dawn had commenced on 3 March 2011 with the air operations starting on 19 March. The British counterpart was Operation ELLAMY, the French was Opération HARMATTAN and Operation MOBILE the Canadian.

36. 'Allied airstrikes continue against Gadhafi forces', CNN, 20 March 2011.

37. 'Libya: US, UK and France attack Gaddafi forces', BBC, 20 March 2011, https://www.bbc.com/news/world-africa-12796972

38. In almost all assessments made by United States and NATO, the Libyan air defences are projected as being very formidable and lethal with state of the art missile systems and integrated network to control the various weapons whereas the Libyan air defences were hardly in a position to offer any resistance to the NATO air forces.

39. As the Libyans were organized on the erstwhile Soviet model, the battalion here refers to a battery.

40. Cordesman, *The North African Military Balance*, Center for Strategic and International Studies, 28 March 2005, accessed at https://csis-prod. s3.amazonaws.com/s3fs-public/legacy_files/files/media/csis/pubs/050328_ norafrimibal5B15D.pdf; and *The Libyan Air Defence System. Libya's Surface to Air Missile (SAM) Network*, (Global Research IMINT & Analysis, 21 March 2011), accessed at https://www.globalresearch.ca/the-libyan-air-defense-system-libya-s-surface-to-air-missile-sam-network/23841

41. Department of Defense (DOD) News Briefing with Vice Adm. Gortney from the Pentagon on Libya Operation Odyssey Dawn by Vice Adm. Bill Gortney, Director of The Joint Staff, US Department of Defence, 19 March 2011, accessed 14 February 2019 http://archive.defense.gov/transcripts/transcript.aspx?transcriptid=4786

42. The absence of any opposition during the conduct of the operations did support the views expressed by O'Connor. (*The Libyan SAM Network* accessed at http:// geimint.blogspot.com/2010/05/libyan-sam-network.html)

43. Bullimer, 'Allies Target Qaddafi's Ground Forces as Libyan Rebels Regroup', *New York Times*, 20 March 2011; Libya live blog: U.S., allies launch missiles against Gadhafi forces, CNN, 20 March 2011 http://news.blogs.cnn.com/2011/03/19/ libya-live-blog-gadhafi-to-obama-sarkozy-butt-out/?hpt=T1

44. 'News Transcript: DOD News Briefing by Vice Adm. Gortney on Operation Odyssey Dawn'. Defense.gov. 21 March 2009.

45. The reason given was 'lack of published knowledge on F-15E manoeuvring with large external store weight imbalances at high altitude' *United States Air Force Aircraft Accident Investigation Board Report – F-15E Strike Eagle, T/N 91-0304* accessed at usaf.aib.law.af.mil.

46. 'Libya: France jet destroys pro-Gaddafi plane' BBC, 24 March 2011, https://www. bbc.com/news/world-africa-12850975

47. 'Operation Unified Protector: Final Mission Stats', NATO.int, 2 November 2011, http:// www.nato.int/nato_static/assets/pdf/pdf_2011_11/20111108_111107-factsheet _up_ factsfigures_en.pdf

48. 'Pentagon Confirms First Predator Drone Strike in Libya', (ABC News, 23 April 2011). https://abcnews.go.com/International/pentagon-confirms-predator-drone-strike-libya/story?id=13442570

49. Walsh, Schulzke, *Drones and Support for the Use of Force*, p. 16.

50. 'Libya: UK Apache helicopters used in NATO attacks', BBC, 4 June 2011; 'NATO uses attack helicopters in Libya', France 24, 4 June 2011 and Dorn (Ed.) *Air Power in UN Operations: Wings for Peace*, p. 275

51. Laidlaw, *Apache Over Libya*, pp. 1–2.

52. Ibid., pp 65–6.

53. Meo, 'Libya: NATO deny Gaddafi troops shot down unmanned drone', *The Daily Telegraph*, 21 June 2011.
54. Chris Hoyle, 'UK eyes Apache modifications after Libyan experience,' *Flight Global*, 26 October 2011.
55. Mueller, and others, *Precision and purpose: airpower in the Libyan Civil War*, p. 46.
56. Most of the SA-7s were never fired, although there were reports in Misrata of loyalist forces trying to use heat-seeking MANPADS against opposition vehicles.

Iraq 1991–2003
1. Nordeen, *Air Warfare in the Missile Age*, (Kindle Edition).
2. Ibid.
3. The figure of fifteen aircraft is given by Nordeen in his book *Air warfare in the Missile Age*, (p. 389) although the other sources mention the claim of the HAWK anti-aircraft missiles having shot down about 22 Iraqi aircraft and one combat helicopter during the invasion. (*Army*, 24 November 2009) accessed at https://web.archive.org/web/20091124195527/http://www.redstone.army.mil/history/systems/HAWK.html)
4. Nordeen, op. cit.
5. The Iraqi Air Force had a mix of combat aircraft, ranging from 190 advanced Mirages, MiG-25s, MiG-29s, and Su-24s to about 300 moderate-quality MiG-23s, Su-7s, Su-25s, Tu-16s and Tu-22s. The majority of the air force, however, comprised older aircraft like the MiG-17s and MiG-21s.
6. Frostic, *Air campaign Against the Iraqi Army in the Kuwaiti Theatre of Operations* (Prepared for the United States Air Force, Project Air Force, RAND Corporation 1994).
7. KARI is Iraq, spelt backwards, in French.
8. *Gulf War Air Power Survey, Volume 4*, Office of the Secretary of the Air Force, 1993.
9. As per Tucker-Jones, Iraq had 7,000 SAM and 6,000 AA guns with the Republican Guard having its own Air Defence System with about 3,000 AA guns and 60 SAM batteries. (Tucker-Jones, *The Gulf War: Operation Desert Storm 1990–1991*, p. 40)
10. P-18 radar which uses metre-length wave in Very High Frequency, has the ability to detect targets at a greater range than centimetre- or millimetre-wave radar which stealth aircraft are optimized against. It was a P-18 radar in Yugoslavia during the Kosovo War that detected an F-117 Nighthawk leading to its shooting down by an SA-3 missile. Similarly, P-12 radar also operates in VHF and can detect the stealth aircraft. Werrell in his book *Archie to SAM* mentions that Iraq had low-frequency radars although this is not mentioned by any other source. Gordon and Trainor, *The Generals' War*, p. 105; and *Gulf War Air Power Survey*, Vol. IV, Operations and Effects and Effectiveness, p. 83.
11. Operation DESERT STORM Evaluation of the Air Campaign, Report to the Ranking Minority Member, Committee on Commerce, House of Representatives, United States General Accounting Office, June 1997, GAO/NSIAD-97-134 Operation Desert Storm Air Campaign, p. 62.
12. *Iraqi Threat to U.S. Forces*, Naval Intelligence Command, (Navy Operational Intelligence Center, December 1990), pp. 3–14.

13. Werrell, op. cit., p. 218.
14. United States Air Force, *History of the Air Campaign*, p. 254.
15. SA-8 and Roland were newer and more advanced than SA-6 but did not have the range and ceiling of the older Kub missile system.
16. *Gulf War Air Power Survey Vol IV, Weapons, Tactics, and Training and Space Operations*, p. 15 accessed at https://media.defense.gov/2010/Sep/27/2001329817/-1/-1/0/AFD-100927-066.pdf
17. Approximately 13 Roland I (clear weather) systems and one hundred Roland II (all weather) systems had been sold to Iraq.
18. *Operation Desert Storm: Evaluation of Air Campaign*, GAO/NSIAD-97-134, June 12, 1997, US General Accounting Office, Washington accessed at https://www.gao.gov/pdfs/NSIAD-97-134
19. The Brigade had 1st Battalion, 2nd ADA (Chaparral), 2nd Battalion, 7th ADA (Patriot), 3rd Battalion, 43rd ADA (Patriot) 2nd Battalion, 1st ADA Task Force and 2-1 ADA (Hawk) and 2-43 ADA (Patriot) in its order of battle in 1990. Of these, the 1st Battalion, 2nd ADA was left behind at Fort Stewart when the brigade deployed. Battery D, 1st Battalion, 7th ADA (Patriot) was attached from 94th ADA Brigade, 32nd AADCOM in Europe, and 2nd Battalion, 43rd ADA was attached from 10th ADA Brigade, 32nd AADCOM.
20. 'Desert Victory', *ADA Journal*, (US Army Air Defence Artillery Yearbook 1991); *The Patriot: Air Defence System*, (US Army Centre for Military History), accessed at https://history.army.mil/books/www/WWWAPENA.HTM
21. 'With The Marine Expeditionary Force In Desert Shield And Desert Storm', *U.S. Marines in the Persian Gulf, 1990–91*, History and Museums Division, Headquarters US Marine Corps, Washington D.C., 1993.
22. 4 LAAM Battalion reverted to its configuration of four batteries consisting of 27 Vulcan and 60 Stinger Teams when it received the Avengers in February 1999; at its full strength the Battalion had six Vulcan platoons, ten Stinger sections and six Avenger platoons. Rob Jagodzinski, 'Marine missiles protect the Gulf', *Stars and Stripes*, 27 October 1990 accessed at https://www.stripes.com/news/marine-missiles-protect-the-gulf-1.12466
23. Tucker-Jones, op. cit., p. 91.
24. Gulf War Air Power Survey, Vol 2, Operations and Effects and Effectiveness, op. cit., p. 118.
25. Task Force 8/43 was formed from units of the 32nd Army Air Defence Command's 69th Air Defence Artillery Brigade. It had four Patriot batteries from the 8th Battalion, 43rd Air Defence Artillery, and two HAWK batteries from the 6th Battalion, 52rd Air Defence Artillery.
26. Schubert and Kraus (General Editors), *The Whirlwind War: The United States Army in Operations DESERT SHIELD and DESERT STORM*, Centre of Military History, US Army, Washington D.C.
27. 'Instant Thunder' was a plan in August 1990 which proposed a massive week-long air attack to 'incapacitate, discredit and isolate [the Saddam] Hussein regime, eliminate Iraqi offensive/defensive capability … [and] create conditions leading to Iraqi withdrawal from Kuwait'. It was never accepted in toto although it was used to

lay the groundwork for final plans for DESERT STORM. The idea of simultaneous targeting the air defence and strategic targets was first given by Col John A. Warden III, USAF. See his book, *The Air Campaign: Planning for Combat.*

28. The target list grew from 10 strategic AD targets and 7 airfields in August 1990 to 56 and 31 respectively by the time the offensive started.

29. Later, an F-111 crashed at a Saudi bomb range while carrying out a low-level practice bomb run. These were amongst the losses before the actual war started.

30. Simpson, *Remembering Gulf War 25 years later*, 20 August 2015 http://fortcampbellcourier.com/news/article_ce783c14-477b-11e5-a088-7704be7a48dc.html

31. Tucker-Jones, op. cit., p. 89.

32. Carrigan, *Desert Storm Air War: The Aerial Campaign against Saddam's Iraq in the 1991 Gulf War*, (Kindle Edition).

33. Lowry, *The Gulf War Chronicles: A Military History of the First War with Iraq*, pp. 3–4.

34. Ibid.

35. Gulf War Air Power Survey, Vol 2, Operations and Effects and Effectiveness, op. cit.

36. Corrigan, op. cit., p. 59.

37. Nordeen, op. cit., pp. 413–14; Norman Friedman, 'Desert Victory: The War for Kuwait', *World Air Power Journal*, Vol IV, No 4, Winter 1992.

38. 'Scud Busters': Patriot Outduels Iraqi Series in Dramatic DESERT STORM Combat Debut', *Air Defense Artillery* (January-February 1991), pp. 5–8; Miles, 'DESERT STORM Rises', *Soldiers* (March 1991), pp. 6, 8–9; McMichael, 'Patriot Passes the Combat Test', *Soldiers* (April 1991), pp. 19–20.

39. Coyne, *Air Power in the Gulf*, pp. 67–71.

40. 'Iraqi missiles strike Israel', *The Guardian*, 18 January 1991 and Pedatzur, 'The Israeli Experience Operating Patriot in the Gulf War', *Federation of American Scientists*, 7 April 1992. Archived from the original on 9 December 2014.

41. Pawlowski, *Gulf War Chronology*; Nordeen, op. cit.

42. Israel had a mix of patriot Batteries – the American batteries, the Israeli batteries and a battery from the Netherlands. In the American batteries all soldiers, including the commanders were American. In the Israeli battery the commanders, the officers and part of the operators were Israeli. The rest of the crew was American. The Dutch battery was comprised of Dutchmen alone (Patriot Missile System, Israel Air Force, http://www.iaf.org.il/241-16912-en/IAF.aspx?indx=1)

43. Kifner, 'WAR IN THE GULF: TEL AVIV; 3 DIE, 96 ARE HURT IN ISRAELI SUBURB', (*The New York Times*, 23 January 1991).

44. Diehl and Claiborne, '*SCUD MISSILE ATTACK ON ISRAEL KILLS 1, INJURES DOZENS*', *Washington Post*, 26 January 1991.

45. Nordeen, op. cit.

46. Cohen, *Gulf War Air Power Survey, Vol II: Operations and Effects and Effectiveness*, op. cit., p. 202.

47. *Conduct of the Persian Gulf War: Final Report to the Congress*, April 1992, Pursuant to Title V of The Persian Gulf Conflict Supplemental Authorization and Personnel Benefits Act of 1991 (Public Law 102–25), Chapters I through VIII.

48. Captain James Crabtree, *Task Force Scorpion: Gulf War Diary* accessed at http://www.angelfire.com/journal2/desertfox/STORM.html
49. 'Avenger's Combat Debut', (*Air Defense Artillery* Magazine, US Army, March–April 1991), pp. 22–4.
50. Crabtree, *Task Force Scorpion: Gulf War Diary* http://www.angelfire.com/journal2/desertfox/STORM.html
51. 'Scud Busters': Patriot Outduels Iraqi Series in Dramatic DESERT STORM Combat Debut', *Air Defense Artillery* (January–February 1991), pp. 5–8; McMichael, 'Patriot Passes the Combat Test', *Soldiers* (April 1991), pp. 19–20.
52. In September 1992 an Army official admitted that electronic signals, or noise, emitted by a variety of United States systems, caused computer problems and accidentally launched Patriot missiles in the first week of the war. In another report, the number of missiles fired is given as 24. Boley, *Patriot Performance Assessment in Desert Storm Roadmap* (U), CAS, Incorporated for United States Army Missile Command, 25 July 1991 (S), p. D-2; Lovece, Joseph, 'Electronic Noise from U.S. Gear Prompted Errant Patriots', *Defense Week*, 28 September 1992, p. 1 (Quoted in 'Information Paper on Iraq's Scud Ballistic Missiles', *Federation of American Scientists*, July 25, 2000, https://fas.org/nuke/guide/iraq/missile/scud_info.html)
53. *The Patriot: Air Defence System*, US Army Center for Military History, https://history.army.mil/books/www/WWWAPENA.HTM. Software Problem Led to System Failure at Dhahran, Saudi Arabia, MTEC-92-26: Published: Feb 4, 1992. Publicly Released: 27 Feb 1992.
54. Werrell gives a figure of 88 at page 212 of *Archie to SAM*. The Federation of American Scientists (FAS) paper gives the tabulated details from various sources. The figures for KTO vary between 42 and 51 and between 39 and 43 for Israel. ('Information Paper on Iraq's Scud Ballistic Missiles', *Federation of American Scientists*, 25 July 2000) https://fas.org/nuke/guide/iraq/missile/scud_info/scud_info_s04.htm#B.TotalScudFiringIncidents
55. *Gulf War Air Power Survey, Command and Control*, Washington, D.C.: GPO, 1993, pp. 248–50; *Gulf War Air Power Survey*, vol. 4, Weapons, Tactics, and Training, pp. 280–1.
56. 'Scud Attack!' *Air Defense Artillery Journal*, US Army, March–April 1991, p. 6.
57. Postol, 'Letter to the Editor', *International Security*, Summer 1992, p. 226. Postol's claims have been widely challenged and disputed as erroneous. One such paper challenging Postol is Zimmerman's 'A Review of the Postol and Lewis Evaluation of the White Sands Missile Range Evaluation of the Suitability of TV Video Tapes to Evaluate Patriot Performance During the Gulf War' published in *Inside The Army*, 16 November 1992, pp. 7–9, accessed at https://web.archive.org/web/20131224183852/http://www.fas.org/spp/starwars/docops/zimmerman.htm
58. Schmitt, 'Israel Plays Down Effectiveness of Patriot Missile', *Washington Post*, 31 October 1991.
59. 'The Israeli Experience Operating Patriot in the Gulf War', Statement of Reuven Pedatzur, Ha'aretz Daily, Tel Aviv, Israel to the Committee on Government Operations, U.S. House of Representatives, 7 April 1992.

60. Ibid.
61. Crabtree, op. cit.
62. Of those 21, 12 were A-10 casualties. A-10s were permitted to operate below 12,000 feet to as low as 4,000 to 7,000 feet on 31 January and thereafter.
63. Bradley 'Gulf War left Iraqi Air Defence Beaten, Not bowed,' *Washington Post*, 6 September 1996.
64. Ibid.
65. Quoted in *The Manchester Guardian*, 2 March 1991. See also Velovich, 'USSR Demands Post-Gulf Air Defense Review', *Flight International*, 13–19 March 1991, p. 5.
66. Lambeth, *Desert Storm and Its Meaning: The View from Moscow*, (RAND Publishing, 1996).
67. Sneider , 'Soviets Assess Their Arsenal After Iraq's Defeat in Gulf', *The Christian Science Monitor*, 8 March 1991.
68. Tucker-Jones, *The Gulf War: Operation Desert Storm 1990–1991*.
69. 'Operation Provide Comfort II', *Global Security*, accessed at https://www. globalsecurity.org/military/ops/provide_comfort_2.htm
70. 'Operation Provide Comfort and Northern Watch', 18 September 2012, https:// www.afhistory.af.mil/FAQs/Fact-Sheets/Article/458953/operation-provide-comfort-and-northern-watch/
71. 'U.S. launches missile strikes against Iraq', *CNN*, 3 September 1996; White, 'Airpower and a Decade of Containment', *Joint Force Quarterly*, Winter 2000– 2001 and *Operation Desert Strike*, United States Air Force Historical Division, 23 August 2011, accessed at https://www.afhistory.af.mil/FAQs/Fact-Sheets/ Article/458974/operation-desert-strike/
72. 'Operation Northern Watch', *Globalsecurity.org*, accessed at https://www. globalsecurity.org/military/ops/northern_watch.htm
73. Gordon, '*After The War: Preliminaries; U.S. Air Raids In '02 Prepared For War in Iraq*', *The New York Times*, 20 July 2003.

Iraqi Freedom 2003

1. 'Analysis: Iraq's air defences', BBC News, 7 March 2003.
2. Ibid.
3. Sharon Otterman in his *IRAQ: Iraq's Prewar Military Capabilities* gives the holding of Iraqi air defences as 850 SAM systems while Cordersman gives a more conservative figure of 380 SAMs remaining at the end of Gulf War I. With sanctions in place, not many SAM systems would have been added in the intervening period. (Otterman, 'IRAQ: Iraq's Prewar Military Capabilities', (*Council for Foreign Relations*, 3 February 2005), accessed at https://www.cfr.org/backgrounder/iraq-iraqs-prewar-military-capabilities)
4. Gordon, 'Threats And Responses: Defenses; Iraq's Air Defense Is Concentrated Around Baghdad', *New York Times*, 17 March 2003; Arkin, 'Iraq's Air Defence will be first hit', *NBC News*, 18 March 2003, http://www.nbcnews.com/id/3070293/ ns/world_news/t/iraqs-air-defense-will-be-first-hit/#.XIzgvxMzZN0
5. 'Analysis: Iraq's air defences', BBC News, 7 March 2003.

6. Only two helicopters were assessed to be 'combat' helicopters. Haulman, *What Happened to the Iraqi Air Force?* Air Force Historical Research Agency 19 October 2015.

7. Hosmer, *Why the Iraqi Resistance to the Coalition Invasion Was So Weak*, pp. 75–6 and Chapman, 'The "War" Before the War', *Air Force Magazine*, February 2004, p. 52.

8. *Army Report Details Patriot Record in Iraq War*, Arms Control Association, accessed at https://www.armscontrol.org/act/2003_11/Patriotmissile

9. In contrast, during DESERT STORM the longer-range SCUD-C allowed response times of about 4.5 minutes.

10. 'Army OIF Report Reveals Emerging Air Defence Challenges, Threats', *Inside The Army*, 27 October 2003.

11. 'Samson, 'The PATRIOT/TORNADO Fratricide: It Could Happen Again', (*Centre for Defence Information*; Graham, 'U.S. Soldiers Cleared in Downing of British Jet', *Washington Post*, 18 May 2004, p. 12; McCarthy, 'Patriot in new "friendly fire" incident', *The Guardian*, 4 April 2003.

12. Bishop, *Apache AH-64 Boeing (McDonnell Douglas) 1976–2005*, pp. 35–7; Bernstein, *AH-64 Apache Units of Operations Enduring Freedom & Iraqi Freedom*, pp. 48–50; Schechter, Erik, 'Choppers On The Chopping Block?', *Jerusalem Post*, 13 June 2003 and Kaplan, 'Chop the Chopper', *Slate*, 23 April 2003.

13. 'Operation Iraqi Freedom – Patriot', *Global Secuirty.Org*, accessed at https://www. globalsecurity.org/space/ops/oif-patriot.htm; *Report of the Defence Science Board Task Force on Patriot System Performance*, accessed at http://www.acq.osd.mil/dsb/reports/2005-01-Patriot_Report_Summary.pdf

14. Ibid.

15. No official explanation is given for why the other nine Iraqi missiles were not fired upon, although the report implied that at least three might have been because their trajectories were judged to be non-threatening. Patriots also did not down any Iraqi cruise missiles. ('Army Report Details Patriot Record in Iraq War', *Arms Control Association*). Report accessed at https://www.armscontrol.org/act/2003_11/Patriotmissile

16. Zucchino, *Thunder Run: The Armored Strike to Capture Baghdad*, pp. 162–71.

17. Ibid.

18. 'Black Hawk, Hornet shot down', CNN, 3 April 2003, accessed at http://edition.cnn.com/2003/WORLD/meast/04/02/sprj.irq.war.main.int/: Iraq Shot down US F/A-18 Hornet, Black Hawk Helicopter, http://en.people.cn/200304/03/eng20030403_114518.shtml

19. Shafran, 'Operation Iraqi Freedom hero shares her story' *United States Air Force History Division*, 18 March 2010; Haag, 'Wounded Warthog: an A-10 Thunderbolt II pilot safely landed her "Warthog" after it sustained significant damage from enemy fire', *Combat Edge*, 2004. Retrieved 2014-12-23 via thefreelibrary.com; 'Kim N. Campbell. Distinguished Flying Cross'. Hall of Valor. *Military Times*. Retrieved 23 December 2014.

20. 'U.S. A-10 Warplane Shot Down Near Baghdad', *Associated Press*, 8 April 2003, https://www.foxnews.com/story/u-s-a-10-warplane-shot-down-near-baghdad;

'30 Apr OIF by the Numbers' UNCLASS.doc (pdf) at globalsecurity.org. Retrieved: 5 March 2010.

21. Cordesman, *Iraq War Note: Iraqi Air Defences and the Battle of Baghdad*.
22. 'Absence of Iraqi Air Defences: A Glimpse at Strategy?' *Stratfor*, 4 April 2003 accessed at https://worldview.stratfor.com/article/absence-iraqi-air-defenses-glimpse-strategy
23. 'Ten feared dead in Hercules crash', BBC News, 1 February 2005); 'US F-16 goes down in Iraq', *Al Jazeera*. 27 November, 2006.
24. 'Helicopters shot down or crashed in Iraq', *USA Today*, 1 August 2004.
25. Harris, 'US helicopters in Iraq face menace of 'aerial bombs', *The Telegraph*, 18 Jan 2006 accessed at https://www.telegraph.co.uk/news/worldnews/middleeast/iraq/1508142/US-helicopters-in-Iraq-face-menace-of-aerial-bombs.html
26. Tyson, 'Copter Attacks In Iraq May Indicate New Battle Strategy,' *Washington Post*, 21 February 2007.
27. Ibid.
28. 'Insurgents Used Cell Phone Geotags to Destroy AH-64s in Iraq', *Military.com*, 15 Mar 2012, accessed at https://www.military.com/defensetech/2012/03/15/insurgents-used-cell-phone-geotags-to-destroy-ah-64s-in-iraq
29. 'General says U.S. Army has lost 130 helicopters in Iraq and Afghanistan', *International Herald Tribune*, 23 March 2007.

Balkans
1. Nordeen, *Air Warfare in the Missile Age* Kindle Edition.
2. Svajncer, 'War for Slovenia 1991', *Slovenska Vojska* (special edition), Ministry of Defence, May 2001, accessed at http://www.slovenija2001.gov.si/10years/path/war/
3. Nordeen mentions the loss of only one helicopter, a Gazelle, at Ljubljana. Though the total number of helicopters lost in the war is 4 as per the *United Nations Security Council Experts report on the Military Structure, Strategy, and tactics of the Warring factions* S/1994/674/Add.2 (Vol. I), 28 December 1994 (page 21). See also, Svajncer, op. cit.
4. Ripley, *Conflict in the Balkans 1991–2000*, Kindle Edition.
5. At least two to three A-2s were reportedly shot down during the war. Cooper, *MiGs Over Croatia*, 28 Oct 2003 from ACIG.org accessed at https://www.scribd.com/document/101566271/MiGs-Over-Croatia
6. United Nations Security Council Experts report on the Military Structure, Strategy, and tactics of the Warring factions, /1994/674/Add.2 (Vol. I), 28 December 1994), p. 22.
7. Shaw, Jr., 'Crisis in Bosnia: Operation Provide Promise', contained in *Short of War: Major USAF Contingency Operations*, edited by Warnock, p. 198.
8. Fisk, 'UN fears aid aircraft was shot down by missile', *Independent*, 22 September 1992, accessed at https://www.independent.co.uk/news/un-fears-aid-aircraft-was-shot-down-by-missile-1549141.html
9. Lidy, Project Leader & Others, *Bosnia Air Drop Study*, (Institute for Defence Analysis, IDA Paper No P-3474), Study conducted for the Deputy Assistant

Secretary of Defense for Peace-keeping and Humanitarian Affairs, Office of the Assistant Secretary of Defense (Special Operations and Low Intensity Conflict), accessed at https://apps.dtic.mil/dtic/tr/fulltext/u2/a368790.pdf

10. Marshall, 'U.S. Airdrop of Aid to Eastern Bosnia Begins', *Los Angeles Times*, 1 March 1993; and Ripley, op. cit.

11. 'NATO Jets told to fire only as last resort', *New York Times*, 12 April 1993. NATO planes in Bosnia were not authorized to bomb anti-aircraft positions or surface-to-air missile sites if the air patrol was attacked by ground fire.

12. Dorn, op. cit., p 206 and Nordeen, op. cit.

13. Owen, *Deliberate Force A Case Study in Effective Air Campaigning*, Final Report of the Air University Balkans Air Campaign Study, p. 21; Cathcart, 'Harrier Pilot Safe', *The Independent*, 17 April 1994.

14. 'United States Air Force and Bosnia', *Air Power History*, Fall 2013, pp. 24–31.

15. Just as the UN feared, the attack on Udbina and a number of additional air strikes against anti-aircraft sites in north-western Bosnia in the weeks afterward to further protect NATO aircraft saw UN hostages taken, including two Czech Army officers who were kidnapped in Sarajevo.

16. 'NATO Handbook: Evolution of the Conflict', (*NATO*, 2010) accessed at http://www.nato.int/docu/handbook/2001/hb050102.htm

17. 'United Nations Protection Force,' Prepared by the Department of Public Information, United Nations - as of September 1996, accessed at https://peacekeeping.un.org/mission/past/unprof_b.htm

18. Bellamy, 'All-American hero's errors bring NATO down to earth', (*The Independent*, 7 July 1995), https://www.independent.co.uk/news/world/all-american-heros-errors-bring-nato-down-to-earth-1590222.html

19. Planning for Deliberate Force began back in September 1994, when NATO defence ministers met in Spain to discuss possibilities for using airpower to stem the ever-worsening Balkan war.

20. Owen, op. cit., p. 134.

21. Hendrickson, 'Crossing the Rubicon', *NATO Review*, Autumn 2005, accessed at https://www.nato.int/docu/review/2005/issue3/english/history.html

22. 'Combatant Forces in the Former Yugoslavia: Volume II–Supporting Analysis', (*National Intelligence Estimate*, Central intelligence Agency, Arlington, July 1993), accessed at https://www.cia.gov/library/readingroom/docs/1993-07-01b.pdf

23. '*Praga Anti-Aircraft Gun System*', http://www.zastava-arms.rs/en/imagetext/1970-1992

24. Owen, USAF, *Deliberate Force: A Case Study in Effective Air Campaigning*, Final Report of the Air University Balkans Air Campaign Study, pp. 134–5.

25. Owen mentions that 14 aircraft performing suppression of enemy air defences (SEAD) struck targets on the Deadeye Southeast list and the targeted SA-6 was located at Sokolac whereas other sources say that a total of 15 SEAD targets were attacked. (Owen, op. cit., p. 135).

26. The pilots managed to eject but were captured by the Serbs and were later repatriated. Galdorisi, Phillips, *Leave No Man Behind: The Saga of Combat Search and Rescue*, p. 209 and 'Mirage shot down during NATO air strikes', *Flight Global*, 6 September 1995.

27. Owen, op. cit., p. 137.
28. Ibid., p. 145.
29. Galdorisi, Phillips, op. cit., p. 209.
30. Owen, op. cit., p.150.
31. Ripley, *Operation Deliberate Force: The UN and NATO Campaign in Bosnia, 1995* p. 279; Owen, op. cit., p. 315.
32. Durham, Strategy and Doctrine Branch, Air Force Special Operations Command (AFSOC), Hurlburt Field, Fla., 'Trip Report, JSOTF2, San Vito dei Normanni AB, IT, 5 Aug–11 Oct 95'. Colonel Durham served as the JSOTF2/J-3 (Operations) during Deliberate Force.
33. Owen, op. cit., pp. 150–5.
34. Report, 'CAOC C-2 Assessment of Operation DEADEYE Part III—10/11 Sep 95' (NATO Secret) Information extracted is unclassified, AFHRA, EUCOM-14 quoted by Owen in *'Deliberate Force : A Case Study in Effective Air Campaigning'*.
35. The details of aircraft held by the Yugoslavian Air Force varies as per different sources with the number of MiG-29s varying between 12 and 16.
36. These figures have been taken from Zaloga, 'The Evolving SAM Threat: Kosovo and Beyond' in *Journal of Electronic Defense*, May 2000.
37. The number of SAMs held by Serbs varies in different sources with some giving a much higher holding. The holding of SAMs as per the *AWOS [Air War Over Serbia] Fact Sheet'* of Headquarters USAFE/SA, 17 December 1999 was 3 SA-2 battalions; 16 SA-3 battalions, each with numerous launchers directed by LOW BLOW fire-control radars; and 5 SA-6 regiments fielding 5 batteries each, for a total of 25 SA-6 batteries directed by STRAIGHT FLUSH radars. See also *The Military Balance, 1998/99*, p. 100. The holding of SAMs was 8 surface-to-air battalions at the start of the war with 24 SA-2 fire units, 16 SA-3 fire units, and 40–60 SA-6 tracked launch vehicles as per Cordesman in *The Effectiveness of the NATO Tactical Air and Missile Campaign Against Serbian Air and Ground Forces in Kosovo.*
38. Unofficial reports suggest that the RL-4 may have been used in action but there is no evidence of RL-2 rounds being fired against NATO aircraft. When hostilities ended, both systems were removed from service. Seymour Johnson, 'Yugoslavia's Secret SAMs', *Jane's Military Review* accessed on 18 February 2019 https://forums.eagle.ru/showthread.php?t=8095
39. Excerpt From: Lambeth. *NATO's Air War for Kosovo: A Strategic and Operational Assessment.*
40. Iraq had been supplied with components of the IADS by Yugoslavia. Iraq very likely shared intelligence with Belgrade on U.S. suppression of enemy air defences (SEAD) tactics, as well as its own experience and recommendations, in subsequent years. Diamond, 'Yugoslavia, Iraq Talked Air Defense Strategy', *Philadelphia Inquirer*, 30 March 1999 and Lambeth, *NATO's Air War for Kosovo: A Strategic and Operational Assessment.*
41. The number of MiG-29s launched is debatable. Some sources say that the Yugoslav Air Force launched 'at least a dozen' MiG-29s (Haulman, 'Manned Aircraft Losses Over The Former Yugoslavia, 1994–1999', *Organizational Histories Branch Air Force Historical Research Agency*, 5 October 2009) but with the total inventory only about 14–16, a dozen MiG-29s seem doubtful. The more likely figure is about 5–6.

See also, Lok, *How Dutch F-16AMs shot down a Mig-29,* janes.com. Retrieved 7 September 2009. Archived 9 July 2006 at the Wayback Machine and Drozdiak, '2 Yugoslav MiG Jets Downed Over Bosnia', *Washington Post*, 27 March 1999.

42. As per Manolache and Chiş in their paper 'Nato Bombing In The Former Republic Of Yugoslavia' presented at the National Defence University, Bucharest, Romania, on 28–30 May 2015, one of the two MiG-29s was shot down by an F-15 while the second managed to return, although damaged. It was later used as a decoy. The second pair of MiG-29s again had one of the aircraft shot down with the second returning but landing at Belgrade where it was kept concealed under a transport aircraft. The fifth MiG-29 was the one shot down by the SA-6 at Niš.

43. Lambeth, *NATO's Air War for Kosovo: A Strategic and Operational Assessment.*

44. Drozdiak, '2 Yugoslav MiG Jets Downed Over Bosnia', *Washington Post*, 27 March 1999.

45. 'Serb discusses downing of stealth', *USA Today*, 26 October 2005.

46. It was speculated that Dani and his crew worked with visual spotters equipped with infra-red and night-vision devices to detect the F-117 and may have used other electromagnetic tools to predict the time and place the F-117 would pass. Even if it were so, there would still have been a need to lock-on to the aircraft.

47. Graham and Drozdiak, 'Allied Action Fails to Stop Serb Brutality', *Washington Post*, 31 March 1999. There was a speculation that a second F-117 was seriously damaged the same night. (Szopa, 'Take down F-117', *Mojeopine*, 2 May 2008) accessed at http://www.mojeopinie.pl/zestrzelic_f117,3,1209735735

48. Palyan, 'Coming of age: B-1 proves itself during Operation Allied Force', Ellsworth Air Force Base, United States Air Force, 27 March 2012, https://www.ellsworth.af.mil/News/Features/Display/Article/217597/coming-of-age-b-1-proves-itself-during-operation-allied-force/

49. Some sources mention that the SAMs were fired during only 30 of the 100 sorties flown by the B-1s of which 10 SAMs actually locked on to them but were all diverted by the ALE-50 decoys. ('N/ALE-50 AAED Advanced Airborne Expendable Decoy', *Global Security*, accessed February 20,2019, quoting *Aviation Week and Space Technology*, 31 May 1999). See also, David Hughes, 'A Pilot's Best Friend', *Aviation Week and Space Technology*, 31 May 1999, p. 25.

50. 'Jumper on Air Power', *Air Force Magazine*, July 2000, p. 43.

51. Cordesman, *The Air and Missile Campaign in Kosovo*, p. 3.

52. Zaloga, 'The Evolving SAM Threat: Kosovo and Beyond', *Journal of Electronic Defence*, May 2000.

53. As claimed by General Clark, the NATO air commander on 27 April (Quoted by Cordesman, op. cit., p. 3).

54. 'Cruise Missiles Not that Precise in Yugoslavia, 20 Downed', *ITAR-TASS*, 30 March 2000.

55. The restrictions were changed later with the forward air controllers flying as low as 5,000 feet and strike aircraft could attack from as low as 8,000 feet, at the pilot's discretion, when necessary. (Grant, 'Nine Myths about Kosovo', *Air Force Magazine*, June 2000).

56. Haun, '*Hit by a SAM*', *A-10s over Kosovo The Victory of Airpower over a Fielded Army as Told by the Airmen Who Fought in Operation Allied Force*.

57. Dana Priest, 'Yugoslav Air Defences Mostly Intact', *Washington Post*, 13 April 1999.

Syria

1. The reports indicated presence of MANPADS but it was not confirmed as none had been used till 2016. Boxx, USAF, 'Observations on the Air War in Syria', *Air & Space Power Journal*, March–April 2013, pp. 147–68); Boxx and White, 'Responding to Assad's Use of Airpower in Syria', *Policy Watch*, 1999, Washington Institute for Near East Policy, 20 November 2012, accessed at http://www .washingtoninstitute. org/policy-analysis/view/responding-to-assads-use-of-Airpower -in-syria.

2. Boxx, USAF, op. cit.

3. Spencer, 'Syrian rebels claim to have shot down Bashar al-Assad MiG fighter jet', *The Telegraph*, 13 August 2012.

4. Boxx, op. cit.

5. Warrick, 'Missiles Boost Rebels' Arsenal', *Washington Post*, 29 November 2012, accessed at http://thewashingtonpostnie.newspaperdirect.com/epaper/viewer. aspx.

6. 'Syrian rebels seize key air base: Activists', CBS News, 11 January 2013, accessed at https://www.cbsnews.com/news/syrian-rebels-seize-key-air-base-activists/

7. At least two OSA-AK mounts were captured from the Syrian Army and used by the rebel factions Jaysh al-Islam and Jaysh al-Ahrar.

8. The SA-8 had also been observed with the rebels as early as 2013 although the first reported use was in January 2014 when it shot down a Syrian Mi-17 helicopter. (Kais, 'Syrian rebels' missile defence system threatens Israel', *Y Net News*, 31 March 2013, accessed at https://www.ynetnews.com/articles/0,7340,L-4412199,00. html); Reed, 'Chinese surface-to-air missiles are being used by Syrian rebels', *Foreign Policy*, 28 February 2013.

9. Lavrov, *The Russian Air Campaign in Syria: A Preliminary Analysis*.

10. At the end of January 2016, Russia deployed its newer Sukhoi Su-35 fighter jets and in February 2016, one Tupolev Tu-214R was reported to have been deployed.

11. 'How many aircraft and pilots Russia has lost in Syria so far', *Pravda*, accessed at http://www.pravdareport.com/world/141651-russia_syria/

12. 'Moscow to deploy S-400 defense missile system to Khmeimim airbase in Syria', *Russia Today*, 25 November 2015 accessed at https://www.rt.com/news/323379-s400-russia-syria-airbase/

13. 'How many aircraft and pilots Russia has lost in Syria so far', *Pravda*; 'How Did al Qaeda In Syria End Up With Anti-Aircraft Missiles?', *Mint Press News*, accessed at https://www.mintpressnews.com/how-did-syrian-rebels-end-up-with-anti-aircraft-missiles-known-as-manpads/237246/

14. Abi-Habib and Meichtry, 'Saudis Agree to Provide Syrian Rebels With Mobile Antiaircraft Missiles', *Wall Street Journal*, 14 February 2014.

15. Haid, 'Does the Syrian opposition have anti-aircraft missiles?', *Atlantic Council*, 14 April 2016.

16. As a precautionary measure, the new Russian air units were equipped with the President-1, a device that interferes with MANPADS' guidance systems. Russian

state news agency TASS, claimed that the effectiveness of the system was 'successfully demonstrated during the fighting for … Palmyra.' (Bennett and Bulos, 'As Russian planes bombard Syrian rebels, debate over anti-aircraft missiles returns', *Los Angeles Times*, 1 May 2016, accessed at https://www.latimes.com/world/middleeast/la-la-fg-syria-downed-planes-20160501-story.html)

17. 'Russian Pantsir-S Goes Hunting In Syrian Skies', 25 August 2017, https://southfront.org/russian-pantsir-s-goes-hunting-in-syrian-skies/ In 2015 an American MQ-1 Predator drone was shot down by an S-125. The manufacturer of the Pantsir-S1 has claimed the system has shot down several Israeli, Turkish and American drones.

18. Roblin, 'Russia Just Might Have the Perfect Weapon to Crush 'Swarm' Attacks', *National Interest*, 20 January 2018, accessed at https://nationalinterest.org/blog/the-buzz/russia-just-might-have-the-perfect-weapon-crush-swarm-24144

19. 'Drone attack on Russia's Syrian air base was elaborate Pentagon operation, says expert', (TASS, 25 October 2018), accessed at http://tass.com/defense/1027834

20. 'No anti-aircraft weapons sent to 'our' Syrian rebels – Pentagon after downing of Russian jet', *Russia Today*, 4 Feb 2018 accessed at https://www.rt.com/usa/417811-pentagon-no-manpads-rebels/

21. Roblin, 'Israeli's Deadly Air Force Has Been Destroying Syria's Russian-Built Air Defence Systems' *National Interest*, 21 May 2018.

22. 'Syrian air defense forces Israeli drone to leave its airspace after downing fighter jet', *Xinhua*, 14 February 2018 accessed at http://www.xinhuanet.com/english/2018-02/15/c_136976608.htm

23. 'Russia claims Syria air defences shot down 71 of 103 missiles' *The Guardian*, 14 April 2017, https://www.theguardian.com/world/2018/apr/14/russia-claims-syria-air-defences-shot-down-majority-missiles

24. Roblin, op. cit.

25. Fomichev, 'Syrian Air Defense System Destroyed by Israel Was Allegedly Unarmed', *Sputnik News*, 12 May 2018.

26. Gross, 'Operation House of Cards,' the IAF mission to cripple Iran's presence in Syria' *Times of Israel*, 10 May 2018.

27. Syrian army says destroyed most of Israeli rockets, Press TV, Damascus, 10 May 2018.

28. Gallagher, 'Russian surveillance plane got shot down by Syria—and Russia blames Israel', *SARS Technica*, 19 September 2018 accessed at https://arstechnica.com/tech-policy/2018/09/russian-surveillance-plane-got-shot-down-by-syria-and-russia-blames-israel/

29. 'Rise in drone attacks on Russian airbase in Syria' *France 24*, 24 August 2018, https://www.france24.com/en/20180824-rise-drone-attacks-russian-airbase-syria-monitor

30. Gallagher, 'Russian surveillance plane got shot down by Syria—and Russia blames Israel', *SARS Technica*, 19 September 2018 accessed at https://arstechnica.com/tech-policy/2018/09/russian-surveillance-plane-got-shot-down-by-syria-and-russia-blames-israel/

31. Russia had supplied Syria with 48 S-200VE launchers of which some were overrun during early days of the civil war and others destroyed by Israel. Pike, 'Syria - Air Force Equipment', *www.globalsecurity.org*. Retrieved 30 September 2018.

32. Frantzman, 'Why Hasn't Syria Used The S-300?', *The Jerusalem Post*, 21 January 2019 accessed at https://www.jpost.com/Arab-Israeli-Conflict/Why-hasnt-Syria-used-the-S-300-578172

33. Ahronheim, 'Russian-made S-300 Missile system active in Syria', *The Jerusalem Post*, 5 February, 2019 accessed at https://www.jpost.com/Arab-Israeli-Conflict/Russian-made-S-300-missile-defense-system - active-in-Syria-579764

34. Harei, 'Israel Hit Several Syrian Air Defense Batteries in Sunday's Strikes', *Haaretz*, 22 January 201 accessed at https://www.haaretz.com/israel-news/.premium-israeli-air-force-hit-eight-syrian-military-batteries-in-sunday-s-strikes-1.6866145

35. Roblin, 'Israel Kamikaze Drones are Destroying Syria's Air Defenses', *National Interest*, 26 January 2019 accessed at https://nationalinterest.org/blog/buzz/israel-kamikaze-drones-are-destroying-syria's-air-defenses-42592

36. Gross, 'Syrian S-300 air defenses 'probably operational', *Times of Israel*, 19 February 2019.

The Other Wars

Grenada

1. Cole, *Operation Urgent Fury: The Planning and Execution of Joint Operations in Grenada*, 12 October-2 November 1983, Joint History Office, Office of the Chairman of the Joint Chiefs of Staff Washington, DC 1997, accessed at https://www.jcs.mil/Portals/36/Documents/History/Monographs/Urgent_Fury.pdf. Clarke, *Operation Urgent Fury: Invasion of Grenada*, October, United States Army.

2. Mendez, *Grenada 1983*, pp. 12–14; Adkin, *Urgent Fury: The Battle for Grenada: The Truth Behind the Largest U.S. Military Operation Since Vietnam*, (Lexington Books, 1989).

3. Ronald, op. cit.

4. Huchthausen, *America's Splendid Little Wars: a short history of US military engagements*, 1975–2000.

5. Cole, op. cit.

6. Clarke, op. cit.

7. Connaughton, 'Grenada 1983', *The RUSI Journal*, Vol. 153, No. 1, 2008; Kukielski, 'How Grenada Reshaped the US Military', *Boston Globe*, 8 September 2013 available at https://www.bostonglobe.com/ideas/2013/09/08/how-grenada-reshaped

Kargil

8. The intrusion began in the early spring of 1999 and was completed by end April/beginning May (Subramanium, 'Kargil Revisited: Air Operations in a High Altitude Conflict', *CLAWS Journal*, Summer 2008. See also, Malik, 'The Kargil War: Some Reflections', *CLAWS Journal*, Summer 2009.

9. The NLI battalions are organized on similar lines as other regular battalions of the Pakistan Army. (Northern Light Infantry, published by the Army Liaison Cell, Army Headquarters, New Delhi). The Pakistani posts had as much firepower as is generally available to a regular infantry battalion. (Kumar, 'What it Took and the Run-up to Operation Vijay', *The Times of India*, 19 July 1999.) The Pakistani troops had carried a number of Stinger and locally produced Anza surface-to-air missiles for air defence, the only air defence weapons that could be carried by the infiltrating troops over the heights. The details of these were not known to the Indians but it was suspected that, in the given terrain, the Pakistanis would be carrying a number of the IR-SAMs.

10. Patrols by the Indian Army's 121 Infantry Brigade first confirmed the infiltration on 5 May. Singh, *Himalayan Eagles: History of the Indian Air Force*, Volume III: World Air Power, p. 108.

11. Subramaniam, op. cit., p. 186.

12. Lambeth, *Airpower at 18,000'*, pp. 9–10.

13. Ibid.

14. The Indian Army's Northern Command had requested the local Air Officer Commanding for Jammu and Kashmir to provide Mi-25 and Mi-35 helicopter gunships and armed Mi-17 helicopters to 'evict a few "intruders" who had stepped across the LoC in the Kargil sector'. This was refused by the AOC on the grounds that if the Army wanted close support, that could be projected to the higher headquarters for approval. The same view was reiterated by the Air Chief. (Lambeth, op. cit, p. 11. See also, Subramanium, op. cit., pp. 183–95).

15. The missile is referred to as Stinger by Tiwari (*Indian Air Force in Wars*) as does the Official IAF website (Operation Safed Sagar, http://indianairforce.nic.in/content/op-safed-sagar) while Lambeth mentions it as a Chinese Anza (quoting Singh, *Himalayan Eagles: History of the Indian Air Force*, op. cit., p. 14).

16. Perumal, 'Missile Strike!', *Bharat Rakshak*, 12 June 2017, https://www.bharat-rakshak.com/IAF/history/kargil/1060-perumal.html. 'Citation for Shaurya Chakra in respect of Wing Cdr Alagaraja Perumal' at Ministry of Defence, Government of India accessed at http://gallantryawards.gov.in/Awardee/wing-commander-alagaraja-perumal

17. Subramanium, op. cit., p. 186; Lambeth, op. cit., p. 13 and Tipnis, 'Operation Safed Sagar', *Force*, New Delhi, October 2006, p. 12.

18. Lambeth, op. cit. and Singh, op. cit., p. 111.

19. Tipnis, op. cit., p. 14.

20. Nachiketa, 'Engine Flameout', *Bharat Rakshak*, 1 December 2009 accessed at https://www.bharat-rakshak.com/IAF/history/kargil/1064-nachiketa.html

21. Subramanium, op. cit., pp. 186–7.

22. His body was subsequently returned bearing fatal bullet wounds and clear signs of brutalization.

23. Subramaniam, op. cit., pp. 186–7.

24. Bedi, 'Tensions heighten after Indian helicopter is shot down by Stinger missile', *Irish Times*, 29 May 1999.

25. Sinha VrC, 'Nubra Formation' *Bharat Rakshak*, 16 October 2009 accessed at https://www.bharat-rakshak.com/IAF/history/kargil/1061-ak-sinha.html
26. Singh, op. cit., p. 152.
27. Tipnis, op. cit., p. 14.
28. Subramaniam, op. cit., p. 187.
29. It is worth recalling that even the most advanced AH-64 Apaches were never used in Kosovo in face of the potential SAM threat. Extract from Operation SAFED SAGAR, Indian Air Force, http://indianairforce.nic.in/content/op-safed-sagar

Georgia
30. Russian reports mention the loss of only 4 aircraft though a paper in *Defence Review* published from Moscow gives the total number of Russian aircraft lost as 6.
31. Watson, 'New Details Surface About Georgia-Russia War', *National Public Radio*, 18 November 2008 accessed at https://www.npr.org/templates/story/story.php?storyId=97008964
32. Cohen & Hamilton, 'The Russian Military And The Georgia War: Lessons And Implications', https://ssi.armywarcollege.edu/pdffiles/pub1069.pdf
33. Cornell, Smith and Starr, *The August 2007 Bombing Incident in Georgia: Implications for the Euro-Atlantic Region*, See also Chivera, 'Georgia-Russia Tension Escalates Over Downed Drone', *The New York Times*, 22 April 2008.
34. The Georgians used the S-75 SAM battalions in the war with Abkhazia in 1992–1993 and shot down a Russian Su-27 fighter near Gudauta on 19 March 1993.
35. Each battery includes two self-propelled launcher mounts and one self-propelled loader-launcher. These were delivered together with 48 9M38M1 surface-to-air missiles. The SIPRI database mentions the sale of two batteries while some sources claim that Georgia was given three batteries.
36. SIPRI Database, http://armstrade.sipri.org/armstrade/page/trade_register.php
37. Georgia had 30 Grom launchers with 100 Grom E2 missiles. Ferguson & Jenzen-Jones, 'Raising Red Flags: An Examination of Arms & Munitions in the Ongoing Conflict in Ukraine, Research Report No 3' *Armament Research Services*, 2014, p. 52.
38. Cohen & Hamilton, op. cit. and Nicolle, ed., 'Russia's Rapid Reaction: But Short War Shows Lack of Modern Systems', (*IISS Strategic Comments*, Vol. 14, Issue 7, September 2008), p. 2. 'Air Power In Russia's Georgian Campaign August 2000', (*Pathfinder* Issue 99, Air Power Development Centre, October 2008.
39. Cohen & Hamilton, 'The Russian Military and the Georgia War: Lessons and Implications', op. cit., p.11, 'Air Power in Russia's Georgian Campaign, August 2000 (*Pathfinder*, No. 99, Air Power Development Centre, October 2008).
40. The figure of 400 is mentioned by Asmus in *A Little War That Shook the World*.
41. This missile attack was broadcast by Russian national television and reported as the shooting down of a Georgian Su-25. Kipp, 'The Russia-Georgia Conflict as Analyzed by the Center of Analysis of Strategies and Technologies in Moscow', *Eurasia Daily Monitor* Volume: 7 Issue: 16, 25 January 2010.
42. 'Analysis of the loss of the Russian air force during the military campaign in Georgia' (*Centre for Strategic Assessment and Forecasts*, 12 July, 2009) http://csef.ru/en/politica-i-geopolitica/423/analiz-poter-rossijskih-vvs-v-hode-voennoj-kampanii-v-gruzii-697

43. Lavrov, *Timeline of Russian-Georgian Hostilities in August 2008*, p. 62.

44. 'Friendly fire downed Russia jets in Georgia', *Reuters*, 8 July 2009, https://www.reuters.com/article/idUSL8262192

45. Cohen & Hamilton, 'The Russian Military and Georgia War: Lessons and Implications'.

Yemen

46. Ghobari, Mukhashaf, 'Moroccan F-16 jet from Saudi-led coalition in Yemen crashes'. *Reuters*, 11 May 2015.

47. Osborne, 'Operation Decisive Storm -- Air Power Over Yemen', *Aviation Week*, 31 March 2015.

48. The rebels converted many of the surviving SA-2 missiles into short-range, surface-to-surface ballistic missiles called the Qaher-1 and 2 (Conqueror-1 and 2).

49. 'Yemeni rebels say they shot down Moroccan jet,' *The Guardian*, 11 May 2015. See also Ghobari and Mukhashaf, op. cit.

50. Nadimi and Knights, *Iran's Support to Houthi Air Defenses in Yemen, Policy Watch Paper 2953*.

51. Knights, 'The Houthi War Machine: From Guerrilla War to State Capture', *CTC Sentinel*, September 2018, Volume 11, Issue 8 accessed at https://ctc.usma.edu/houthi-war-machine-guerrilla-war-state-capture/

52. The coalition claimed that one of the F-16s, a Jordanian aircraft, crashed due to a technical malfunction.

53. 'Twelve Saudi soldiers die in Yemen "friendly fire" helicopter crash,' BBC, 18 April 2017) accessed at https://www.bbc.com/news/world-middle-east-39633701 and '12 Saudis die in "friendly fire" helicopter crash in Yemen', *Middle Eastern Monitor*, 18 April 2017.

54. Shaw, 'US MQ-9 drone shot down in Yemen', *Navy Times*, 2 October 2017.

55. No confirmation was ever given for the shooting down of the F-15 and it remains an 'unverified' claim of the Houthis.

56. The US-made FLIR sights were delivered to Yemen back in 2008. ('Houthi's do it Yourself Air defences' at *War is Boring* https://warisboring.com/the-houthis-do-it-yourself-air-defenses/)

57. The Sayyad (Hunter) series includes three medium-range (75–120km), high-altitude (27km) missiles: the Sayyad-1, a domestic copy of the Chinese HQ-2, itself a copy of the SA-2; the Sayyad-2, based on the 1970s U.S. RIM-66 SM-1; and the Sayyad-3, a longer-range version of the Sayyad-2. Compared to the AA-10's relatively small 35kg warhead, the Sayyad-2 has a more destructive 195kg warhead. The virtual radar receiver passively gathers air traffic control signals given off by military and commercial aircraft and can help track all aircraft within a radius of over 250km. (Nadimi and Knights, op. cit.)

58. 'Yemeni rebels enhance ballistic missile campaign', *Jane's Intelligence Review* accessed at https://www.janes.com/images/assets/330/72330/Yemeni_rebels_enhance_ballistic_missile_campaign.pdf. See also, Neuman, Scott, 'Saudis Shoot Down Scud Missile Fired By Houthi Rebels In Yemen', NPR, 6 June 2015 accessed at https://www.npr.org/sections/thetwo-way/2015/06/06/412451669/saudis-shoot-down-scud-missile-fired-by-houthi-rebels-in-yemen

59. It is likely that the missiles came into the Houthis' hands from North Korea via Iran. Ghoshal, 'Houthi Missile Attacks and the Many Influences on Yemen's Conflict', *Terrorism Monitor* Volume: 16 Issue: 5, *The Jamestown Foundation*, 9 March 2018.

60. Ghoshal, op. cit.

61. Qaef-1 is identical to the Iranian Ababil-T, manufactured by the Iran Aircraft Manufacturing Industries and is assembled from Iranian components. The attacks targeted the air defences in the initial phase and were soon carried out at other targets also; the command and control centre and the front-line troops. Knights, 'The Houthi War Machine: From Guerrilla War to State Capture', *CTC Sentinel*, September 2018, Volume 11, Issue 8, https://ctc.usma.edu/houthi-war-machine-guerrilla-war-state-capture/; Nadimi and Knights, 'Iran's Support to Houthi Air Defences in Yemen'.

62. Stein, 'Low-Tech, High-Reward: The Houthi Drone Attack', *Foreign Policy Initiative*, 11 January 2019.

63. Brennan, 'Did U.S. Made Saudi Missile Defenses Fail during Yemen Rocket Attack?', *Newsweek*, 26 March 2018; 'Saudi air defences foil Houthi missile attack on Riyadh', *Arab News*, 25 June 2018.

Conclusion

1. Cohen, *Military Misfortunes: The Anatomy of Failure in War*.

2. Luttwak and Horowitz, *The Israeli Army*, p. 302.

3. Futrell, *Ideas, Concepts, Doctrine: Basic Thinking in the United States Air Force 1961–1984*, Volume II, p. 484.

4. Cohen, *Israel's Best Defence: The First Full Story of the Israeli Air Force*, trans. Cordis, p. 314.

5. Carter, *Airpower and the Cult of the Offensive*, accessed at *https://apps.dtic.mil/dtic/tr/fulltext/u2/a391659.pdf*

6. Kreis, *Air Warfare and Air Base Air Defence, 1914–1973*, https://apps.dtic.mil/dtic/tr/fulltext/u2/a208631.pdf

7. Doyle, *The Yom Kippur War and the Shaping of the United States Air Force*, Drew Paper No. 31, (Curtis E. LeMay Centre for Doctrine Development and Education, Air University Press, Maxwell Air Force Base, Alabama).

8. Chiles, 'Raptors Uncaged' (*Air & Space Magazine*, February 2016). https://www.airspacemag.com/military-aviation/raptor-strikes-180957782/

9. '2C38 Derivatsiya-PVO or why Air Defence Guns are still relevant' (*Ack-Ack: All About Air Defence*), http://www.airdefence.in/weapons/2c38-derivatsiya-pvo-or-why-air-defence-guns-are-still-relevant/

10. Bronk, 'Russia's Air Defence Challenge in Syria', *RUSI Defence Systems*, 29 June 2017 accessed at https://rusi.org/publication/rusi-defence-systems/russiaE28099s-air-defence-challenge-syria

11. Evans, *National Air Defense: Challenges, Solution Profiles, and Technology Needs*.

12. Leventoploulos, *Ground-Based Air Defence System: Challenges and Perspective*, Research Paper No. 175 July- August 2018.

Bibliography

Adkin, Mark, *Urgent Fury: The Battle for Grenada: The Truth Behind the Largest U.S. Military Operation Since Vietnam*, (Lexington Books, 1989)

'Air Power in Russia's Georgian Campaign August 2008', *Pathfinder* Issue 99, (Air Power Development Centre, Washington D.C., October 2008)

Alam, Air Commodore M. Mahmood, Pakistan Air Force, 'Tactical Air Power Evolution and Employment from an Historical-Analytical Perspective', *Islamic Defence Review* 6, No. 2 (1981)

Al-Sadat, Anwar, *In Search of Identity*, (Harper & Row, New York, 1978)

Alexiev, Alexander, *Inside the Soviet Army in Afghanistan*, (Rand, Santa Monica, California, 1988)

Aloni, Shlomo, *Arab-Israeli Air Wars*: *Combat Aircraft* (Osprey Publishing, Oxford, 2001)

—— *Israeli Mirage and Nesher Aces* (Osprey Publishing, Oxford, 2004)

—— *Israeli Phantom II Aces* (Osprey Publishing, Oxford, 2004)

—— *Israeli A-4 Skyhawk Units in Combat* (Osprey Publishing, Oxford, 2009)

Armitage, M.J., and R.A. Mason, *Air Power in the Nuclear Age* (University of Chicago Press, 1985)

Arnett, Peter, *Live from the Battlefield. From Vietnam to Baghdad 35 Years in the World's War Zones*, (Simon & Schuster, New York, 1994)

Avidror, Zvi, *Hammers – Israel's Long-Range Heavy Bomber Arm: The Story of 69Squadron* (Schiffer Publishing, Atglen, Pennsylvania, 2010)

Bar-Joseph, Uri, *The Watchman Fell Asleep: The Surprise of Yom Kippur and Its Sources* (SUNY Press, New York, 2012)

—— 'The Wealth of Information and the Poverty of Comprehension: Israel's Intelligence Failure of 1973 Revisited', (*Intelligence and National Security 10, No. 4,* October 1995)

Bar-Siman-Tov, Y., 'The Myth of Strategic Bombing: Israeli Deep-Penetration Air Raids in the War of Attrition, 1969–70' (*Journal of Contemporary History*, Sage Publishers, California, 1984)

Begquist, Ronald E., *The Role of Airpower in Iran-Iraq War* (University Press of the Pacific, 2002)

Bishop, Farzad, and Tom Cooper, *Iranian F-4 Phantom II Units in Combat* (Combat Aircraft Book 37; Osprey Publishing, Oxford, 2012)

Black, Ian, and Benny Morris, *Israel's Secret Wars: A History of Israel's Intelligence Services* (Grove Press, New York, 1991)

Blackman, Tony, *Vulcan Boys: From the Cold War to the Falklands: True Tales of the Iconic Delta V Bomber* (Grub Street Publishing, London, 2015)

Boyne, Walter J., 'El Dorado Canyon' (*Air Force Magazine*, March 1999)

Braithwaite, Rodric, *Afgantsy: The Russians in Afghanistan 1979–89* (Oxford University Press, Oxford, 2011)

Brower, Kenneth S., *The Israel Defense Forces, 1948–2017* (Mideast Security and Policy Studies No. 150; The Begin-Sadat Center for Strategic Studies, Bar-Ilan University)

Brown, David, *The Royal Navy and Falklands War* (Pen & Sword Books, Barnsley, 1987)

Callwell, C.E., *Small Wars* (University of Nebraska Press, Lincoln, 1996)

Chant, Chris, *Air War in the Falklands 1982* (Osprey Publishing, Oxford, 2013)

Chivvis, Christopher S., *Toppling Qaddafi: Libya and the Limits of Liberal Intervention* (Cambridge University Press, 2013)

Clark, Robert, *Symmetrical Warfare and Lessons for Future War: The Case of the Iran-Iraq Conflict*, (Canadian Forces College, Advanced Military Studies Course 3, 2000)

Cohen, Ariel, & Robert E. Hamilton, *The Russian Military And The Georgia War: Lessons And Implications* (Strategic Studies Institute, US Army War College, Pennsylvania, June 2011)

Cohen, Col Eliezer 'Cheetah', *Israel's Best Defence: The First Full Story of the Israeli Air Force*, trans. Jonathan Cordis (Orion Books, New York, 1993)

Cohen, Eliot A., *Military Misfortunes: The Anatomy of Failure in War* (Free Press, 2006)

Coll, Steve, *Ghost Wars: The Secret History of the CIA, Afghanistan, and Bin Laden, from the Soviet Invasion to Sept. 10, 2001*, (Penguin Books, New York, 2004)

Cordesman, Anthony H., *Iraq War Note: Iraqi Air Defences and the Battle of Baghdad* (Centre for Strategic & International Studies, Washington D.C., 1 April 2003)

—— 'The Sixth Arab-Israeli Conflict: Lessons Learned for American Defense Planning', (*Armed Forces Journal International*, Springfield, Virginia, August 1982

—— *The Gulf and the West: Strategic Relations and Military Realities*, Boulder, Colo.: Westview Press, 1988

—— The Middle East Military Balance: Force Development in North Africa, (Center for Strategic and International Studies, Washington D.C., 28 March 2005)

Cordesman, Anthony & Abraham Wagner, *The Lessons of Modern War: Volume I: The Arab-Israeli conflicts, 1973–1989*, (Westview Press, Boulder and San Francisco, 1990)

—— *The Lessons of Modern War: Volume II, The Iran-Iraq War*, (Westview Press, Boulder and San Francisco, 1990)

—— *The Lessons of Modern War: Volume III, The Afghan and Falklands Conflicts* (Westview Press, Boulder and San Francisco, 1990)

—— *The Lessons of Modern War: Volume IV, The Gulf War* (Westview Press, Boulder and San Francisco, 1996)

Corum, James S., 'Argentine Airpower in the Falklands War: An Operational View' (USAF School of Advanced Airpower Studies)

Corum, James, and Johnson, Wray, *Airpower in Small Wars: Fighting Insurgents and Terrorists* (University Press of Kansas, 2003)

Corrigan, Jim, *Desert Storm Air War: The Aerial Campaign against Saddam's Iraq in the 1991 Gulf War* (Stackpole Books, Mechanicsburg, PA, 2017)

Dick, C. J., *Mujahideen tactics in the Soviet-Afghan War* (Conflict Studies Research Centre, January 2002)

Donnelly, Christopher, *Red Banner: The Soviet Military System in Peace and War* (Jane's Information Group, Surrey, 1994)

Dorn, A. Walter, *Air Power in UN Operations* (Ashgate Publishing Ltd, Surrey, 2014)

Doyle, Joseph S., Squadron Leader (Royal Air Force), *The Yom Kippur War and the Shaping of the United States Air Force*, Drew Paper No. 31, (Curtis E. LeMay Center for Doctrine Development and Education, Air University Press, Maxwell Air Force Base, Alabama)

Dunstan, Simon, *The Yom Kippur War 1973: The Golan Heights Campaign* (Osprey Publishing, Oxford, 2003)

Dupuy, Trevor N., and Paul Martell, *Flawed Victory: The Arab-Israeli Conflict and the 1982 War in Lebanon* (Hero Books, Fairfax, VA, 1986)

El Badri, Maj. Gen. Hassan, Maj. Gen. Taha El Magdoub, and Maj. Gen. Mohammad Dia El Din Zohdy, *Decision and Concept. The Ramadan War* (Dunn Loring, VA: T.N. Dupuy Associates Inc., 1978)

El-Gamasy, Mohammad Abdel Gahni, *The October War* (American University in Cairo Press, Cairo, 1993)

Engelbrekt, Kjell, Marcus Mohlin, Charlotte Wagnsson (Eds), *The NATO Intervention in Libya: Lessons learned from the campaign* (Routledge, New York, 2014)

Evron, Yair, *War and Intervention in Lebanon: The Israeli-Syrian Deterrence Dialogue* (The Johns Hopkins University Press, 1987)

Farrar-Hockley, Major General A.H., 'The October War', *Adelphi Paper #111*, Winter 1974–75, (International Institute of Strategic Studies, London, Winter 1975)

Farrokh, Kaveh, *Iran at War: 1500–1988* (Osprey Publishing, Oxford, 2011)

Flintham, Victor, *Air Wars and Aircraft: A Detailed Record of Air Combat, 1945–Present* (Arms and Armour Press, London, 1989)

Freedman, Sir Lawrence, *The Official History of the Falklands Campaign, Volume II* (Abingdon, 2005)

Freedman, Lawrence, and Efraim Karsh, *The Gulf Conflict, 1990–1991: Diplomacy and War in the New World Order* (Princeton University Press, 1995)

Frostic, Fred, *Air campaign Against the Iraqi Army in the Kuwaiti Theatre of Operations* (Prepared for the United States Air Force, Project Air Force, RAND Corporation, 1994)

Futrell, Robert Frank, *Ideas, Concepts, Doctrine: Basic Thinking in the United States Air Force 1961–1984*, Vol. II (Alabama, 1989)

Gabriel, Richard A., *Operation Peace for Galilee: The Israeli-PLO War in Lebanon* (Hill and Wang, London, 1984)

Gordon, Shmuel, and Trainor, *The Generals' War*, (Back Bay Books, 1995)

Gordon, Shmuel (2008). *Thirty hours in October* (in Hebrew), Ma'ariv Book Guild, 2008)

Gordon, Yefim, *Russian Gunship Helicopters*, (Pen and Sword Aviation, Barnsley, 2013)

Grant, Rebecca, 'The Bekaa Valley War', (*Air Force Magazine*, June 2002)

Grau, Lester W., and Michael A. Gress, *The Soviet-Afghan War: How a Superpower Fought and Lost*, (University Press of Kansas, 2001)

Grau, Lester W., T*he Bear Went Over the Mountain: Soviet Combat Tactics in Afghanistan*, (National Defence University Press, Washington D.C., 2005)

—— 'Breaking Contact Without Leaving Chaos: The Soviet Withdrawal from Afghanistan' (*Journal of Slavic Military Studies*, Vol. 20, No. 2)

—— 'The Battle for Hill 3234: Last Ditch Defense in the Mountains of Afghanistan' (*Journal of Slavic Military Studies*), Vol. 24, (2011)

Gray, Colin (2012) Airpower For Strategic Effect. Maxwell Air Force Base: Air University Press

Greenleaf, Major Jason R., USAF, 'The Air War in Libya', *Air & Space Power Journal* (March-April 2013)

Gulf War Air Power Survey, Command and Control (Goverment Publishing Office, Washington, D.C., 1993)

Handel, M. I., 'The Yom Kippur War and the Inevitability of Surprise', *International Studies Quarterly* 21(3), 461–502 1977

Hefez, Nir, and Gadi Bloom, *The Shepherd: The Life Story of Ariel Sharon* (in Hebrew) (Tel-Aviv: Yediot Aharonot; Sifrey Hemed. ISBN 978-965-511-202-3. (English: Hefez, Nir; Gadi Bloom, (2006).

Heikal, Mohamed, *The Road to Ramadan* (William Collins Sons, London, 1975)

Herzog, Chaim, *The War of Atonement, October 1973* (Boston: Little, Brown and Company, 1975

—— *The Arab-Israeli Wars*, (New York: Random House Inc., 1982)

—— *The War of Atonement: The Inside Story of the Yom Kippur War*, (London: Greenhill Books, 2003)

Higham, Robin, John Greenwood, and Von Hardesty (Eds), *Russian Aviation and Air Power in the Twentieth Century* (Routledge, London, 1998)

Hiro, Dilip, *The Longest War: The Iran-Iraq Military Conflict* (Routledge, Chapman and Hall, Inc., New York, 1991)

Hosmer, Stephen T., *Why the Iraqi Resistance to the Coalition Invasion Was So Weak* (RAND Corporation, 2007)

Huchthausen, Peter A., *America's Splendid Little Wars: a short history of US military engagements*, 1975–2000, (Penguin, New York, 2003)

Hurley, Matthew M., 'The BEKAA Valley Air Battle, June 1982: Lessons Mislearned?' (*Airpower Journal*, Winter 1989)

Isby, David, *Russia's War in Afghanistan*, (Osprey Publishing, Oxford, 1986)

Jalali, Ali, and Grau, Lester, *Afghan Guerilla Warfare: In the Words of the Mujahideen Fighters* (MBI Publishing, Minneapolis, 2001)

Kreis, John F., *Air Warfare and Air Base Air Defense, 1914–1973* (Office of Air Force History, United States Air Force, Washington D. C., 1988)

Kumaraswamy, P. R., *Revisiting the Yom Kippur War* (Routledge, Abingdon, UK, 2013)

Kuperman, Alan, 'The Stinger Missile and U.S. Intervention in Afghanistan' (*Political Science Quarterly*, Vol. 114, No. 2, 1999)

Lambeth, Benjamin S., *Moscow's Lessons from the 1982 Lebanon Air War* (Rand Corporation, Santa Monica, California, September 1984)

—— *The Transformation of American Air Power* (Cornell University Press, 2000)

—— *NATO's Air War for Kosovo: A Strategic and Operational Assessment* (Apple Books, 2001)

—— *Airpower at 18,000* (Carnegie Endowment for International Peace, Washington 2012)

Laidlaw, Will, *Apache Over Libya*, (Pen & Sword Books, Barnsley, 2016)

Laur, Timothy M & Llanso, Steven L, *Encyclopaedia of modern U.S. military weapons*, (Berkley Books, New York, 1995)

Lavrov, Anton, *The Russian Air Campaign in Syria: A Preliminary Analysis*, (Centre for Analysis of Strategies and Technologies, Moscow, June 2018)

Livingston, Alastair, 'Israeli Air Power 1973–1982: How Did the Israeli Air Force Recover after the October War?' 20 May 2013, https://www.e-ir.info/2013/05/20/israeli-air-power-1973-1982-how-did-the-israeli-air-force-recover-after-the-october-war/

Lowry, Richard S., *The Gulf War Chronicles: A Military History of the First War with Iraq*, (iUniverse, 2008)

Luttwak, Edward, and Dan Horowitz, *The Israeli Army* (Dehra Dun, 1983)

Martin, David C., and John Walcott, *Best Laid Plans: The Inside Story of America's War Against Terrorism* (Harper & Row Publishers, New York, 1981)

Martin, Mike, *Afghanistan: Inside a Rebel Stronghold* (Blandford Press, Poole, UK, 1984)

McMichael, Scott R., *Stumbling Bear: Soviet Military Performance in Afghanistan* (Brassey's, London, 1991)

Middlebrook, Martin, *Argentine Fight for the Falklands*, (Pen and Sword Books, Barnsley, 2009)

Miller, Marshal Lee, 'The Soviet Air Force View of the Bekaa Valley Debacle' (*Armed Forces Journal International*, June 1987)

Morison, Samuel L., 'Falklands(Malvinas) Campaign: A Chronology' (*United States Naval Institute Proceedings*, June 1983)

Morris, Benny, *Righteous Victims: A History of the Zionist-Arab Conflict, 1881–2001* (Vintage, 2001)

Mueller, Karl P. (Ed.), *Precision and Purpose: Airpower in the Libyan Civil War* (RAND Publications, New York, 2015)

'Mujahideen Tactics in the Soviet-Afghan War' (Foreign Military Studies Office, Fort Leavenworth, Kansas)

Murray, Douglas J. and Paul R. Viotti (Eds), *The Defense Policies of Nations*, (The Johns Hopkins University Press, Baltimore, 1994)

Nordeen, Lon, *Air Warfare in the Missile Age*, (Smithsonian Institution Press, Washington D.C., 2002)

—— *Fighters Over Israel: The Story of the Israeli Air Force from the War of Independence to the Bekaa Valley*, Crown Books, 1990)

Norton, William 'Bill', *Air War on the Edge – A History of the Israel Air Force and its Aircraft since 1947* (Midland Publishing, 2004)

Osborne, Tony, 'Operation Decisive Storm -- Air Power Over Yemen', (*Aviation Week*, 31 March, 2015)

O'Ballance, Edgar, *Electronic War in the Middle East* (Anchor Books, Hamden, Conn, 1974)

O'Neill, Bard E., 'The October War: A Political-Military Assessment' (*Air University Review* 25, July-August 1974)

—— *No Victor, No Vanquished: The Yom Kippur War* (Barrie & Jenkins Publishing, 1979) 'Soviet Tactics in Afghanistan', *Military Review*, vol. LX no. 8, (Fort Leavenworth, Kansas, 1980)

—— *The Gulf War* (Brassey's, London, 1988)

—— *Afghan Wars 1839–1992. What Britain Gave Up and the Soviet Union Lost* (Brassey's, London, 1993)

Owen, Col Robert C., *Deliberate Force A Case Study in Effective Air Campaigning*, Final Report of the Air University Balkans Air Campaign Study, (Air University Press Maxwell Air Force Base, Alabama, January 2000)

Palit, Major General D.K, *Return to Sinai* (Compton Russell Ltd, Salisbury, 1974)

Panagiotis, Dimitrakis, *The Secret War in Afghanistan: The Soviet Union, China and Anglo-American Intelligence in the Afghan War* (Bloomsbury, London, 2013)

Perman, Stacy, *Spies, Inc.: Business Innovation from Israel's Masters of Espionage* (FT Tess, 2004, Kindle Edition)

Pierre, Razouk, *Iran Iraq War* (Harvard University Press, 2015)

Pollock, Kenneth M., *Arabs at War: Military Effectiveness, 1948–1991*, (Bison Books, 2004)

Pook, Jerry, *RAF Harrier Ground Attack-Falklands* (Pen & Sword Books, Barnsley, 2007)

Privratsky, Kenneth L., *Logistics in the Falklands War* (Pen and Sword Military, Barnsley, 2015)

Riedel, Bruce, 'Comparing the U.S. and Soviet Experiences in Afghanistan' (Combating Terrorism Centre (CTC) *Sentinel*, Volume 2, Issue 5, US Military Academy, West Point, 2009)

Ripley, Tim, *Operation Deliberate Force: The UN and NATO Campaign in Bosnia*, 1995 (Centre for Defence and International Studies, 1999

—— *Conflict in the Balkans 1991–2000*, (Osprey Publishing, Oxford, 2010)

Rubright, Richard W.,*The Role and Limitations of Technology in U.S. Counterinsurgency Warfare*, (Potomac Books, University of Nebraska Press, Lincoln, 2015)

Russell, Lee; Mendez, Albert, *Grenada 1983* (Osprey Publishing Ltd, Oxford, 2012)

Schiff, Ze'ev & Ehud Ya'ari, *Israel's Lebanon War*, (Touchstone, 1985)

Schubert, Frank N., and Theresa L. Kraus (General Editors), *The Whirlwind War: The United States Army in Operations DESERT SHIELD and DESERT STORM* (Center for Military History, US Army, Washington, D.C.)

Seale, Patrick, *Assad: The Struggle for the Middle East* (University of California Press)

Segal, David, 'The Iran-Iraq War: A Military Analysis' (*Foreign Affairs*, Summer 1988)

Sherman, Arnold, *When God Judged and Men Died: A Battle Report of the Yom Kippur War* (Bantam Books, New York, 1973)

Singh, Pushpindar, *Himalayan Eagles: History of the Indian Air Force, Volume III*: World Air Power (The Society for Aerospace Studies, New Delhi, 2007)

Sneider, Daniel, 'Soviets Assess Their Arsenal After Iraq's Defeat in Gulf' (*The Christian Science Monitor*, 8 March 1991)

Stein, Aaron, 'Low-Tech, High-Reward: The Houthi Drone Attack' (*Foreign Policy Initiative*, 11 January 2019)

Subramaniam, Air Commodore Arjun, IAF, 'Kargil Revisited: Air Operations in a High-Altitude Conflict' *CLAWS Journal* (New Delhi, Summer 2008)

Svante, E., Cornell, David J. Smith and S. Frederick Starr, 'The August 2007 Bombing Incident in Georgia: Implications for the Euro–Atlantic Region' (The Central Asia-Caucasus Institute, School of Advanced International Studies, Washington, D.C, October 2007)

Trainor, Michael R., *The Generals' War: The Inside Story of the Conflict in the Gulf* (Little, Brown, New York, 1995)

Trevor N. Dupuy and Paul Martell, *Flawed Victory: The Arab-Israeli Conflict and the 1982 War in Lebanon* (Hero Books, Fairfax, VA, 1986)

Tucker-Jones, Anthony, *The Gulf War: Operation Desert Storm 1990–1991* (Pen and Sword, Barnsley, 2014)

Urban, Mark, *War in Afghanistan* (Macmillan Press Valenta, 1998)

Valenta, Jiri, 'From Prague to Kabul: The Soviet Style of Invasion' (*International Security*, Vol. 5 No. 2, Fall 1980)

Van Der Bijl, Nick, *Victory in the Falklands* (Pen and Sword, Barnsley, 2007)

Walter J Boyne, 'El Dorado Canyon', (*Air Force Magazine*, March 1999)

Werrell, Kenneth P., *Archie to SAM: A Short Operational History of Ground Based Air Defence* (Air University Press, Washington DC, 2005)

Westermann, Edward B., *The Limits of Soviet Airpower: The Bear versus the Mujahideen in Afghanistan, 1979–1989* (BiblioScholar, 2012)

—— 'The Limits of Soviet Airpower: The Failure of Military Coercion in Afghanistan, 1979–89' (*Journal of Conflict Studies*, Vol. XIX No. 2, Fall, 1999)

Williamson, Murray, and Kevin M. Woods, *The Iran-Iraq War: A Military and Strategic History* (Cambridge University Press, 2012)

Williamson, Murray, and Robert H. Scales, *The Iraq War*, (Belknap Press, An Imprint of Harvard University Press, 2005)

Withington, Thomas, 'The Experiences of the Soviet Air Force in Afghanistan 1979–1989' (*Air Power Review*, 8:1, 2005)

Woods, Kevin M. & Ors, *Saddam's War: An Iraqi military Perspective of Iran-Iraq War*, McNair paper 70 (Institute for National Strategic Studies, National Defence University, Washington, D.C., 2009)

—— *Saddam's Generals: Perspectives of the Iran-Iraq War* (Institute for Defense Analyses, Alexandria, VA, 2011)

Yefim Gordon, *Russian Gunship Helicopters*, (Pen and Sword Aviation, 2013)

Yousaf, Mohamed, and Adkin, Mark, *Afghanistan, The Bear Trap: The Defeat of a Superpower* (Pen & Sword Books, Barnsley, 2001)

Zucchino, David, *Thunder Run: The Armored Strike to Capture Baghdad* (Grove Press, 2004)

Index